THINKING MATTER

Consciousness from Aristotle to Putnam and Sartre

Joseph S. Catalano

Routledge · New York and London

Published in 2000 by
Routledge
29 West 35th Street
New York, NY 10001

Published in Great Britain by
Routledge
11 New Fetter Lane
London EC4P 4EE

Library of Congress Cataloging-in-Publication Data

Catalano, Joseph S.
    Thinking matter: consciousness from Aristotle to Putnam and Sartre / Joseph S. Catalano.
        p.   cm.
    Includes bibliographical references and index.
    ISBN 0-415-92664-5 (HB) — ISBN 0-415-92665-3 (PB)
    1. Consciousness. 2. Matter. I. Title.
B808.9 .C38 2000
110—dc21

                                                                    99-049935

In Memory of Stellario
and Evelyn Marchese

Contents

A c k n o w l e d g m e n t s

William L. McBride graciously read and commented upon every version of this manuscript, and, in a very special way, I wish to acknowledge my gratitude. A few of his observations resulted in my moving some of the material into the two appendixes of this final version. The usual caveat is, I suppose, nevertheless, appropriate: I alone am responsible for both the format and the content of this book. Gayatri Patnaik of Routledge greatly eased the difficult task of creating a book out of a manuscript. I wish to thank her for her gracious efficiency.

The Perspective

Thinking about trees and stars, many philosophers today consider both the thought and the tree as material and yet as separate. That is, even though these philosophers are materialists, they are also realists: they do not identify the consciousness of a tree with the tree but give each its separate existence. I begin by noting my general agreement with this realist and materialist perspective.

At this point, someone who is not a materialist might want to stop reading. I may be able to keep the dialogue going by denying my materialism, even as I affirm it. The ambiguity arises from the present-day notion of matter. If I claim allegiance with materialism, it might seem that I am accepting the general contemporary tendency to view matter and consciousness scientifically and quantitatively, and I do not do so. Also, I do not concentrate on the brain alone as the organ of thought. Rather, I take the view that the whole body thinks, and I take the body in its fleshy, organic nature.

Further, in opposition to most materialist conceptions of the world, I consider that our body gives us a unique bond to the world: the world is the way it is because our bodies are the way they are. For example, there is color in the world simply because our consciousness can occur through fleshy eyes. Thus, the world is visible regardless of whether anyone is actually perceiving things. On this level, the proper question to ask about sight does not concern the degree to which we may each see things differently, but what our world would be like if all human bodies lacked eyes. The proper answer to this question is that consciousness as sight makes things visible. Further, this revealing of the world is also our knowledge of the world as visible.

Our bond to the world is thus both a knowledge of the world and a making of the world. Our world, however, is not made out of some primordial goo. We make matter into a world because our senses highlight and discriminate matter in the particular ways that give us our common-sense world. It will be my main task in this work to clarify these claims. Here, however, I wish to expand a little further about my ambiguous stance on materialism and realism.

When I press the issue of what I mean by materialism, I cannot, for the most part, find my understanding reflected in the contemporary literature. To repeat, I might deny being a materialist. My middle-of-the-road approach is to qualify my materialism by describing it as both nonreductive and anthropocentric. I regard reductive materialism to be a narrow scientific materialism with the following two general characteristics: first, it attempts to reduce quality to quantity, and second, it frequently follows through by attempting to reduce the consciousness of quality to quantitative relations.

In the first instance, the sound of a voice becomes the pattern and the form of its waves as they travel through the air. Consequently, if a tree falls and there are no organisms with ears to hear the sound, the quality, sound, according to scientific or reductive materialists, does not exist. Nevertheless, they would agree that there is a disturbance in the air that can cause the quality sound in some potential listener. Thus, while scientific materialists deny the objective existence of qualities, such as sound, they are realist to the extent that they claim that the causes for our hearing sound exist in the world.

As regards consciousness, this scientific materialism, in its most radical form, offers us a neurophilosophical explanation of the entire realm of our awareness of the world and of our self-awareness. We are to view consciousness as a complex interaction among neurons and electrical impulses. Thus, both on the part of the world and on the part of our awareness of the world, much of contemporary materialism attempts to eliminate the reality of anything except quantity. It is true, of course, that quantum mechanics has somewhat loosened our present scientific view of the world from the obvious picturelike aspect of its quantitative perspective. However, from the general viewpoint that motivates scientific materialists, it will become clear that, philosophically, their picture of the world remains fundamentally a quantitative one.

My nonreductive materialism claims that qualities exist in the world and that our consciousness is a unique experience irreducible to quantitative relations. However, my nonreductive claim is relational: in relation to human eyes and ears, the qualities of color and sound exist in the world. And, in relation to our entire fleshy body as a perceptual organism, our consciousness and self-consciousness are not reducible to quantitative relations.

However, both consciousness and qualities have quantitative aspects: sound is a wavelength, and our consciousness can, no doubt, be regarded as a sophisticated computer. I regard these truths to be relational. In relation to our scientific theories and instruments, both qualities and consciousness can be regarded quantitatively.

The claim that truth is relational is *not* equivalent to affirming that truth is relative. Relational realism merely requires us to keep attentive to the way structure and meaning come about through our own organic existence, and through our collective historical practices. I should note that, throughout this work, I take structure to be what is objective and meaning to be what happens in us when we become aware of structure. For the purpose of making my general points about materialism and realism, I do not regard as necessary extreme precision about either structure or meaning. However, I should note that I presuppose the acceptance that all structure and meaning imply some degree of continuity over time. Even to speak or refer to *chance* is to imply that the word at least exists with sufficient continuity to be referred to as *chance*. With this in mind, my implicit claim is that all continuity over time arises in things by their relation to our fleshy body and its historical practices. (I will not, however, develop this background claim in this work, but I plan to return to it in a future study.)

In a sense, few thinkers would deny my claims about qualities. They would, however, privilege the quantitative aspects by relying on them to be the explanations of the things. They would grant that water has a nourishing and refreshing aspect, but they would insist that water is essentially H_2O.[1] This philosophical move is not as innocent as it might appear. In the final analysis, the qualitative aspects of things become second-class citizens whose rights can be eliminated with proper discourse.

Since I regard the sense organs, and, indeed, the entire fleshy body as a collective organ of thought, my materialism is thus opposed to the contemporary brain-body dualism that characterizes much of our present materialistic thought. For me, speaking, listening, writing, and reading are forms of thought, but so are such activities as dance, music, painting, and political gatherings. All these are forms of thought precisely because they are accomplished by the entire body acting through this or that fleshy sense organ or fleshy limb.

I discuss the difference between a reductive and a nonreductive materialism mainly in the first two chapters, which then prepare the way for the more challenging anthropocentric aspect of my materialism. Nevertheless, it will become clear that both the nonreductive and the anthropocentric aspects are related: they are different ways of explaining how the world comes to be through matter's relation to our human body. I emphasize the human body over other organic bodies because that is what we know best, and because it seems that only the human body allows us to propose the question of its relation to the world.

Throughout this work, my intent is not to anthropomorphize our relation to the world but to anthropocentrize it. The question I propose is *not* how you and I personally view the world; but, rather, how the world is made *our* world by its relation to the fleshy organic body. Thus, in place of the disinterested scientific observer, who views the world through scientific theories, I place the human body, and I place our body in the center of things, precisely as it is a unity of organic parts. The human body is a unity that feels, sees, hears, smells, tastes, and reflects. The thoughts of our body are not only its concepts and reflections but the entire range of its sensuous and fleshy activities.

My anthropocentric realism views the world to be the way it is because of matter's relation to our fleshy body, and it views that we craft the tools to understand the world thus differentiated. For example, because our consciousness takes the form of seeing through fleshy eyes, things are revealed as visible with various shades of color. This revealing is a non-thetic awareness of color; it is a nonconceptual knowing of the essence of color. It is true that historically we have crafted the conceptual and linguistic tools to explicate our bond to the world, but the bond and the tools to understand the bond are of one anthropocentric piece. This claim represents the general direction of my thought, and it is most explicitly formulated beginning in chapter 4.

The use of the terms *know* and *essence* in relation to our sense awareness of things may grate upon philosophically trained ears. I could introduce other terms. However, I think communication is facilitated, wherever possible, by rethinking our relation to the world through traditional philosophical concepts and terms. Part of my task is thus to trace the historical roots of our thinking about the world. Specifically, I will sketch how our philosophical heritage separated sense awareness from the true knowledge of things, and how it forged a view of knowledge as "pure knowledge."

Indeed, the separation of sense awareness from the true understanding of things is rooted not only in Plato's dualistic view that clearly separates the world of sense from the world of reason. It is also to be found in Aristotle's attempt to unite the objects of reason and sense in our one material world. Aristotelian realism is the father of classical realism. In this realism, true knowledge of the world is had when we know the way the world would be even if we were never there to view it: the universe of stars and galaxies; the Earth filled with minerals, plants, and animals of all sorts exist and have always existed independently of any relation to human existence. Except for the fleeting quality of being aware of it for a relatively short period of time, the classical realist considers that our existence adds nothing to the universe.

This claim that true knowledge merely reflects the way things are independent of our existence is a statement of the correspondence theory of truth, and this theory is the foundation of classical realism. Of course, classical realism would admit that, for example, we do alter the atmosphere of the Earth, but for better or worse, we merely add our personal touch to what has been there independently of a relation to our existence.

The history of philosophy has made it clear that the correspondence theory of truth requires a guarantee that our thoughts can mesh with things. To be more exact, the correspondence theory of truth requires us to believe that we do not, for the most part, impose human intentions on the world. Part of the complexity of my anthropocentric realism is that I agree that the world does not come about by imposing human intentions upon some amorphous matter. In chapter 3, I will sharpen my perspective by comparing it with that of such thinkers as Hilary Putnam, Nelson Goodman, and W. V. O. Quine. Although these thinkers consider themselves realists, they depart from the correspondence theory of truth, and thus from classical realism.

I interpret the history of philosophy to have shown that traditional realism, based as it is upon the correspondence theory of truth, implies the existence of a transcendent mind that can ground the meshing of thought to thing. Frequently, classical realists attempt to hide from this requirement by appealing to some transcendent mysterious Entity—Being, Nature, or Chance. I personally see no substantive difference between such appeals and the traditional belief that, since God created us to live in the world, He was kind enough to allow us to be able to have knowledge of it. From the perspective of our bond to the world, the result is the same: our consciousness is not bonded *to* things but is merely a reflection *of* things.

Another way of summarizing how the correspondence theory of truth views our connection to the world is to note that our relation to the world is external in two senses that are relevant for my discussion: First, to be known adds nothing to what is known. Second, the fleshy organic constitution of the body, the way consciousness appears through eyes, through nose, through ears, through the mouth and tongue, is incidental to our acquiring true knowledge of things. In this context, the ideal examples are from mathematics: the natural numbers 1, 2, 3, 4, etc. are supposed to be meaningful apart from any particular expression of them, such as the alternate form I, II, III, IV, and the truth of their relations are independent of any particular marks or sounds that express them, such as the marks 2+2=4. Making marks or uttering sounds is something done by a fleshy body, but we are supposed to believe that all this is incidental to mathematical truth. In particular, the use of the mathematical zero as an emptiness allowing us to give numbers a place value is supposed to be a discovery of what was always there awaiting to be found and not, as I consider it to be in chapters 6 and 7, a human invention. In these last two chapters, I will be making the case that our universal concepts and terms are objective in the sense that they emerge from a long history of crafting matter into meaning. Still, I should note that I consider the general claims of my relational realism to be independent from some of the strong claims I make in these last two chapters. For example, I personally consider my views on language to be a logical consequence of my anthropocentrism. However, I can understand that someone might be willing to accept my general anthropocentric views, but not my notion of crafting marks into meanings that I discuss in chapter 7.

However, since I am a realist and a materialist, I must be careful in rejecting the view that our relation to the world is by way of external relations; that is, by way of relations that do not constitute the world. Traditionally, internal relations are the mark of idealism. Internal relations concern the constitution of a thing, and idealists claim that, in some way, we constitute the world by our relation to it. To be a brother or sister is to be in relation to another, and the relation is essential to being a brother or sister. In a similar way, an idealist would have us see that a star is a star because of its relation to our consciousness.

Nevertheless, traditional idealism shares an essential feature with traditional realism, and that is why I reject both. Although realism stresses our external relation to the world and idealism our internal relation, both agree that the fleshy organic nature of our consciousness is not an essential component of our bond to the world. In traditional realism, the world is the way it is independently of the fact of our existence; in traditional idealism, the world is the way it is independently of the fact of our organic existence. The internal relation that idealism stresses is one of thought, mind, or spirit to matter, but not one of the fleshy body to the world, and that is precisely the relation that I wish to stress.

Sketching realism and idealism in this manner thus allows me to frame my own position as sharing insights with both and yet as disagreeing with both. First, to repeat, I am a realist: stars exist independently of our personal conceptions or linguistic expressions about them. On the other hand, if human consciousness never existed in the unity and differentiation of its organic fleshy structure, then neither stars nor galaxies would exist. Thus, stars exist independently of whether you and I are thinking about them but not independently of matter's relation to our fleshy body.

My anthropocentric nonreductive materialism is thus a relational realism. Truth is relational, and to repeat, I accept matter's relation to our scientific theories and instruments. In this work, however, I want to counterbalance the contemporary emphasis on the scientific structure of things by putting forward the general claims of common sense as equally valid. My insistence that the insights of common sense are a true knowledge of the world summarizes a substantial part of the import of my work.

Another way of expressing my view of common sense is to note that my anthropocentric perspective is distinguished from humanisms and pragmatisms because my claims are ontological. By this I mean that a tree is a tree because it is a relation to the human body and its practices. I regard this claim to be no more mysterious than the claim that a hat arises from a relation to a head and yet can exist by itself hanging on a coatrack. Or, at least, the existence of trees and stars, wetness and color, are not much more mysterious than the existence of a hat: we do not make hats out of any kind of matter and we do not make stars out of primordial goo. It is a question of differentiating and highlighting matter through our thinking organs of feeling, seeing, hearing, smelling, tasting, internal reflections, as well as through our theories and instruments. Further, this claim of relational existence does not deny the possibility of novelty. On the contrary, novelty arises because matter is structured in relation to our fleshy, organic body in this way rather than in some other way.

I personally become mystified when someone, like Richard Rorty, tells me that a tree is a tree because of our pragmatic or linguistic ways of dealing with that part of matter. I am inclined to think that there is something hidden beneath the appearance of a tree that I should not ask about, namely the tree in itself. Pragmatists, of course, would reject the view that things have hidden natures; their view, however, frequently creates the condition for just such a wonder about things. For me, however, a tree is just the way this part of matter should be in relation to a thinking fleshy organism, and it is so essentially.

I thus regard my holding on to the notion of essences as demystifying. Essences revealed to common sense are modest and earthy things; they are just the way matter should be in relation to a fleshy organism. Indeed, demystification is an important part of my project. I refer not only to essences but also to archetypes, to mind, and to transcendence, and, in each case, I attempt to root these notions in our fleshy bodies and in the historical practices of our bodies.

The claims I make for common sense are strong, and yet they are modest. I do not offer any new categories of thought or any new ways of perceiving the world. My aim is to reveal how our everyday knowledge points to our bond to the world and to our worldmaking. This relation of matter to our fleshy consciousness does not, of itself, give us all that there is to know about the world. It does, however, reveal the tie between the features of our commonsense world and our body; for example, the relation between the woody and leafy character of a tree and the fact that our consciousness is in the form of flesh. I admit, of course, that all these bonds have various interpretations in different cultures. I will clarify this stance on common sense throughout, but particularly in my discussion of the "given" in chapter 2.

My critique of ahistorical thinking is also central to my perspective. It may come as a surprise that I consider linguistic pragmatism, such as represented by Rorty, as ahistorical. Rorty certainly does take history seriously, but this history is not one in which we have effectively wed structure to matter. It is not a history in which we have successfully crafted structure into meaning. Thus, even if we keep to language as a formal system, I view this system to have been constituted by our historical efforts in such a way that it connects language to things. I discuss this in chapter 7, where I focus on our crafting of the written word, and in appendix II, where I sketch a nominalism that points to our anthropocentric ties with matter.

On the other hand, an important aspect of linguistic pragmatism, such as advocated by Rorty, is on the mark, namely its movement toward relation. But language, particularly language as the spoken or written word, is too lean to provide support for trees and stars, or even for wetness. If we break with our notion of language as a formal system, if we consider the movements of the total fleshy human organic body and the history of its practices as language, then I would agree that language is the basis of our worldmaking. This healthy expansion of the use of *language,* however, would make my discourse too difficult to handle, or, at least, too difficult for me to handle, and it would seem to remove me further from the possibility of dialogue. Thus, I accept a more restricted use of *language* as spoken and written language, and with this usage, I distinguish my ontological relational realism from linguistic pragmatism, even as I sympathetically note our common relational perspectives on reality.

My emphasis on the concrete fleshy body brings me to reflect on the proper way to begin a philosophical investigation. Do we attempt to clarify our definitions, or do we first begin to understand our body and its relation to the world? Aristotle's thought is important because he introduces us to both perspectives. Nevertheless, to me he seems to have developed, at least in his major philosophical works, the wrong approach, namely the definitional one, and I discuss this in some detail in appendix I. Here I will simply note that a definitional approach to rationality, for example, would attempt to clarify its meaning and then look to see what things embodied that meaning—questioning whether computers might embody rationality. I see this definitional approach to consciousness as characteristic not only of reductionists but of linguistic pragmatists. An ontic approach, however, looks first to the things that are archetypes of embodied meanings, and then it raises the question of whether the quality found there can also be found in other beings. For example, I view the human fleshy organism to be the archetype of thought and all forms of reason, and I then extend the notion of reason to Nature and to the world of artifacts. In chapter 7, for example, I extend the notion of our fleshy thought to *mind*—something that exists in the world, transcending us, even though it was produced by us.

Throughout this work, I argue that there is a connection between a definitional approach to reality and an ahistorical approach. Thus, I suggest that, despite the appearances to the contrary, Descartes's cogito has its roots in Aristotle's definitional approach to our philosophical understanding of things. Still, I would note that Plato does not allow the distinction to arise in any substantive way, and, in this sense, we must credit Aristotle with an effort at naturalization.

Raising the point about the definitional versus the ontic may help forestall objections about my lack of discussion of thinkers who seem to be making claims that are similar to mine. Thus Donald Davidson's anomalous monism and his general affirmation of our commonsense views seem to approach my own nonreductive materialism and relational realism. However, even if I could abstract from Davidson's overly linguistic bent—a bent that, as far as I can see, is formally linguistic in the sense of privileging the spoken and written word—he separates himself radically from my own efforts by his definitional approach to rationality. He writes:

> The question is what animals are rational? Of course I do not intend to name names, even names of species or other groups. I shall not try to decide whether dolphins, apes, human embryos or politicians are rational, or even whether all that prevents computers from being rational is their genesis. My question is what makes an animal (or anything else, if one wants) rational?[2]

I thank Davidson for being so clear. My general point is that even though Davidson may, at times, be making claims that seem similar to mine, I think that there is a substantive difference in our views. For example, one can claim, as Davidson does, that "mind matters," because our discourse about mind cannot be reduced to the way we refer to the rest of the world. But I consider this to be a mere linguistic distinction that, for me, at least, mystifies rather than clarifies the nonreductive materiality of the fleshy human body in its anthropocentric relation to the world.[3]

I should also note why there is very little formal discussion of Edmund Husserl and none of Maurice Merleau-Ponty. I have enjoyed reading and teaching Merleau-Ponty's thought, and I have learned a great deal from him. But in the large anthropocentric context in which I am working, Merleau-Ponty's views on ambiguity and flesh are, for me, too mystifying. Sartre's clean anthropocentrism is more to my taste. Or perhaps I should simply note that for my purposes Sartre is more useful for the philosophical points I wish to make.[4]

Husserl's thought permeates this work, but again, for me, it is a thought that has already been altered by Sartre. Husserl must be credited for noting that essences are relational. Nevertheless, he undermined this very insight by reinstating essences as a relation to a transcendental ego, a relation that effectively made essences absolute, or, at least, absolute in relation to my anthropocentrism. Still, if we were to substitute the human fleshy body and its historical practices for the transcendental ego, we would be close to the relational realism I sketch here. (We would also be close to my anthropocentrism, if we substituted the unity of our fleshy organism and the differentiating power of its senses for the Kantian categories.) In Husserl's later thought, he attempts to reinstate the world of common sense by emphasizing what he calls the "lived-world." However, Husserl's context is anything but anthropocentric, and it is not relational in my sense.[5]

I am concerned with making a philosophical point, and the people I discuss are either longtime friends, like Aristotle, Aquinas, Sartre, Putnam, and Rorty, who have helped shape my thought, and with whom I am on familiar terms, or, like Patricia and Paul Churchland, they are chosen because they represent a kind of ahistorical and scientific thinking that I oppose but which I still use to shape my own anthropocentric perspective.

By focusing on the fleshy body and its practices, I find structures and meanings on the surfaces of things—in tutored flesh, in the qualities and relational natures of things, in the general way the world arranges itself about our fleshy body, and in the way we craft structure and meaning. Although the structures and meanings that I refer to are on the surfaces of things, I do not deny that we can form a project of discovering the interior nature of things, as we do in science. But this project has been adequately noted. It is the surface structures and meanings that have become mystified. As I indicate in chapters 6 and 7, surface structures and meanings have roots not only in the organic structure of the body, but in the long prehistory and history of the way our body makes matter immaterial and forges mind out of the stuff of the world.

PART ONE

The Body
and the World

Chapter 1

Matter   and
Pure   Enquiry

The introductory remarks framed my anthropocentric perspective: our knowledge of the world is one with our bond to things, and this bond is itself a worldmaking. This worldmaking is such that things exist independently of our conceptions and linguistic expressions about them, but not independently of their relation to the fact of our organic conscious existence. Thus, the world arises primarily from matter's relation to our fleshy organism and secondarily from matter's relation to our theories and instruments.

There is no way to prove this anthropocentric claim about the world, for there is no neutral position from which I can survey the world. Indeed, one of the points of this chapter is to establish that any quest for a seemingly neutral, bird's-eye perspective on things already finesses flesh from thought, and thus attempts to remake knowledge and reality to fit our so-called neutral thoughts.

Still, I must give some justification for my own ontological claim. I am tempted simply to ask the reader to be aware of the necessity of his or her organic and fleshy body. Reading this script presupposes the use of eyes, or fingers as in braille, and whereas it seems natural to pass through these fleshy and material constituents to something seemingly immaterial called *meanings,* the obvious fact of our fleshy eyes and fingers remain. No doubt our brain is also important. However, in this work I wish to challenge the brain-body dualism that I see replacing the old Cartesian mind-body dualism, and thus I emphasize the entire fleshy and organically differentiated body.

One way of indicating the significance of the way our bond to the world is through organs is to imagine what the world would be like if we did not have sight. The blind live in a world constituted by those of us who see. Suppose, however, that consciousness had emerged in such a way that its organic structure did not include vision. I claim that not even our wildest science fiction or thought experiments could sketch what such a world and such an awareness of the world would be like. The world in which we live is structured in relation to an organism for whom sight is an essential bond to matter. Reciprocally, the only consciousness that we know about is one in which sight is an essential aspect, for blindness is the privation of sight. And what is true of sight is true of the other sense organs, including the fleshy texture of the entire body. Regardless of so-called illusions or errors of perception, regardless of interpretations, regardless of how the entire weight of culture bears down on our sense impressions, the world, in its basic differentiation into things, is the way it is because our body is the way it is. And, regardless of whether our science might manufacture a nonfleshy consciousness, that production would be brought about by our fleshy organism and in imitation of it. Consequently, my ontological perspective on knowledge and consciousness regards sense organs not only as revealing the world but also as differentiating matter into a world. We have trees and stars because our body is fleshy and organic in just the way it is. Once given in relation to our body, "natural" things are there to be discovered and investigated. These claims give the general direction of my thought as developed in this work.

It is difficult to highlight the importance of our fleshy bodies because, when they function well, we pass through them in use: seeing, we appear not to have eyes but to be in contact with the world as visible. Still, we do have eyes, and, to repeat, as consciousness takes the form of sight, things are not only revealed to be visible but they are made visible. If we add the relation of matter to our entire body, we have the universe as it is for the most part given to us by our common sense.

It is thus important for me to note that I take the so-called "hard" question of consciousness that is commented upon in much contemporary literature to refer to a secondary explication of our bond to the world. I am only minimally interested in reflecting upon the extent to which our consciousness is unique because it is a self-awareness. That is, I am only incidentally interested in subjectivity. I do not deny the uniqueness of subjectivity; for the most part, I take it for granted. For example, in explaining "our experience of red," I am not very interested in whether the "experience" may be unique but, rather, to what extent "red" exists in the world as a unique quality, precisely because of its relation to sight. Some scientific materialists do attempt to go all the way and reduce both red and the experience of red to quantitative relations, and I will consider some of their views in the next chapter. Nevertheless, thinkers who normally tend to reduce quality to quantity are usually willing to grant some irreducibility to consciousness. I consider this position not only insufficient but inconsistent. My implied and, to some extent, explicit view is that consciousness can be both material and irreducible to quantity only if qualities such as red exist in the world irreducible to quantity. *Indeed, if red can exist in the world as a quality irreducible to quantity, then consciousness is itself a quality irreducible to quantity.* The general reason for the connection is my relational realism: if red is a unique quality in the world because of its relation to consciousness as sight, then consciousness as sight has itself a unique quality irreducible to quantity. From this aspect, my relational realism is one with my nonreductive materialism. Of course, I must add that I agree that, in relation to our scientific theories and instruments, both red and the consciousness of red can be perfectly explained quantitatively. To repeat, I am mainly interested in asserting the relative but valid claims of our commonsense experience and the world it reveals.

My goal then is to show that our consciousness *of* the world is first and foremost our bond *with* the world. I thus place the human fleshy body in the center of the universe, and I must clarify why this anthropocentrism is not an anthropomorphism. The task is difficult because, having displaced the Earth from the center of the universe, we conceived this feat to be the outcome of our ability to acquire pure knowledge about things. To reinsert the human body within the center of things now seems to be a return to a Ptolemaic, anthropomorphic view of the world. I find it thus necessary to reexamine some of the broad features of our conception of ourselves as minds capable of pure knowledge. Specifically, how did we get the notion that we had a spiritual mind or a body that was like a complicated machine? How did we go about divorcing flesh from knowledge? This effort of unveiling the roots of our view of ourselves as being capable of pure knowledge fitted more for angels than humans is philosophy as demystification, and if it is not my only effort, it is one of my main tasks.

I want to begin by examining some of the origins of our so-called pure knowledge. I am concerned with our belief that knowledge about things should be aimed at grasping how they would be even if we never existed. Although I start with some general reflections on Plato and Aristotle, my main point is to introduce René Descartes as the father of our present scientific thinking about thought and matter. My formal discussion of Aristotle is scattered throughout the later chapters, but it is centered in appendix I.

The direction of my critique of Descartes is to note that he eliminated flesh from thought by abstracting from the long historical practices that forged language and numbers into webs of meanings. He thus began his reflection by encountering a world of meanings that seemed to exist a priori, and he regarded his main task to be one of sifting through these notions. For me, then, the condition for Descartes's dualism is already given in his ahistorical outlook on knowledge.

MOLDING THE KNOWER TO THE KNOWN

Historically, philosophers like Plato, Aristotle, and Descartes have assumed that something like an absolute conception of reality must be possible, a conception in which things are known as they are in themselves, independently from any relation to human existence. One way of understanding this effort is to view it as an attempt to mold both the knower and reality in a way that makes pure knowledge possible. Thus, for Plato, the seeker after truth could not be the ugly flesh and bones that was the appearance of Socrates, and, reciprocally, the truth could not be found in the world in which that body lived. The true nature of things exists, rather, in an immaterial realm, and the real knower is itself immaterial: Socrates *is* a soul, imprisoned in a body. Plato, at least in the traditional interpretation that has come down to us and influenced our Western thinking about ourselves, easily fits the knower to the known by making them both immaterial. Thus, Plato can easily ground our universal notions about mathematics and justice both by placing their objects in another world and by making the knower a true resident of an immaterial realm that exists apart from matter.

If Plato's inclination to put truth in an immaterial realm arose from the primacy he attributed to mathematics, in which universal truths appeared to have no human source, Aristotle's naturalistic bent, his interest in physics and biology, can be said to have motivated his search for a truth that existed in this material world. Aristotle then had the task of molding the knower in such a way that it could obtain its universal knowledge from this world. Since we are able to know that an elm is a tree, or in more contemporary language, since we can classify tokens that are different specimens of trees into the general type "tree," Aristotle begins his philosophical thinking with the belief that both the token and the type must, in some sense, be real.

Thus the naturalistic tendencies of Aristotle inclined him to insist that only individuals exist as entities; there is no quasi-angelic twoness or pure justice existing in some other world. Rather, we obtain our knowledge of numbers and justice by reflecting upon both material things and concrete acts of justice. Still, the shade of his teacher remained. Aristotle followed Plato to the extent that he felt compelled to look for an a priori grounding for our universal notions. There had to be some connection between the individual tree that could be felled by lightning and the universal claim that all trees are plants. In some sense, *this* tree must be all trees. The qualification *in some sense* led to Aristotle's insistence that something like Platonic Forms exist, but only in matter, as coprinciples of material things. Thus, each material thing was to be seen as a composite of matter and form, somewhat the way a shaped piece of wax is a composite of the wax and the shape.

Aristotle molded the knower to the known in such a way that our universal notions came from matter and yet were not completely reducible to matter, or at least not reducible to the matter of observable things. Aristotle accepted from Plato that some of our universal notions were not totally the result of our historical activities, but were a priori, in the sense that our abstractive powers got in touch with the eternally true natures of things. Predications of the type "Socrates is a rational animal" and "Two and two are four" are, for Aristotle, true, because we abstract fourness from the way two sets of two things form one quantitative arrangement, and because we can dig below Socrates's appearances and get to know the special way his matter embodies his soul.

If Aristotle was not able to note the historical formation of our ideas, he did recognize that universality *as such* is a human product; that is, precisely as *tree* and *four* are classes containing individual examples of things, they exist only in the human intellect. This claim, however, leaves open the question of how to explain the workability of our judgements of the type "This tree is a plant," since the subject is singular and the predicate is universal. More generally, the Aristotelian notion of abstraction requires us to explain just how our universal notions that exist formally only in the intellect conform to the singular things that exist in the material world.

The Aristotelian answer is "I think," most clearly seen in Thomas Aquinas's explicit formulation. The correspondence between *this tree* and *a plant* is grounded, for Aquinas, in the indifference of the nature of *plant* to having either a singular or universal mode of existence. The predication "This tree is a plant" expresses a truth, even though the subject, "this tree" is individual and the predicate "plant" is universal: the strain is taken off the "is" because the identity carried by "is" refers to the nature of plant as such, a nature indifferently singular or universal.[1]

There is, however, a price to pay for molding our thought so that it grasps the essence of things as they are in themselves. It is a price that I suspect Aristotle would be willing to pay, for it provides the proper foundation for his notion of abstraction. To see what is at stake, we simply have to ask what great fortune allows us to believe that the nature that exists as individual in matter is the same that our mind abstracts.

Aquinas forces us to face honestly the foundation of the correspondence theory of truth. The general Aristotelian-Thomistic answer to the workability of knowledge is that knowers and natures are part of a grand totality, Nature. In Nature, we find a hierarchy from minerals to plants to animals and then to animals that can think. The forms in each, while individual, are also less "material" as we go up the ladder. The human form, or soul, is so immaterial that it can be united with other forms, can *be* other forms, without the soul losing its identity as *this* form in *this* matter. Abstraction is thus a natural process like digestion, and like digestion, knowledge is guided by the same laws that keep all things working harmoniously together.

If we press further and ask why Nature should work in such harmony with the human intellect, Aristotle has recourse to separated substances, which guide, however loosely, the working of the material universe. And if we are in a stubborn mood and continue asking what directs the separated substances, Aristotle gives us the Prime Mover, Who, by being actuality rather than merely possessing it, supposedly answers an infinite series of whys.

Although Aristotle seemed to hedge on the spiritual makeup of the human soul and the personhood of the Prime Mover, this doubt gave Aquinas enough logical space in which to describe the form of Socrates as so immaterial that it was spiritual, immortal, and ripe for baptism, and the Prime Mover as the caring God. Nevertheless, Aquinas remains an Aristotelian to the extent that he insists that the form of Socrates is not Socrates. For a Platonist like Augustine, a good Christian prays for Socrates that he might arrive in heaven; but for an Aristotelian, like Aquinas, one prays for the soul of Socrates and looks for the resurrection of the body in order for Socrates to live whole again as an individual.

Thus, for Aquinas, the body is essential to the human reality, and yet, the soul can exist apart from the human body. The knower is molded to the known in a way that neatly fits Christian beliefs: the human knower is half spiritual, and that half is the more important half, for it is the seat of our abstractive faculties; correspondingly, truth is half spiritual, for the ultimate bedrock of all true judgments is found in the Mind of God. Thus, logical truth, the truth of judgments, is founded on ontological truth, the truth of a thing having a nature, and this, in turn, is founded on the Idea of that nature in God's Mind, and from this perspective, one has to ask, "How far have we really progressed from Plato?"

When Descartes attempts both to weave his way through this hierarchy of forms provided by his Jesuit scholastic training and to fit his thought within the context of the rising Copernican and Galilean science, he sees the need to mold the knower and the known in a simpler way. Descartes thus returns to Plato's vision of the apparently obvious truths of mathematics.

> Above all I delighted in mathematics, because of the certainty and self-evidence of its reasonings. But I did not yet notice its real use; and since I thought it was of service only in the mechanical arts, I was surprised that nothing more exalted had been built upon such firm and solid foundations. . . . Reflecting too, that of all those who have hitherto sought after truth in the sciences, mathematicians alone have been able to find any demonstrations—that is to say, certain and evident reasonings—I had no doubt that I should begin with the very things that they studied.[2]

If knowledge is to be possible, that is, if it is to be truthful, then it must be like the most indubitable of all knowledge, mathematics. Descartes's absolute conception of reality demands acquiring the kind of certitude that one has when it is known that a triangle is a three-sided plane figure; that is, the predicate, "three-sided plane figure," must be seen clearly and distinctly to contain the subject, "triangle." But what must knowledge and reality be like if such pure enquiry is to be possible for humans? We must be capable of having clear and distinct ideas, and reality must be able to mesh with such ideas; it certainly seems that we do have clear and distinct ideas. The idea of a triangle as a three-sided plane figure seems both clear—we know exactly what it means—and distinct—we know how it is distinguished from other ideas; for example, a triangle is not a square.

Or is this judgment about a triangle all that clear? What exactly do we mean when we speak about a plane figure? The surface of a three-dimensional object is not a plane as such. Mathematics may refer to a three-dimensional object as being composed of an infinite number of planes, but as far as clarity goes, that seems to make matters worse. And, if we forgo these kinds of objections to the status of mathematical objects, we can still question to what extent this knowledge is natural rather than the result of a historical process of refinement that led to the formation of geometry. I think that this point is crucial and, wherever appropriate, I shall be making it throughout this work, but particularly in the last chapter, where I consider the nature of writing and hint that a similar situation exists in regard to the natural numbers. Here I will anticipate by noting that the mathematical zero (0) has about the same place in the furniture of the universe as an electric lightbulb. The electric lightbulb exists as the end of a long search for separating light from heat; and zero, precisely as the emptiness that moves arithmetic operations along by allowing us to give positional value to numbers, is the inventive termination of the long search to simplify these operations.[3] In general my claim is that what appears to be the spontaneous agreement among mathematicians about a mathematical proof is an historical achievement, a victory won in the name of abstraction.

Thus I claim that the initial delusion sets in when Descartes thinks he is being critical about historical influences on his thought. In fact, he is bracketing from his reflections the entire realm of the historical formation of our notions. He thinks critically about what he considers "accepted opinions," but not about the formation of clear and distinct notions.

> In order to philosophize seriously and search out the truth about all things that are capable of being known, we must first of all lay aside all our preconceived opinions, or at least we must take the greatest care not to put our trust in any of the opinions accepted by us in the past until we have first scrutinized them afresh and confirmed their truth.[4]

But this scrutiny is from afar, or at least Descartes wants us to believe that it arises from a pure mind thinking about its own ideas. When

Descartes looks into his mind, he finds there the realm of mathematics. All the abstractive refinement of mathematics is simply there, waiting to be recognized. He thinks that all that he has to do is to put aside "accepted opinion," and that ideas will then shine forth in their clarity as the sun in a clear sky. And Descartes wonders, as indeed he should, what kind of being could know, by the natural power of its own individual intellect, the high degree of universality and clarity that is evidenced in mathematical truths.

Descartes is right to conclude that no being whose knowledge was essentially acquired through flesh and blood could recognize and formulate mathematical truths by itself, *a novo*. This is the sort of work suited for an angel. Descartes's dualism, his split of the human reality into a pure mind and a mechanical body, is the result of a mistaken belief about inquiry as an ahistorical phenomenon. Descartes pays no heed to the great effort it took Socrates to get his disciples to suspect that spirit might be more than a shade, and he also does not see the discovery of the alphabet as an historical achievement. Or, to be more exact, he no doubt recognizes them, but like most contemporary mathematicians, Descartes thinks that these vagabond efforts are incidental to mathematical truth, whereas they are constitutive of it, and, indeed, of all truth. When Descartes passes through all these historical efforts he is, of course, amazed by the power of his own mind.

> But what am I to say about this mind, or about myself? (So far, remember, I am not admitting that there is anything else in me except a mind.) What, I ask, is this "I" which seems to perceive the wax so distinctly? Surely my awareness of my own self is not merely much truer and more certain than my awareness of the wax, but also much more distinct and evident.[5]

In the *Meditations*, Descartes invites us to seat ourselves comfortably in a dark, quiet room and, paying attention to our thoughts, realize that we could be still thinking, even if we had no body. Putting aside for the present the need to posture our body so that we are not very aware of it, one suspects that an ancient Egyptian, so positioned in comfort, would find in his reflections the anguish of a shade that fears to lose itself if the body is not embalmed for eternity. The *I* that Descartes finds in his thoughts is already a cultured *I*, an *I* loaded with all the meaning of a Greco-Roman-Judaic-Christian culture. About that *I*, one can indeed wonder if *it* needs a body.

Having made the choice to ignore the history of the formation of language and thought, Descartes thinks he knows his own mind more clearly than he knows the existence of his body. But, if he is not to flout common sense completely, he must now offer us proof that his and other bodies exist. He has to give us reasons for the existence of bodies; he must offer us explanations of the meaning of qualities, and these can exist only if they conform to the reasons why they should exist. Descartes wants us to believe that the existence of bodies awaits the outcome of a logical duel.

> I see that without any effort I have now finally got back to where
> I wanted. I now know that even bodies are not strictly perceived
> by the sense or the faculty of imagination but by the intellect
> alone, and that this perception derives not from their being
> touched or seen but from being understood; and in view of this
> I know plainly that I can achieve an easier and more evident per-
> ception of my own mind than of anything else.[6]

Descartes has now placed himself in the strange position of needing to prove that what his senses clearly perceive to exist does in fact exist. This table which looks solid, and which seems to be of a mahogany-colored wood and which feels like wood, and sounds like wood, may, in principle, not be what it seems to be. Descartes has to first turn to his idea of body, his idea of color, his idea of hardness to see whether they are clear and distinct, and thus worthy to represent reality.

The path from the mind to matter is even more devious than simply going from clear and distinct ideas to the objects of these notions. Descartes has to resort to God to guarantee that his clear and distinct perceptions reflect the things perceived. We feel the table and then reason as follows: this solid object clearly seems to exist, and since a good and wise

God would not create faculties that could go astray even when they focused on clear objects, therefore the table exists.

The connection between our mind and matter is, for Descartes, accomplished through logic with the guarantee of God, but not even God can make the *real* hardness of the table seem more dense to the sense of touch than an *apparent* hardness might seem. The logical conviction that the table exists does not make it feel any more material than it would feel if it were merely a false idea about the world. No wonder Bishop Berkeley followed this logic with the invitation to just keep the appearance and forget the useless object which is supposed to correspond to it. This line of reasoning is interesting to reflect upon because I will claim in the next chapter that remnants of it are preserved by reductionists. Thus, D. M. Armstrong claims that causality connects us to the world. But if God cannot make a seeming solidity feel any more solid than a real solidity, then neither can a causal relation.

Descartes thus bypasses Aristotle's naturalistic efforts and breathes new life into Plato's shade, resurrecting a dualistic view of the knower and the known. Now, however, the division is even sharper. A pure spiritual mind knows its ideas and is connected to other minds and to the material world by a proper chain of reasonings about both. In particular, our reasoning about the world tells us that qualities exist only in our spiritual mind, and that the world is an arrangement of pure quantity and solidity. What appears to be a living body of flesh and blood is a complex machine made by God, and the soul guides the movements of this body by working through the pineal gland to produce what we call sensations.

Descartes has thus accomplished what today is called a complete reduction of qualitites to quantity, and the reduction is one of identity: apart from our subjective interpretation, heat is *only* moving particles. What we feel to be heat is in fact a mental interpretation of fast moving particles as they interact with our mechanical body. Thus, the very nature of explanation changes: the explanation of the quality perceived cannot be in terms of the quality itself. Explanations must fit the realm of what can be explained, and this realm is that of what can be put in clear propositional form. Indeed, Descartes is explicit about what he means by explanation:

> If you find it strange that in explaining these elements I do not
> use the qualities called "heat," "cold," "moisture" and "dryness"—
> as the philosophers do—I shall say to you that these qualities
> themselves seem to me to need explanation.[7]

In fairness to Descartes, I think that Aristotle and Aquinas were mistaken in their attempt to mold a hierarchy of knowers in which the human knower was simply rather high up on the ladder, but not on top. Nevertheless, their transcendent view of things enabled them to accept that qualities, such as heat, cold, color, and sound, as well as the textures and gradations of things are, for the most part, the way they appear to be. They regarded the knower to be confronted with certain facts or givens, and thus sound was sound, whatever else one might say about it.

What is Descartes doing to qualities when he demands that they be explained in clear and distinct ideas? The issue is complex. First, there is nothing wrong with wanting to understand the world conceptually and through propositional claims about it. Second, our perceptions are indeed laden with cultural interpretations. Still, there is a jump from these general claims about knowledge to the demand that qualities, such as heat and color, need philosophical explanations of the type provided by Descartes. These qualities can be given the kind of explanation that Descartes is searching for, the kind that packages them together with quantity and mathematics. However, I see this as historically constituted and a relative perspective on knowledge and the world: in relation to our historically constituted theories and crafted instruments, the knower is mechanical and the world is pure quantity.

Descartes believes that his dualism is the result of a neutral, unbiased stance on the nature of thought. He sees himself to have proved that the mind is a spirit and the body a machine. When Thomas Hobbes insists that thought should be looked upon in a more material way, Descartes responds that his own view is the result of a proof that originates from a neutral conception of thought, one that supposedly transcends matter and spirit.[8] But again, something has been palmed by Descartes, namely the entire prehistory and history of our efforts to forge the basic notions not only of mathematics but of common sense as well. However, I wish to approach this claim a little more slowly.

THE DEMAND FOR CERTAINTY

Both Richard Rorty and Bernard Williams remark that Descartes's dualism results from his demand for certainty and truth.[9] Williams puts the emphasis on Descartes's formal doubt: if the project of pure enquiry is to succeed, we must have knowledge that can withstand any attempt to doubt that it might not be true. Rorty puts the emphasis on the way the demand for indubitable knowledge leads to assimilating states such as pain into the mental area usually reserved for abstract thoughts. But my anthropocentric point attacks Descartes's project at a different level than either Williams's or Rorty's observations, without contradicting them.

In my view, the foundation for Descartes's dualism begins much earlier than the demand for incorrigible knowledge as formally expressed by Descartes. To understand what I am getting at, it is important to see that too much is handed over to Descartes when Rorty says:

> Granted that the "argument from doubt" has no merit, I think that nevertheless it is one of those cases of "finding bad reasons for what we believe on instinct" which serves as a clue to the instincts which actually do the convincing. The hunch in question here was, I think, that the indubitably known mathematical truths (once their proofs had been worked through so as to make them clearly and distinctly perceived with a sort of "phenomenal" vividness and nondiscursiveness) and the indubitable momentary states of consciousness had something in common—something permitting them to be packaged inside of one substance.[10]

Rorty is probably right in his astute observation that, by giving phenomena such as pain the mark of being indubitable, Descartes helps invent the modern notion of consciousness. But beyond this, it is important to see how much we grant Descartes when we hand over to him the clarity and certainty of mathematical truths. To repeat, the canonical formulations of mathematical proofs have a long history, and it is not clear exactly what they mean apart from that history. Further, the universal acceptance of mathematical discoveries, such as Descartes's own coupling of geometry and arithmetic, implies a worldwide community of mathematicians who have tacitly agreed that, in certain fundamental areas, questions about the foundation of mathematics should be relegated to the periphery of the discipline.

However, there is no a priori reason why this should be so. It takes no great imagination to imagine a world in which the demand for clarity and certainty in mathematics implied, for example, that one had to know exactly what it meant to call something a natural number before proceeding to expand the number system. In our imaginary world, one might be able to calculate with irrational and imaginary numbers, but such calculation would not be seen to be of any great moment nor would it be accepted as worthy of the name *mathematics*. Indeed, I suspect that pure mathematicians today feel exactly like this about their subject matter. The objective status not only of nondenumerable numbers, but even of natural numbers is still in question, as is, in fact, the very notion of a class. For example, not every mathematician would accept Quine's claim that objectivity demands that we "posit" the existence of mathematical classes as well as the existence of trees and stars. One could thus very easily imagine a world in which the true mathematician, as opposed to the mere technician, could not logically proceed even to the real number system, since the mathematical status of the so-called natural numbers remains questionable.

The foundation of the Cartesian dualism is already set in Descartes's ahistorical outlook on language and mathematical symbols: the entire corpus of achieved mathematical truths and other views on the world are all present for Descartes to contemplate, and he thinks that his only task is to sift through them and decide which are clear and distinct. Descartes is not aware of the efforts needed to bring about even the possibility of thinking abstractly, for example, of thinking about justice as something that concretely applies to everyone equally, or of thinking about numbers as abstract entities. My critique of Descartes is thus different from Williams's own observation that the "I think" could, and perhaps should be, "We think."

> In these last considerations, I have been taking the "first person" to mean the first person *singular*. Yet earlier I spoke of "our" representations; why should *"we,"* even under Pure Enquiry, contract to "I"? Might not Pure Enquiry be a collective enterprise? For Descartes, certainly, it is not. . . . When we turn from knowledge to the activity central to Pure Enquiry of self-criticism, it is very obvious that *our* self-criticism may essentially involve many selves. That fact in itself is enough to cast some doubt on the program for the theory of knowledge which ties it to the first person singular.[11]

Williams is right in his claim that pure enquiry is a collective enterprise, although for me, and not for Williams, this collective effort constitutes pure enquiry as one among many philosophically valid perspectives on reality. Thus, in chapter 6, "The Transcendence of Mind," and in chapter 7, "The Written Word," I will make a case that the disinterested view of the world is not so much an error as a particular result of our efforts at molding reason.

Nevertheless, here I focus on these collective efforts from a different perspective. I wish to draw attention to the degree to which even our most private thoughts and reflections carry the weight of history, of clarifications achieved and of distinctions lost, of hierarchies built and dismantled, of elitisms and repressions—in effect, of an entire view of what it means to be human, and, in particular, what it means to be a private human with the kind of thoughts that Descartes thought he was born with. Our language, even the language in which we speak our most private thoughts to ourselves, has been molded, for better or worse, by our history of victories and defeats. (Of whose victories and of whose defeats is another question.)

Williams thus concedes too much to Descartes. Williams acknowledges that the notion of incorrigibility is not necessary for true knowledge, but he still wants to keep the notion of pure enquiry:

> Knowledge does have a problematical character, and does have something in it which offers a standing invitation to skepticism.

Attempts to uncover this just in terms of the relations between the concepts knowledge, doubt, certainty and so forth seem nevertheless to fail. . . . The source of the invitation lies deeper. What exactly it is, is a difficult question; I will try to sketch an approach which seems to me to lead in the direction of the source. This starts from a very basic thought, that if knowledge is what it claims to be, then it is knowledge of a reality which exists independently of that knowledge, and indeed . . . independently of any thought or experience. Knowledge is of what is there *anyway*.[12]

If true knowledge is to be possible, then, for Williams, we need to know the way the world really is apart from any human intervention. It is this view of knowledge and reality more than anything else that has led philosophers to believe that knowledge cannot be the function of the workings of the flesh and blood body as such, for how can a being essentially constituted of flesh and blood have an a priori bird's-eye view of reality? To repeat, in the last two chapters I will make a case that we have, in fact, constituted a kind of knowledge that is "pure enquiry." However, this is another matter; it is then a question of the results of our efforts, and its meaning as "knowledge" is thus quite different from Williams's a priori ability to know the world as it would be apart from any relation to us. Indeed, if the heuristic formula that requires compatibility between knower and known is true, as I think it obviously is, then the only kind of objectivity and truth suitable to a fleshy conscious organism is one that constantly shows the evidence of flesh and bones, even where, as in mathematics, it seems to be hidden.

NEUTRAL THINKING

Behind both Descartes's and Williams's belief that we have an a priori capacity for pure enquiry is the conviction that we can take a neutral, bird's-eye stance on knowledge itself, a stance that is apart from our fleshy nature. At least Descartes is explicit about the aspect of pure enquiry focusing on thought itself: the query about the nature of knowledge is to be solved by adopting a conception of thinking, apparently neutral to matter or spirit, which then becomes the springboard for proving that only a spiritual knower could make knowledge possible.

Present-day materialists, such as Armstrong (I consider Armstrong to be a particularly clear and honest example of such thinking), follow in Descartes's path to the extent that they also claim to be beginning their investigations with a neutral conception of what knowledge and the world are like. In principle, the knower, for Armstrong, could be a spiritual substance; it is a contingent fact that the knower is a complex of neurons. And because the knower is a complex of neurons, the world is appropriately a complex of moving particles and waves. We are essentially back to Descartes, and once again it is important to see exactly what is involved in claiming to begin one's philosophical investigations with a so-called neutral, unbiased, or ahistorical conception of thought:

> Inside the context of our theory, somebody who asserts the logical possibility of a disembodied mind is only asserting that mental states (which are states of the person apt for the bringing about of certain sorts of behavior) are not really states of the brain, but are states of a spiritual substance capable of existence after the dissolution of the body. And since we have allowed the logical possibility of nonphysical substance, and since for Central-state Materialism it is a mere contingent fact that the mind is the brain, there is no bar to such a logical possibility. It is incompatible with the truth of Central-state Materialism, but that theory is, at best, only contingently true.[13]

But is such a starting point really neutral? What does it mean to claim that it is contingently true that consciousness is material? That a consciousness exists may be contingent, but is it contingent that it exists as matter? If a mental state could, in the abstract, be either material or spiritual, does not that possibility shape beforehand the nature of consciousness? I think that it does. A neutral conception of thinking finesses the fleshy human body as well as the history of its practices in forging reason to be reasonable. Such a stance shapes the condition for the possibility of consciousness being either a pure mind or a mechanistic system, and it shapes the world accordingly.

Further, a neutral conception of knowledge is not an ahistorical notion. At the very least, we need at hand the notions of spirit and matter, and these notions are an historical achievement. To the extent that Armstrong gives the impression that these notions have always been there, waiting to be used, he passes through the same history of human efforts as does Descartes. I think it thus no surprise that his Central-state Materialism seems as removed from human history as Descartes's claim that mind is spiritual. If we might be spirits or pure machines, then we can always find the logic to sway us one way or the other. In either case we have wrenched thinking from the flesh and bones of the body, and once that has been done, it is impossible to heal the breach.

FUNCTIONALISM

Functionalism is a slight variation on the attempt to think about thought from a neutral perspective. Functionalists, such as the early Putnam, do not attempt to extend the notion of thought to spirit, but rather limit it to matter. Thought has to be enmattered, to use an Aristotelian term, but it might be enmattered in flesh and blood or in the mechanism of a computer. Thus Martha Craven Nussbaum finds precedence for functionalist thinking in Aristotle's thought. In her study of Aristotle's *On the Motion of Animals*, she has Aristotle, in an imaginary conversation, respond to Democritus:

> But living beings are necessarily enmattered. Although the account of what it is to be a man or animal should not make the mistake of supposing that the flesh and bones in which such creatures always, in our experience, turn up are necessary parts of their essence (for if we found tomorrow a creature made of string and wood who performed all the functions mentioned in our formal account of what it is to be human, we could not rule him out simply on material grounds), it should at the same time recognize that *some* sort of matter is necessary for the performance of these functions. . . .[14]

On the one hand, Nussbaum turns our attention to the biological works of Aristotle in order to show us his concern with the individuality of things. On the other hand, we are supposed to regard these biological specimens functionally, that is, not precisely as they are—beings of flesh and bone. But, if a horse is not of flesh and bone, what is it? Are hunger and pain incidental to being a horse? Still, if one is looking for it, one can find a basis for Nussbaum's functional interpretation of Aristotle in a much quoted text from the *Metaphysics*:

> In the case of things which are found to occur in specifically different materials, as a circle may exist in bronze or stone or wood, it seems plain that these, the bronze or the stone, are no part of the essence of the circle, since it is found apart from them. Of things which are *not* seen to exist apart, there is no reason why the same may not be true, e.g. even if all circles that had ever been seen were of bronze (for none the less the bronze would be no part of the form); but it is hard to effect this severance in thought. E.g. the form of man is always found in flesh and bones and parts of this kind; are these then also parts of the form and the formula? No, they are matter; but because man is not found in other matters we are unable to affect the severance.[15]

In appendix I, I will show that there are other ways of glossing this text, but here I simply note that Nussbaum pays a high price to update Aristotle and make him palatable to aspects of contemporary thought. For if it is true that thought merely requires some kind of matter in which to exist, then how far has Aristotle departed from Plato's notion that the human soul merely participates in matter, and how far are we from Descartes's notion that thought is a spiritual substance that interacts with the pineal gland of a mechanical body? For this minimal contact, the soul can just as well be a pure mind, and we have thus jettisoned the entire Aristotelian belief that things are a composite of matter and form.[16]

Functionalist thought becomes possible because the universe has already been reduced by the scientist to a mechanistic complex of matter and motion. We start by seeing the relation of color to scientific equipment to be more objective than its relation to the human eye, and we conclude by understanding the essence of color to be the way it relates quantitatively to our scientific theories. We then mold the knower to fit this essence, and it is not surprising that it becomes as mechanistic or as spiritualistic as its object.

A neutral conception of thought has a place in the world that is not too dissimilar to artifacts: if both thought and the world appear to be less material than flesh and blood, this itself is an achievement of our own collective efforts at making matter to be immaterial. Compared to a roaring fire, an electric lightbulb is an immaterial source of light; it is the present-day culmination of a long search to separate light from heat, a search that took us from torch to candle to gas lamp to the electric lightbulb itself. Because of these historical efforts, the ideal of "pure light" without heat now exists in the world. The ideal is not evaporated into our subjective or our historical interpretations because it arose from our socially placed efforts. In a similar way, my goal is to show that immateriality, whether in obvious artifacts, such as chairs, or in less obvious artifacts, such as numbers and just acts, are no less objective for being relational.[17] We have made our thinking thoughts to be immaterial, and we have constituted a world to which these thoughts can correspond.

Moving Matter,
Thinking Thoughts

The implication in the preceding chapter amounts to the claim that, if we give our interior states a privileged position in regard to certitude, then the path is laid for leading us into either a mechanistic materialism or a dualism of matter and spirit. However, if we reestablish, within the center of our relation to the world, the total human thinking organism in its fleshy and organic constitution, then our bond to the qualitatively rich world is recognized to be as genuine as it appears to be. This second chapter thus continues my efforts to lay the ground for my relational realism that claims that the world arises from matter's relation to our organically differentiated body. I do not deny the validity of matter's relation to our scientific theories and instruments or to our historical linguistic practices. However, to repeat, these claims have been amply made by others, and my purpose is, rather, to put forward the claims of common sense as equally justifiable.

The basis for my relational realism is that I claim that our senses, working as aspects of our total fleshy conscious body, not only reveal the world but make the world. The aim of the following chapters is thus to indicate the reasonableness of the view that the qualities and things that constitute our commonsense world are, for the most part, the way they are because our body is the way it is. On this level, our relation to the world is both a bond to it and a nonconceptual knowledge of it: seeing things to be colored is a revealing of matter as visible through colors, and this revealing is a knowledge of the world as visible through colors.

In this and the following chapter I will prepare the way for this anthropocentric and relational realism by showing in some detail how the privileging of our interior states is tied to the ambiguous search for hidden qualities that effectively turn out to be the scientific structure of things. In particular, I want to develop more fully the tie between the privileging of our interior states and adopting a neutral, bird's-eye perspective on reality, a perspective from which we apparently look down on our own thinking thoughts and the world's moving matter from an unbiased vantage point. In Richard Rorty's terms, the ideal of knowing thereby comes to "mirror nature." To be more precise, given a neutral perspective on things, knowing becomes the correspondence of thought to reality, where reality is the way things are independent of our existence. After this critique of the correspondence theory of truth, I will gradually build a case in the following chapters for an anthropocentric, nonreductive materialism, one that both distinguishes flesh from the rest of the world and also shows how the world arises in relation to our fleshy body.

While the distinction between the flesh of the body and the wood of a tree, for example, is itself a type of dualism, I claim that it is philosophically harmless insofar as it is a dualism that remains materialistic and basically returns to us our commonsense world and clarifies our relation to it. More specifically, the distinction between flesh and the rest of the world's matter does not encounter the embarrassments of traditional dualisms that arise from a transcendent perspective on the body and the world. If I have a dualism, it is one that arises from the perspective of the fleshy body itself. Further, as organisms, we are already part of the world, and the issues that concern most dualisms, such as how to connect the two parts of reality or how to move from thought to thing, do not arise. Further, although this anthropocentric and nonreductive materialism may seem to be

Cartesian insofar as it begins from the individual, the substitution of the conscious fleshy body for a thought that first turns upon itself as well as my emphasis on the effectiveness of the way we collectively craft matter into meanings, will, as I proceed, initiate a radical rupture from Descartes's philosophy.

MATERIALISM AND MEANING

Behind the contemporary materialists' picture of the world is the claim that, in principle, one must be able to reduce both qualities and our experiences of qualities to quantitative relations. Our scientific materialist tells us to look upon the eye as a camera: just as light enters through a lens and interacts with the chemicals in a film, so too light passes through the mechanism of the eye and sparks certain fibers of the brain. But where is color as color, where is the shade of the red rose that I perceive? The question is equally ambiguous if we ask our materialist the same question about the camera and its so-called color prints. Is the color in the developed film? No! we will be told. The color print is an arrangement of quantities, waves, or quanta absorbed or emitted here and there. The color print, apart from its interpretation, is black and white. But how does one interpret a black and white print as colored? We are, of course, offered explanations of this appearance, some of which I will examine in this chapter.

The same question arises when one tries to look for color in the eye and the brain. Is the color of a rose in the brain? Is the quality red, red? If she is to avoid being a dualist, the materialist, such as Patricia Churchland, must answer "No!" This red of this rose, precisely as it is the color I experience to be in the world, is not in the brain any more than it is in the world. The redness of the rose, as it is in the brain, is, again, colorless matter in motion. The brain too, she would say, is itself a quantitative network of fibers, each of which lacks color or any other quality.

Descartes, on the other hand, houses our perceptions of qualities in the mind. Red is an idea about things, a foggy idea that does not correspond to reality, but red nevertheless exists in the mind. Many contemporary materialists—indeed, the ones that I regard as the most consistent—

cannot give qualities even this tenuous existence. Rather, our scientific understanding of the world attempts to educate us to understand first that the red we perceive to be in the world is only a wave length or a quanta of energy, and second that the perception of red itself is reducible to a neurological process. We are actually supposed to perceive the interiorized quality, or what is frequently termed "quale," as it is explained by scientific theory. We are to educate our sense of sight so that the seeing of color itself becomes the experience of an arrangement of colorless matter interacting with our brain, which we also then perceive to be complexities of colorless matter. At least this is one extreme but consistent view.

This contemporary slant on materialism that I will soon examine is not, strictly speaking, Cartesian, and yet its roots are indeed in Descartes's cogito. Descartes started us on the path of thinking about matter as an idea. He wanted the reflections of his mind to deliver to him the truth about matter, and this truth was to be in the form of clear and distinct ideas about matter. To protect himself against reasoning about matter erroneously, Descartes postulated the existence of an imaginary demon bent on deceiving him, and his task became to outwit it.

> I will suppose therefore that not God, who is supremely good
> and the source of truth, but rather some malicious demon of the
> utmost power and cunning has employed all his energies in
> order to deceive me. I shall think that the sky, the air, the earth,
> colors, shapes, sounds, and all external things are merely the
> delusions of dreams which he has devised to ensnare my judge-
> ment. I shall consider myself as not having hands or eyes, or
> flesh, or blood or senses, but as falsely believing that I have all
> these things.[1]

It is crucial to grasp that not even Descartes's evil demon could eliminate the appearances of things. In the beginning of the meditation, the world appears to Descartes to be filled with colors, sounds, odors, and textures. This may not be the way the world really is. In fact, there may be no world. But no demon can change the fact that the world with all its qualities appears to exist. If the appearance of the world dissolved away,

Descartes could never return to the world, even through a chain of logic. He connects himself to the world because he thinks a particular appearance, namely quantity, is clear and distinct, whereas colors and the like are not. God can thus guarantee the truth of the former but not the latter.

For Descartes, the determination of the essence of matter is a conceptual enterprise. Still, no intellectual comprehension of the world is supposed to make the world seem to be other than it seems to be. The same can be said for Plato, Buddha, Christ, or Berkeley, none of whom would deny the appearance of things: Plato's and Berkeley's tree *seems* as real as Aristotle's tree.

According to the scientific materialist's picture of the world, however, common sense misleads us in a way that far exceeds the power of Descartes's demon. Present-day scientific materialists, such as Patricia and Paul Churchland, want to push us through the appearance so that we actually perceive the world to be the way it is supposed to be essentially, namely, in its scientific structure. What is behind their motivation?

These materialists would have us reflect that every aspect of our experience is the result of some kind of interpretation. Thus, if the issue concerns the nature of color, we must be referring to an interpreted phenomenon; and, if we must have interpretation, then why not have the best we can have, namely, the most advanced scientific explanation about color. The allusion to so-called givens, such as color, we will be told is a philosophical myth. I want to leave my own discussion of the given to the end of this chapter, but here I want to examine some of the reasons for considering that everything that appears to be a fact to common sense is an interpretation.

THE OLD FOLKS

Many reductionists like to assume that the reduction of light and sound to waves is settled, and that the only question remaining is how to reduce a mental phenomenon to a scientific explanation about it. Paul Churchland gives this impression as he sums up the scientific materialist's program:

Consider sound. We now know that sound is just a train of compression waves traveling through the air, and that the property of being high pitched is identical with the property of having a high oscillatory frequency. We have learned that light is just electromagnetic waves. . . . We now appreciate that the warmth or coolness of a body is just the energy of motion of the molecules that make it up. . . . What we now think of as "mental states," argues the identity theorist, are identical with brain states in exactly the same way.[2]

Well, if one could grant that sound and light are just waves and that warmth is just molecules in motion then, molding the knower to the known, we could grant that the mental is just mechanical brain states. But if this is true and if our perceptions get us in contact with the true world, then why do we not actually see quanta, hear waves, and perceive moving molecules, rather than see colors, hear sounds, and feel warmth or coldness? I, for one, do not. But let us grant that I am backward; I am not yet free of these commonsense beliefs. Surely I have learned how to perceive the sun revolving about the earth? I am ashamed to confess that I am backwards even there. In my youth I was an amateur astronomer, and I indeed know that, from the perspective of being situated appropriately in space, the earth revolves about the sun, the sun about the center of our galaxy, the galaxy about other galaxies, and our present theories seem to indicate that our cluster of galaxies is moving away from other clusters of galaxies. The uniformity of the background radiation as well as the shift in the spectrum of stars and galaxies indicate that we live in an expanding universe.

Still, I enjoy the *setting* of the sun, and I think that this enjoyment arises from a true perception of things. In relation to my fleshy body with its fleshy eyes, and in relation to my being situated on Earth, the sun *sets*. Paul Churchland, however, contends that our basic perceptions about the world are part of a folk psychology, and that this has been inherited from the Greeks. Thus, he views the past twenty-five hundred years to have been an era of stagnation awaiting the discovery and advancement of science.[3] Aside from the obvious fact that most of the world was not influenced by *our* Greek heritage, Churchland confuses the theory-laden aspect of science both with cultural interpretations and with the basic relation of things to the organic differentiation of the body, distinctions that I will clarify toward the end of this chapter. Still, what is immediately evident is the strangeness of the reductionist's view of the world. This strangeness surfaces when we consider a particular example of how "science" is supposed to replace common sense.

> Reflect on the common ability to catch an outfield fly ball on the run, or hit a moving car with a snowball. . . . On these and many other mental phenomena, [folk psychology] sheds negligible light.[4]

I think that "folk psychology" does indeed explain what any outfielder needs to know about catching a fly on the run or getting a base hit. I did both in Brooklyn before I even heard about mental phenomena. Churchland wants a scientific explanation to count as the only valid one; but then it is tautologically true that our present science should replace folk psychology. Of course, knowing how every fiber of the body moves and knowing the corresponding mechanics of a moving baseball might indeed influence the playing of the game of baseball, but this is merely to say that the meaning of the game might change over time. Without this knowledge, the game of baseball is perfectly understood as the game that is played. Are we to say, for example, because he did not master the mechanics of a moving baseball and did not have expert knowledge about tissue construction of his muscles, that Babe Ruth did not *know* how to play baseball? Further, it is always clear how to learn to play baseball—practice with someone who knows how to play the game.

In activities such as sports, and in all commonsense activities such as knowing how to walk, knowing how to do something implies a comprehension of the meaning of the act. (Implicitly, my relational realism that takes knowledge to be a worldmaking breaks with most traditional distinctions between "knowing how," and "knowing that." Also, for me, knowledge as worldmaking is on a different level than distinctions between knowing, on the one hand, and comprehending or interpreting, on the other hand.) True, someone who merely knows the rules and techniques of a sport can teach someone to perform the action; but only a Cartesian prejudice could prevent us from granting the status of true knowledge to the person who competently performs the action. The pianist is the archetype of one who knows the meaning of piano playing.

Patricia Churchland also leads us along the path of rejecting the claims of common sense. She first assures us that reduction, after all, concerns only a relation among theories.

> Reduction is first and foremost a relation between *theories*.
> Simply put, one theory is said to reduce to another theory when the first is explained in terms of the second. . . . For example, when it is claimed that light has been reduced to electromagnetic energy, what this means is that (a) the theory of optics has been reduced to the theory of electromagnetic radiation, and (b) the theory of optics is reduced in such a way that it is appropriate to identify light with electromagnetic radiation.[5]

Well, of course, if common sense is indeed theory-laden, and if science can provide a better theory, then the former reduces to the latter. Temporarily forgetting about this big "if," this move seems to appease our doubts about the reductionist's program: if reduction is only about reducing one theory to another, who could object to that?

But what does this theoretic reduction have to do with the fact that we hear sounds and not sound waves? The emphasis on theory is actually introduced to distract us from the sleight-of-hand substitution of quantity for quality. As with most magic, the trick is revealed if you can keep your eyes on both hands.

It is not easy. Patricia Churchland soothes our misgivings that there might be something amiss in attempting to dissolve color into a wavelength, even if there is nothing wrong in claiming that color *has* a wavelength aspect. This move seems to reassure us that reduction concerns only theories. Churchland, however, knows that she needs more, but this "more" comes in very quietly through the back door, or, rather, through several back doors.

We are told that theories explain properties and that properties can be reduced to theories. But how do theories explain properties? Why, of course, scientific theories explain properties scientifically. But who in their right mind would object to the fact that it is convenient for physics to explain a red color as a quantum or sound as a wavelength? What about color as color or sound as sound? What about H_2O as that wet thing that cools us in summer or as that wondrous thing that quenches thirst? We are, according to Churchland, close to explaining all these phenomena, although admittedly the detailed mathematics may not be forthcoming.[6]

But in what sense could science explain the coolness or wetness of water? Hydrogen and oxygen are gases whose properties are radically different from water. Of course, chemists attribute this difference to the formation of a molecule, H_2O, from the union of two hydrogen atoms and an oxygen atom. As a chemical explanation of water, this is fine. But there is a jump from the claim that water is a liquid that feels wet and satisfies thirst to the claim that it is basically the union of two hydrogen atoms and one oxygen atom. I am not saying that we cannot explain the relation between these two essential aspects of water, the one arising from the relation of water to our fleshy body, the other arising from the relation of water to our socially constructed theories and instruments. We must retain *both* the reality of the commonsense qualities *and* the reality of their scientific makeup, without privileging either, and without reducing one to the other. As I see it, that is just what a relational realism attempts to do.

The Churchlands believe that the only way to explain how water is experienced by common sense is either to rely on science or some "spooky" qualities in matter.[7] But these qualities are spooky only to someone who needs to reduce all experience to science. There is nothing spooky about the quality of quenching thirst when this quality is viewed in relation to a fleshy organism that needs water, and there is nothing wrong with the explanation that, in relation to the fleshy body, water *is* just that. But spooky or not, neither Patricia Churchland nor professional chemists truly explain why H_2O should *feel* wet to us or why sound waves are heard by us as sound.

The Churchlands can avoid facing the world as it is revealed to common sense because they would have us focus on the hand holding out the theory-laden aspect of science. But what is true of the Churchlands is true, in the main, for other scientific materialists. Stephen Stitch, who has reservations with the Churchlands' extreme claims about the primitiveness of common sense, still concludes:

> Our everyday use of folk psychological concepts to explain and predict the behavior of our fellows clearly presupposes some rough-and-ready laws which detail the dynamics of belief and desire formation and connect these states to behavior. Collectively they surely count as a commonsense theory.[8]

What is evident is that common sense has these laws, that is, the laws that science is looking for, only if one interrogates common sense about them from a scientific perspective. But this is to bring common sense into the realm of science. The family of farmers that today still tills the soil with oxen and plants rice, and that wonders whether its children will continue farming or leave to live in town, is carrying the weight of history in its attitudes, beliefs, and speech. But whether a set of rules exists in these attitudes, in the sense that neurobiology looks for sets of rules, is another question. It would be strange if a prescientific, commonsense attitude possessed rules in anything like the scientific sense of "rule." Perhaps an educated person like Stitch can see rules in his common sense. Still, I would suspect that, in his fleshy commonsense attitude to the world, he reacts much the same as all of us: he sees the hues of colors, and he hears the tenor, bass, or soprano quality of a human voice.

In their more sober moments, reductionists admit that when they are referring to common sense, it is the common sense of the very educated. This sobriety, however, is soon forgotten, and this elitist notion of common sense becomes everyone's common sense. Presumably, at one time, everybody thought that heat was phlogistons. Subsequently, this "commonsense" theory has proven to be so wrong that it has had to be jettisoned completely. Our commonsense belief in respect to heat was thus not revised but eliminated. In the words of Paul Churchland:

> The phlogiston theory of combustion is one such example. Here the correction required was so massive that it seemed appropri-

ate to think of the old ontology as displaced entirely by the new theoretical ontology; that is, we now say that there is no such thing as phlogiston, not that phlogiston reduced to some compound containing oxygen.[9]

Paul Churchland is trying to make a case that neurobiology will replace folk psychology in the way that our contemporary molecular theory replaced the phlogiston theory. When folk psychology refers to beliefs and pains, neurobiology will teach us to refer to the firing of C-fibers or some such. But there is an extreme elitist view of common sense at work here that is never explicated. What portion of the world's population ever believed that heat was phlogistons? I think one thousandth of one percent would be a generous estimate. A handful of very cultured people had this notion that, when you burned yourself and said "ouch," it was because phlogistons were afoot. Now we believe that atoms or quanta are afoot. I don't know what this has to do about anybody's common sense, except that of philosophers who read too much. Most peoples' common sense tells them nothing about phlogistons or atoms but, rather, a great deal about painful things to avoid, whether caused by phlogistons, atoms, or a vengeful god—all of which one person may be very concerned about, and another not at all.

Paul Churchland admits that we do, in fact, have a problem seeing the world the way that science tells us that we should see it. "Our minds, perhaps, have been freed from the tyranny of a flat immobile Earth, but our *eyes* remain in bondage."[10] He shows in great detail how to situate ourselves so that we can actually *see* the proper movements of the planets.

> I urge the reader not to judge the matter from my own spare sketches. Judge it in the flesh some suitable planeted twilight. A vertiginous feeling will signal success.[11]

Well, I want very much to judge "in the flesh," but I doubt that Churchland is doing just that. If vertigo is the criteria, Ptolemaic epicycles win the day, and they could, I suspect, be seen by placing oneself in a position, if not identical, at least similar to the one recommended by Churchland. But suppose we grant Paul Churchland his point. One still has to put one's body in a certain posture, tilting one's head just so, to see the world "as it really is." Strange, that so awkward a posture is needed to give us the world as it really is.

In fact, the Churchlands have to arbitrarily stop this game to get at the world "as it really is." The sun moves about the galaxy, the galaxy about other galaxies; how do we twist our necks to see this? Even if we could see all this movement, our walking would still be straight ahead, upward, or downward, depending upon the relation of our fleshy body to our earthy terrain. Further, in relation to this body, the sun would indeed set, and the world would be more or less how it appears to be to our commonsense perceptions.

PERCEPTION AND THE ESSENCE OF MATTER

We are all familiar with so-called illusions, such as the reflection of light on a road that makes it appear wet or a stick half in water that appears bent. I think that these so-called illusions can be handled by simply claiming that, while we do in fact see color, we never see wetness as such, which is more properly the object of our sense of touch. More radically, however, I would here begin the formulation of my relational realism that encourages us to reinsert the organic body in our relation to the world. Thus, in relation to the sense of sight, a stick half in water is indeed bent; it appears just the way it is supposed to appear in this situation, and it appears this way to every-one looking at it from this perspective. D. M. Armstrong, however, wants to use these illusions to explain how we perceive color when only wavelengths exist. What distinguishes Armstrong's position is its honesty in at least see-ing that the supposed reduction of quality to quantity does present us with a real problem of interpreting our perceptions about the world.

> If we consult perception, then its verdict is clear. The green color
> is a property of the vine leaves. . . . It is an intrinsic property of the
> leaves. In what follows I will hold fast to this perceptual deliver-
> ance. . . . It is the surface of the leaf which is green, sounds fill the
> room, smells hang around in them, tastes can inhere in the tasty
> body, water can be hot or cold, just as perception delivers.[12]

Common sense could not want a stronger advocate. Or so it would seem. But Armstrong wants qualities, such as colors, odors, tastes, and temperatures—qualities that, since John Locke, have been referred to as secondary—to be reduced to the primary qualities of extended matter. Thus, the "is" of the claim, "It *is* the surface of the leaf which is green...," becomes, as we read on, *seems.*

The problem begins when Armstrong attempts to give us scientific reasons and conjectures that are aimed at explaining how the eye could be mislead to see a leaf as green, when the leaf is really not green. Or, to be more exact, he begins to define anew the essential meaning of the claim that a leaf is green. Gradually, the quality green becomes the answer to a scientific question, and once again green becomes a quantitative phenomenon. Color as a quality becomes a case of mistaken identity, an illusion caused by quantity being placed just *so.*

> My suggestion is that the illusion of concrete secondary quality
> is created in the following way. Phenomenologically, the sec-
> ondary qualities lack structure, they do not appear to have any
> "grain" as Wilfrid Sellars puts it. Nevertheless, they have a huge
> multitude of systematic resemblances and differences *to each*
> *other....* The immensely complex dimensional classification of
> the secondary qualities, with all its degrees of resemblance, is a
> matter of perception of resemblances without grasping the basis
> of the resemblance in the primary qualities.[13]

Armstrong is here on far more dangerous ground than Descartes was with his postulate of an evil demon whom we had to appease before we could acquire certitude about what part of the world actually was the way it appeared to be. For like the Churchlands, Armstrong wants us to see through the way the world appears to the way it actually is. That is, we are not supposed to be content with Descartes's intellectual conviction that color is a mere appearance, but we are supposed to actually *perceive* color as a wavelength rather than as a color. Armstrong takes this position because he is aware that Berkeley showed that, if color is subjective, then quantity must be subjective also, for we *never perceive pure quantity.*

Rather, we always experience quantity through its so-called secondary qualities. But if qualities are the product of illusions, then perhaps primary qualities are in the same sinking boat.

> Here again I would simply allow this speculation. Contemporary physics suggests that we should give an account of color, sound, taste, smell, heat, and cold in terms of the "executive" primary properties. But who knows if the latter are fundamental? (Why should middle-sized creatures like ourselves be in perceptual touch with the fundamental properties of the world, if there are any?) A deeper physics might give an account of the current list of primary qualities in terms of properties which we can neither perceive nor image.[14]

And presumably all of physics might be explained best through a set of mathematical functions which are perfectly understandable by a pure mind. But we do not really have to await a possible future result; the reduction of physics to mathematics is, to a great extent, true now. If we are after *the* truth of perception, why not dissolve matter into mathematical formulae about matter? Aside from this observation, it is difficult to see how Armstrong has preserved the original intrinsic quality of the greenness of the leaf. Further, how can quantity stand, when qualities are the product of illusions?

Why does Armstrong go to such lengths to reduce color to quantity (or, to what Locke calls "primary qualities")? The answer is that he does not know what to do with the awareness of qualities such as red *as* red. But this problem arises for him from the same source as it arises for Descartes. If you begin with a mechanistic view of the body, the perception of quality then becomes itself a strange quality. For Armstrong and other scientific materialists, the choice is between a mechanistic notion of matter or a form of dualism of matter and spirit.

To some extent, Armstrong's desire to reduce qualities such as color to quantity arises also because he does not wish to get caught in affirming the existence of any brute givens. The objects of our perceptions may or may not be belief structures as some think, but perception, for him, is clearly theory-laden:

Whether we should actually *reduce* perceptions to a certain species of acquiring of beliefs (and so the having of images to a species of entertaining thoughts) is a further question. I incline to favor such a reduction, but it is controversial among philosophers of perception. What is perhaps a little less controversial, because weaker, and so may secure wider agreement, is this: perceptions are propositional in structure.[15]

Materialists, such as the Churchlands and Stitch, take the perceptions of common sense to be belief structures that can themselves be reduced to calculative thinking, which in turn is reducible to a neurological understanding of the firing of C-fibers or some such. Armstrong's position is hardly less extreme. Perception, for him, is propositional in structure. Does Armstrong mean subject-verb-predicate proposition? What about the perceptions of the Chinese whose language is presumably nonpropositional in a Western sense of that term? Even if we grant that Chinese thinking is implicitly propositional, I still do not know in what sense any perception is propositional. A proposition is a formal construct; it bears the weight of our historical linguistic clarifications. Armstrong is being elitist, and he confuses philosophical and linguistic clarifications with the ambiguous cultural-laden aspect of common sense; but I will soon examine this distinction in more detail. At least Armstrong seems willing to admit that perceptions do deliver to us a qualitatively rich world, even if he takes the rug from under our feet afterward.

To all of my objections, a reductionist will no doubt reply that it is still true that light *is* an electromagnetic wave, and that it is explained by electromagnetic theory. The "is" in the reduction means that color is essentially colorless matter in motion, whatever common sense may tell us. This move to give over to science the essential insight into things is unfortunately taken not only by reductionists such as Armstrong, the Churchlands, and Stitch, but frequently, by antireductionists such as Putnam and Saul Kripke. In a sense, Quine is a reductionist; but I will show why I think that his ontological indeterminacy puts him in a unique position. Goodman appears to be one of the few who, although rooted in the analytic tradition, holds out to the end against giving science a privileged perspective on reality. However, I will leave the consideration of these matters to the following chapter.

This claim that science gives us the essence of things faces several embarrassing consequences. It seems clear that we have no right to expect that the future may not look upon our present scientific efforts as naive. We are then in a position of claiming that science gives the essence only in the sense of a Peircean limit: the essence of reality is an ideal limit that we approximate, but never reach. Aside from the question of how we are ever to know that we are approaching rather than receding from the ideal, this view resurrects the Kantian thing-in-itself—reality is essentially unknowable by the human intelligence. Kant, however, was able to turn to God as the Being who did know reality as it was in itself, and presumably science does not wish to move in that direction.

Also, reductionism arbitrarily stops at a convenient plane of reality. Why not go all the way and claim "Heat *is* a mathematical function?" Why not dissolve the world in a system of pure relations? We may not have the technique, but if what one wants is theory, mathematics wins the day. Patricia and Paul Churchland choose to stop at neurons, but they seem unaware of it as a choice. Quine chooses to stop at the behavioral inputs that we receive from the world, but at least he knows that this is his choice.

The basic answer to the existence of qualities is disarmingly simple: there are colors because there are fleshy eyes. Our eyes discriminate among the countless aspects of matter, highlighting those that we call color. Without the existence of eyes, the world would not be colored. Still, the existence of colors in the world does not depend upon my perceptions or your perceptions of them. The simple existence of the sense of sight in any organism is itself a relational bond with matter as colored.

There is no need for the Churchlands, Armstrong, or any other scientific materialist to take the extreme position that only scientific explanations are explanations. If the Churchlands wish to attempt a neurological or mechanically material explanation of perception, they have every right to do so. There is simply no reason, except shock value and publicity, to attempt to reduce commonsense claims and explanations to scientific entities and theories.

No doubt, Rorty would respond to Armstrong, the Churchlands, and Stitch, as well as to my objections against them, that we are all attempting to make an ontological issue where there is only a question of language use. Rorty was an eliminativist materialist, that is, one who holds that qualities and mental states can be eliminated by a proper materialistic explanation. However, in *Philosophy and the Mirror of Nature*, he rejects this for an even more subtle form of materialism. For Rorty, the scientific materialist's explanation of such things as sensations, thoughts, and beliefs are neither a reduction nor an explanation of a false belief. Rather, they are merely different explanations. And if we should be tempted to ask, "Different explanations of *what*?," Rorty would say that we should stop trying to find an ultimate ontological answer and accept the different explanations as simply capable of working in different areas. He invites us to imagine that:

> Far away, on the other side of our galaxy, there was a planet on which lived beings like ourselves—featherless bipeds who built houses and bombs, and wrote poems and computer programs. These beings did not know that they had minds. They had notions like "wanting to" and "intending to" and "believing that" and "feeling terrible" and "feeling marvelous." But they had no notion that these signified *mental* states—states of a peculiar and distinct sort—quite different from "sitting down," "having a cold," and "being sexually aroused.". . .
>
> In most respects, then, the language, life technology, and philosophy of this race were much like ours. But there was one important difference. Neurology and biochemistry had been the first disciplines in which technological breakthroughs had been achieved, and a large part of the conversation of these people concerned the states of their nerves. When their infants veered toward hot stoves, mothers cried out, "He'll stimulate his C-fibers!" When people were given clever visual illusions to look at, they said, "How odd! It makes neuronic bundle G-14 quiver, but when I look at it from the side I can see that it's not a red rectangle at all."[16]

When an expedition from Earth lands on the planet of the Antipodeans, a heated philosophical discussion among the Earth philosophers ensues. The issue centers around whether the Antipodeans *feel* pain when they report that their C-fibers are firing. Their behavior in this regard is identical to the behavior of the Earth visitors. The Antipodeans tend to shun circumstances that might induce the firing of C-fibers, and they think that it is terrible to have their C-fibers stimulated. "It's my C-fibers again—you know, the ones that go off every time you get burned or hit or have a tooth pulled. It's just awful."[17]

Many of the Earth philosophers still insist that the Antipodeans cannot be having the same *sensation* of pain as they are having. The firing of C-fibers cannot *be* the awareness of pain. These Earth philosophers have no trouble accepting that the Antipodean culture could have trained them to *report* their feeling as the firing of C-fibers, but they insist that the firing of C-fibers, as such, cannot be the phenomenal quality that is pain. Still, no examination nor intricate test is able to get the Antipodeans to see that a sensation could not *be* the firing of C-fibers, although, of course, the firing of C-fibers might accompany a sensation.

Indeed, even when the brain of an Earth neurologist is wired to that of an Antipodean so that the input from the brain of the Earthling goes to that of the Antipodean and vice versa, there are no interesting results. When the Antipodean receives the input from the Earthling's brain, he still does not understand what "feeling" is supposed to be like. Whenever the Earthling talks in terms of pain, the Antipodean still talks in terms of the firing of C-fibers. They agree only that both pain and the firing of C-fibers are terrible to have. And the same situation occurs in relation to other sensations, such a seeing colors. The Earthling insists that it is the quality *red* that is being seen, whereas the Antipodean reports that it is very clearly C-692 that is being stimulated.

For Rorty, the substitution of the firing of C-fibers for sensations does not correct common sense by delivering to us the essence of raw feelings; science merely gives us another way of talking about what we now call pain and color. We are not to take these different ways of talking about things to be different ways of talking about some fundamental phenomenon, whether C-fibers or felt qualities. What we take to be a noninferential report is merely a case of familiarity. Thus, if we could divorce our beliefs about feelings and sensations from the notions of our glassy essence and privileged access, and if we could similarly divorce the notion of the firing of C-fibers from that of giving us the true essence of our feelings, then both ways of talking would be pragmatically equal.

Rorty's position is thus not that of scientific realism; neither mode of conversation gives the essence of things. This lack, for Rorty, is not a defect, because to give the essence of something is to continue the attempt to present consciousness as a mirror of nature reflecting the way things are in themselves, apart from all human intervention. What is wrong with scientific realism is that it continues within this tradition and merely gives us another supposedly true answer for the one provided by common sense.

But, if Rorty is not a scientific realist, he is also no longer an eliminativist materialist. The point about the Antipodeans is that, while *they* have eliminated feeling from their discourse, they are not inclined to say that we should follow in their footsteps. It is the Earthling philosophers who want to make an issue of the difference, because they are hung up on the conviction that ways of talking should "limn the real." There is, for Rorty, no more difference between talking about feelings or talking about C-fibers than between talking about nations and individuals. You could get very excited about whether a nation is an entity or whether a nation should be reduced to the individuals that compose it, but this excitement is again nothing more than taking the notion of glassy essence seriously, and thus continuing the empty debate of previous philosophers about how the mind corresponds to reality. Why not just say that, at times, it is fruitful to talk about nations as such, and at other times, it is more useful to speak about the individuals that constitute nations.[8]

LEADING THE WITNESS

I find it difficult to formulate my objection to Rorty because I agree with his and Armstrong's claim that we do not have a privileged access to the meaning of our interior states. Further, like Rorty I also reject the notion that knowledge mirrors the way things are in themselves, apart from any human existence. Still, Rorty leaves me with the conviction that he also has an elitist notion of common sense, and that he is making things more mysterious than they have to be. Finally, I am always suspect when one attempts to illustrate a position by having recourse to science fiction.

I think that it is useful to view Rorty's questioning of the Antipodeans and the Earthlings like a lawyer leading a witness, even if we are not quite sure who the witness is. It seems that Rorty would have us believe that the witness is the ordinary person, whether Antipodean or Earthling. I think it safe to say that the ordinary Earthling has no particular philosophical or scientific training. This average person reports "feeling" pain. Rorty says that we know what he means, and that there is no need to reduce his report to anything ontologically more basic. A neurologist may, of course, talk in terms of C-fibers, and the average person could have been trained to speak this way. We were not so trained, according to Rorty, simply because our history developed notions like mind, consciousness, and awareness, along with the kinds of things that were supposed to be in our conscious minds.

However, I am not sure to whom Rorty is referring, or to what history he is referring. Why does Rorty refer to Antipodeans and not the Chinese, for example? Until recently, the history of China proceeded along for thousands of years with little influence from our Greek heritage.

In brief, there is no indication that the average Chinese encounters the kind of problem talking to an American as Rorty suggests, and there is no indication that children born from such "mixed" marriages face a dilemma between accepting various cultural interpretations of pain. The attitude toward the pain might be different, but this has nothing to do with a particular philosophical interpretation of pain, or a scientific interpretation of a sunset. On the level of common sense, pain and a sunset have something to do with flesh, and we recognize this flesh to be basically the same for all people of Earth. True, one can be trained to experience pain differently and to give different interpretations to a sunset. Nothing is culturally neutral. Nevertheless, it is the pain of the flesh and the perception of the sun by fleshy eyes that are culturally laden. If Antipodeans *looked* so different from us that we could not determine whether they were made of flesh or of some other matter (whether they were thinking plants or thinking puffs of air), then we would have good commonsense reasons to wonder about the similarity of their feeling and ours. This emphasis on flesh is most obvious in screams of pain. Is a scream a reporting of pain? Rorty seems to fudge the issue.

> More generally, we can note that the way in which the prelinguistic infant knows that it has a pain is the way in which the record-changer knows the spindle is empty, the plant the direction of the sun, and the amoeba the temperature of the water. But this way has no connection with what a language user knows when he knows what a pain is—that it is mental rather than physical, typically produced by injured tissues, etc.[19]

This is a very strange passage. We are presented with a dichotomy between language users on the one hand, and babies and phonograph needles on the other. What sort of language users does Rorty have in mind, and what kinds of questions about the reports of pain are being implied by the distinction itself? Let us accept for the sake of argument Rorty's lumping together of crying babies and the movement of plants to water. The question still remains, "Who are these language users?" Are they the average person or the very well educated? Does the average person throughout the world typically talk in terms of damaged tissues? I think not. Indeed, who is Rorty questioning? Once again, it seems that Rorty is referring to the average person. In the opening paragraphs of *Philisophy and the Mirror of Nature,* he says:

> Discussions in the philosophy of mind usually start off by assuming that everybody has always known how to divide the world into the mental and the physical—that this distinction is commonsensical and intuitive, even if that between two sorts of "stuff," material and immaterial, is philosophical and baffling. . . .
>
> We seem to have no doubt that pains, moods, images, and sentences which "flash before the mind," dreams, hallucinations, beliefs, attitudes, desires, and intentions all count as "mental"

whereas the contractions of the stomach which cause the pain, the neural processes which accompany it, and everything else which can be given a firm location within the body count as nonmental. . . .

These purported intuitions serve to keep something like Cartesian dualism alive.[20]

Rorty seems to safeguard himself by calling these intuitions of the mental "purported." Is the distinction between the physical and the mental then not truly commonsensical? Is the distinction itself foisted on us by the philosophers of mind? As one reads on, Rorty's position becomes fairly clear: there *is* some kind of commonsense distinction between the physical and the mental, but this distinction does not point to any ontological gap between the physical and the mental. Nor does the commonsense distinction point to any neutral substance that can be either physical or mental. The commonsense distinction between the physical and the mental is as pragmatically useful as the distinction between nations and individuals. We are involved with two different ways of talking about things, and there is no ontological issue to be made about these discourses.

The philosophers of mind are, for Rorty, the ones who attempt to give ontological weight to the distinction. Of itself, the distinction between the physical and the mental functions perfectly well within language. For Rorty, we do not have to give ontological significance either to language or to what language supposedly represents. He claims that we don't have to take seriously the view of consciousness as a glassy essence or the correspondence notion of truth which goes along with this notion. The so-called "intuitions" of common sense are not a privileged access to any given. Rather, these intuitions are learned, and they are merely what we have become accustomed to, just as a scientist can be accustomed to reporting the movement of particles within a cloud chamber.

Thus, Rorty's twist on eliminative materialism: everything materialism says is probably perfectly true as a global explanation of things; it just does not rule out local differences that can only be explained by another vocabulary. Thus, also, Rorty's desire is to have the Antipodean's vocabulary equivalent to ours, without implying any reduction. So far so good.

Once again, however, I think that we have a right to press for a little clarification on the extension of Rorty's "we." Who are these commonsense language users? Since commonsense intuitions are, for Rorty, a question of familiarity, the report of pain as a feeling rather than as the firing of C-fibers is due to our cultural training. But whose culture? Who is this average person? The freshman crossing the campus of Princeton or the freshman I meet at my state college? The Madison Avenue shopper or the homeless person? Those born in the West or those born in the East? Are we confusing Woody Allen's upper-middle-class angst, the "privilege of suffering" (which most people would give their right arm to have) with the pains of the starving or half-starving peoples of the world? Rorty's commonsense person is educated enough to understand what the history of anatomy and medicine has won for us, namely, the world of the damaged tissues and organs.[21] Most of the people of the world do not know about tissues and organs as such. The starving people of the world are hungry; *they* are hungry, not their stomachs. And in *their* pain, they are as far removed from the medical world of deficient vitamins and damaged tissues as they are from the Antipodean world of the firing of C-fibers.

THE MYTH OF THE "MYTH OF THE GIVEN"

This attempt to reduce quality to quantity, to eliminate it in favor of quantity, or to consider our references to quality to be merely socially pragmatic or linguistic ways of coping with the world, all these are allied with the critique of so-called givens, or facts. These givens were first taken to be the data received by the senses, such as patches of color. Later, they became forms of thought supposedly best expressed by mathematical logic. Finally, in what Richard Rorty calls "the linguistic turn," the given became language itself.[22] In each case, the move to base our reflections in some bedrock foundation encountered not only the difficulties of justifying a correspondence theory of truth, but the degree to which every so-called given, fact, or datum is layered with interpretation.

However, I think that the situation in regard to the given is far more complex than is usually assumed. I believe that we can distinguish at least three different ways in which something can be viewed as a fact, and I claim that one of them is indeed genuine, although it is nevertheless relational.

The two senses in which I regard the given to be indeed a myth are the one assumed by the logical positivists, such as Rudolph Carnap, and the cultural one that, after G. W. F. Hegel's wedding of thought and history, has become part of our thinking. I wish to generalize the attempt of the positivists to include all philosophical and scientific attempts to ground a correspondence theory of truth upon some given that supposedly exists independently of human existence. This attempt is characterized by the neutral, or bird's-eye, thinking discussed above, and I will refer to it as simply the *philosophical given*. I will generalize the second sense of the given, the Hegelian one, to include whatever is culturally interpreted, including language, gestures, and beliefs. This I term the *cultural given*.

Although the philosophical given is a myth, it is so differently than the cultural given. The existence of an atom as something given by nature and merely waiting out there to be discovered is a myth apart from its relation to our scientific concerns, theories, and instruments. And the use of a handshake to signify friendship as something underlying different cultures is also a myth. But the myths are different because the origin of the givens are different. The philosophical given, such as an atom, arises from the specific historical occurrence of science within the West. An atom is a myth apart from its relation to that specific scientific program. The cultural given, such as a handshake, is more dependent upon the general history that gave us our language and gestures. The attempt to see these two givens and their consequent myths as the same is one with the attempt to see science as the natural outcome of common sense. But I take that to be historically false. I see no reason why we could not have continued historically along lines laid down by China or India. We would, of course, have had technology, but not science.

Finally, I put forward a third sense of the given, the *organic relational given*, and I do not regard this given to be a myth. We indeed have the givens of the human body—the organic fleshy body with these senses and not others. The givens of the senses both reveal and make the world; for example, they both reveal and make matter visible and tangible. More generally, the givens of our senses, together with our whole fleshy organism, differentiate matter into the things of this world rather than some other possible world. Again, I ask the reader to try to imagine a world in which consciousness had never emerged as having sight. I claim that such a feat is impossible, and that more basic than any possible errors of judgments that sight can lead us to make is the way that sight reveals the world to be visible in just the basic colors that we see it to have.

I do not regard the world of colors, sounds, and textures, as well as the world of trees and stars—those things that twinkle in the heavens and that, for centuries, have been useful for navigation—to be a myth, even though I agree that any particular expression of this world is intertwined with at least one of the other myths about the given. Still, I think the separation of the first two myths from the organically given is at least possible to indicate, for only the organically given is a worldmaking.

I consider my own critique of a neutral, bird's-eye, and an ahistorical perception of reality that was given in this chapter to sufficiently dispose of the philosophically given. Nevertheless, it is also important to note W. V. O. Quine's internal criticism, both because of its intrinsic value and because of its influence on contemporary analytic thinking. Although I will expand on this in my formal discussion of Quine in the next chapter, it is useful for my view of the given to note here Quine's basic critique.

Quine critiques the traditional model of our understanding of giving something a name. Simple pointing and giving a thing a name was supposed to show how language hooked up with the primary data of perception. From this foundation, one was supposed to be able to judge the relation of any theory to experience, the degree to which it explained or did not explain our commonsense experience. Quine, however, showed that language had to be treated holistically and that, when language was handled this way, there was no unequivocal object. To use Quine's example, saying "rabbit," you might seem to be pointing to a whole rabbit but actually intend a temporal stage of rabbithood, and I might be pointing to the same rabbit and mean the rabbit legs I want for dinner. If I try to be more specific, the associated meaning in my language also adjusts, and perfect translation from my pointing and linguistic framework to yours becomes impossible. In fact, this critique of Quine gave rise to the specific label of the given as a "myth."

However, to repeat, it is important to distinguish this philosophical notion of the given from the culturally given, and both from the genuine notion of the given related to the organic body. Whatever history led to the formation of the sound "rabbit" to mean either the whole organic rabbit or its legs or its temporal parts, this cultural history is surely not one with the philosophical or scientific program that leads us to believe in the given implied by the correspondence theory of truth. Specifically, the long, sophisticated history of many cultures, such as that of classical China never gave rise to a science or a philosophy in the Western senses of those terms.

This distinction between the philosophically given and the culturally given is one with my earlier view that the traditional criticism leveled against Descartes concedes too much to the spirit of Cartesianism by granting to him that a meaning can be a priori clear and distinct, regardless of whether it corresponds to reality. Also, this distinction between the philosophical and cultural givens underlies my view that philosophers such as the Churchlands frequently confuse an elitist notion of common sense with an everyday one.

The point is that, while the philosophical given is frequently recognized for the myth that it is, the culturally given is usually bypassed. Thus our usual critique of the given overlooks the cultural formation of concepts and terms such as "spirit" and "body," as well as all the cultural formation of notions associated with mathematics, such as "natural number." We tend to assume that philosophical and mathematical notions are simply given, and that we merely have to determine their relation to the world. (In this way we divorce the cultural formation of these terms from their behavioral content, and from the way in which they *forge* the correspondence of language and thing.)

The third sense, that of the genuine given, works within the recognition of the first two myths, and it focuses on the relation of our organic fleshy body to the world. To repeat, I claim that, in relation to our fleshy eyes, the perception of the *setting* of the sun is a given. Of course, I am assuming that we are viewing the sun from the planet Earth, but, since we have to be somewhere, and at this time in history most of us are on the planet Earth, this is not a particularly noteworthy assumption.

However, I have not forgotten about the first two senses in which the given is a myth. I agree that all our perceptions are culturally interpreted. There is no such phenomenon involving the simple setting of the sun. To each person, the setting sun appears in just this particular way, a way that is always layered with particular interpretations. We are immersed in a culture. Still, we all have basically the same fleshy, organic body, and with healthy organs, our body discriminates the qualities of the world for each of us in basically the same way. For the blind, the sun does not set in the same way as it does for those of us who have sight. If no human consciousness were gifted with organs of sight, then there would be no setting of the sun.

Thus, in relation to all formal systems and all cultural history, the perception of a *setting* sun is a given, as is a body ravished by hunger. No matter how we philosophically or culturally attempt to restructure our fleshy body or the sun, we will continue to need food and water and to perceive a setting sun from the Earth.

We cannot interpret away the fleshy organic body, and when we attempt to do this we interpret away the world. Color, sound, odor, the bitter and sweet, temperatures, and textures are givens to our senses, and perceptual objects such as a sunset are givens in relation to our commonsense perceptions of the world. True, these objects are relational, and they are each impregnated with cultural interpretations; there is no such thing as a pure rabbit, unhued red, or an uninterpreted sun. Still, a bright red is not the sound of a trumpet, even though we might describe it as such to a blind person; and the warmth received from the sun is not its light, even though we may tell the blind that the light and warmth of the sun are connected. The following chapters are devoted to sketching this anthropocentric relational realism that centers about the fleshy body. However, the following example, which I owe to one of my students, may serve as a useful introduction.

The sound of our voice is indeed relative, relative to our ears, the ears of others, the equipment of a telephone or recorder. Nevertheless, these relations are in the world, and they each specify an essential way our voice can exist in the world. Still, there is no neutrally given voice beneath these appearances. Although our voice sounds differently to ourselves, to others, over the phone, and in a recording, and although the response to our voice is always individually and culturally interpreted, we always hear a voice and not a sound wave. Further, there is no a priori reason to privilege the way our voice sounds to us or to others or how it sounds when it is electronically reconstituted. Circumstances may indeed lead us to privilege one aspect over another, but that is another matter. Finally, although we always have to use language to refer to our voice, the different ways our voice appears in the world are not reducible to our linguistic expressions about our voice.

The correct way to think about matter is be more expansive in our view. Granting that qualities and consciousness itself are material, we must be open to see that there are perspectives from which the materiality of both is revealed to be *essentially* irreducible to quantitative relations. If we adopt such a view of matter, we must also be expansive in our notion of what constitutes an explanation. The description of a quality may very well be the only kind of explanation that can retain its distinctiveness. Or, what I would regard as a more precise and more challenging claim, we must be open to recognize that consciousness first and foremost goes out to matter, revealing and making a world. On the level in which revealing a world is making a world, our bond to matter is a nonthetic knowing of matter-made-world: seeing blue is knowing the essence of blue. I will not develop in detail these claims about sense knowledge as a knowledge of essences. However, in chapters 6 and 7, as well as in appendix II, I will briefly describe how to interpret our general linguistic expressions along the lines of a dialectical and relational nominalism, a nominalism that preserves an anthropocentric and relational realism.

The issue of getting hold of the uniqueness of consciousness is more complex, but it is not my main concern. However, I will consider it briefly in chapter 6. Here I would, again, simply note that we "make" our interiority through the way our consciousness goes "out" to the world and to other people. The realm of "others" adds a complexity to our attempt to describe the uniqueness of consciousness in general. Nevertheless, although initially this awareness is nonreflective and nonconceptual, I would insist that in seeing blue we simultaneously become aware of blue as a unique quality existing in the world and of our own consciousness as a unique materiality irreducible to matter as quantity.

Chapter 3

Knowledge as

Worldmaking

Hilary Putnam's internal realism, Nelson Goodman's worldmaking, and W. V. Quine's linguistic holism are all useful in framing my own more ontological worldmaking. Each of these critique the correspondence theory of truth, and I wish to introduce these views by once again reflecting upon our conception of a pure knowledge. If we put aside the issue of reducing qualities, such as colors and sounds, to quantities, such as wavelengths, the scientific materialist's picture of the world faces the broader realist issue of explaining how our perception and concepts of things should match the world. To the extent that this realist question is faced, and more frequently it is not, two kinds of answers are offered.

One may side with D. M. Armstrong and admit that, in principle, we have no theoretical guarantee that our knowledge reflects the way the world truly is. Science seems to work, and one lets it go at that. Once acknowledged, however, this skeptical glance at the foundation of the correspondence theory of truth—the theory that maintains that our ideas about the world reflect the way the world truly is independently of our own existence—is soon forgotten. In practice, Armstrong and others rely on causality to ground the way our perceptions seem to match onto the world. However, if pressed they would admit that we cannot justify the causal connection itself. In effect, they don't press the issue, and they proceed as if the foundation of causality is somehow given.

The other general move to avoid the knotty issue of correspondence, what Richard Rorty calls our glassy essence—our ability to reflect the way the world is in itself—is to claim, as Daniel C. Dennett does, that teleology disappears when we push the mechanistic picture deep enough.

> AI homunculi talk to each other, wrest control from each other, volunteer, subcontract, supervise, and even kill. There seems no better way of describing what is going on. . . . One *discharges* fancy homunculi from one's scheme by organizing armies of such idiots to do the work.[1]

Of course, this army of idiots is organized by us. We have simply taken a complicated job and broken it down so that it can be done in simpler steps. Teleology is not eliminated; it is merely pushed back to the operation of human consciousness. Dennett obviously is not suggesting that there is a Divine Consciousness guiding the erratic movements of matter toward meaningful ends, but if this is not his implication, his analogy of a computer with human consciousness limps badly. However, there is no need to press this issue. Let us take a closer look at Dennett's suggestion that nature is continuing to build up intentionally operating organisms by an army of "idiot" particles moving hither and thither.

> Darwin explains a world of final causes and teleological laws with a principle that is, to be sure, mechanistic but—more fundamentally—utterly independent of "meaning" or "purpose." It assumes a world that is *absurd* in the existentialist's meaning of the term: not ludicrous but pointless, and this assumption is a necessary condition of any non-begging-account of *purpose*.[2]

Darwin's world is not absurd in the existentialist's sense of that term. For Jean-Paul Sartre, from whom I cull many of my anthropocentric views, absurdity means that, without a relation to human existence, continuity over time would not exist.[3] But without continuity over time, no move-ment, idiotic or not, could ever get started. Dennett is actually projecting human purpose in nature and then attempting to negate that this projec-tion has taken place.

This move to project ourselves into the world and then negate the pro-jection is admitted but dismissed as harmless by Richard Sorabji. It is, however, to Sorabji's credit that he approaches the problem at its root, namely the issue of continuity over time.

> Little is involved in imagining an event in the personless situa-tion becoming past. We need only imagine the universe bereft of conscious life, while further imagining that, if there *had* after all been an intelligent being present, he *would* have been able to say: "so and so is earlier (or later) than this time." Once again this is not to imagine conscious beings both present and absent. It is rather to imagine a counterfactual situation within a counterfac-tual situation: having imagined that conscious beings might have been absent, we further imagine what could have been said by one of them, if one had after all been present.[4]

Sorabji is right on the mark. The continuity of things over time, their before and after, presupposes our presence in the world, at least counter-factually. But Sorabji's attempt to recognize this counterfactual situation and then pass it off as innocent is nothing but an effort at magic. In this context, I regard David Lewis's notion of plural worlds, which I will exam-ine in the following chapter, extravagant but more honest in its approach to counterfactuals, and I will postpone my formal study of modality for that chapter.

Dennett is, of course, correct in noting that we break up large prob-lems into small ones; but we have to have some idea where we are going, some notion of the problem to be solved. Like Armstrong and the Churchlands, Dennett puts reason in matter and then makes a case that matter just happens to hit upon teleology. Ironically, all these thinkers pre-sent us with a materialism that borders on idealism: matter dissolves into a set of scientific explanations about matter.

With the exception of Jean-Paul Sartre, whose thought I will consider in the next three chapters, no line of thought comes as close to the nonreductive anthropocentric materialism that I am sketching than Hilary Putnam's internal realism.

Putnam's internal realism seems to have been initially elaborated as part of his attempt to clarify the notion of meaning as detailed in his lengthy article "The Meaning of 'Meaning.'"[5] In the first part of that article, Putnam directed his attention to showing that meanings are not linked to concepts that reside in our minds. The thrust of Putnam's remarks are that the two crucial notions used to clarify this mental view of meaning—namely, *extension* and *intention*—are themselves ambiguous. Thus, conceptual meanings, meanings in our head, are supposed to be universal; that is, they are supposed to refer to a group, or set, of objects (extension), and they also are supposed to designate essential features of the objects (intention).

Putnam's general point was that both extension and intention are determined by our public linguistic practices, but in different ways that are incompatible with a mentalist view of meanings. In particular, there is, to use Putnam's expression, "a division of linguistic labor." Thus, our commonsense use of terms such as *elm, beech, water,* or *gold* can have a definite extension,we can identify the objects these terms refer to—even though we do not have scientific knowledge of the essential features of these objects. The appropriate experts in the field can, more or less, inform us of these essential features. Putnam astutely qualifies his view of the division of linguistic labor by noting, first, that the linguistic division presupposes a nonlinguistic division, that the division does not concern all objects (for example, chairs are excluded), and that it is relative to the times.[6] I agree with all of Punam's own qualifications on the notion of a linguistic division of labor, but these qualifications have more weight for me than they have for Putnam.

In a very broad sense, two sets of problems arise from Putnam's attention to the distinction between the extension and intention of terms. Those that arise from attending to the extension of terms can be said to lead us to examine the "sufficiently good epistemic condition" for asserting that an object belongs to the extension of a concept. Those that arise from attending to intention lead us to examine what constitutes objects, and this, in turn, leads to a notion of "natural-kinds." That is, the problems arising from attending to the extension of terms lead us to reflect upon truth, and those that concern the intention lead us to reflect upon how we divide the world.

Although Putnam's program is to show us that meanings are not in the head, it is the second set of problems, those that arise from the intention of terms, that more clearly do the job of emptying the mind of meanings. Indeed, from 1975 until the present (1999), Putnam gradually moves away from questions concerning truth conditions to questions concerning worldmaking. Thus, in *Reading Putnam*, in his reply to Simon Blackburn, Putnam remarks about his program:

> The point of the picture was to combine realism with a concession to moderate verificationism (a concession I would no longer make, by the way). . . . Yet there are reasonable and unreasonable, warranted and unwarranted, ways of using words. I continue to think of truth, like warrant, as fundamentally a normative notion. A second claim of "internal realism"—one I have not at all given up; the one I have increasingly emphasized in my writing, and the one at which most of Blackburn's fire is directed—concerns notions like "object," "entity," "property," and "existence." I have argued that it makes no sense to think of the world as dividing itself up into "objects" (or entities) independently of our use of language.[7]

In his efforts to show how we divide the world through our language, Putnam used two science-fiction examples in the classic essay "The Meaning of 'Meaning.'" The first concerned a twin Earth on which molybdenum was as common as aluminum is on our Earth, and the second concerned a twin Earth in which "water" existed that resembled our water, but had a different chemical constitution. This latter example was to attract the most attention, and it is the one that I will soon consider. Here, I simply wish to note again how Putnam's thought has moved away from being concerned about epistemic conditions to those concerning the way we divide the world. In his introduction to *The Twin Earth Chronicles: Twenty Years' Reflection on Hilary Putnam's "The Meaning of 'Meaning'"*, Putnam remarks:

> Unfortunately, more than one author has misread the essay by overlooking the fact that it asserted that there are additional factors involved in meanings. "The Meaning of 'Meanings'" also contains the beginning of a theory of natural-kind words.[8]

Putnam here and elsewhere urges that we reflect upon his notion of "stereotype" to clarify the notion of natural kinds. However, I will not follow his suggestion, for it would distract from my more general and more modest program. (I might note that I would deflate Putnam's "natural kinds" to a relatively few things—color, sound, trees, animals, and the like.) I do not deny the place of language. I simply insist that the linguistic division of labor needs, first and foremost, the ontological foundation of a relation to the organic differentiation of the fleshy body, and, secondarily, a relation to the set of scientific instruments and laws that are in our books. I think that attention to these relations help clarify Putnam's own praiseworthy efforts to empty our head of meanings. For, while Putnam is clear that meanings are not primarily in the head, he is not clear on where they should be. "I don't mean to say that some *other* objects are the meanings of words in a public language; in my view, meanings aren't objects at all."[9] Of course, "meaning" is, in this sense, a technical word, arising from our reflective attempts to clarify language. It is almost tautologically true that the real questions about language should remain within the domain of language. Still, the interesting issues about meanings are realist ones, and Putnam is a realist. Therefore, even if meanings are formally within the web of language and are to be clarifed by issues such as synonymy, and even if we reject a correspondence notion of how language maps on to the world, we still have to ask, "Are there natural kinds *in* the world?" However, before sketching Putnam's answer to this important question, and, in particular, before examining the twin Earth example of different "waters," I want to sketch Putnam's more general views on how we empty our minds into matter, while still keeping within a realist program.

In his *Many Faces of Realism*, Putnam questions the Cartesian view of the world.

The Cartesian picture is confused. It exhibits both modern phys-
icalist and medieval "tendency-ist" forms of explanation in an
unhappy coexistence. The new image of nature—the World
Machine—ought to have no place for the classical "tendencies.". . .
To analyze the dispositional idiom, we need an analysis of the
phrase "under normal conditions," or something similar. . . . .
But the currently most fashionable of theses—the notion of
"similarity" of possible worlds—only illustrates the distance
of counterfactual (and dispositional) talk from the world picture
of physics—illustrates it by introducing a metaphysical primi-
tive, which sticks out like a sore thumb.[10]

Putnam is right to note that the appeal to so-called tendencies and
possible worlds indicates that the mechanistic picture cannot stand on its
own foundation. Indeed, idealism slips into the scientific materialists' picture of the world, because they must defend their view of materialism by
giving theoretical reasons why the purposeful organization of matter
should exist. But if Descartes has taught us anything it is that, once we
allow philosophical or scientific explanations about the existence of matter to mediate our pragmatic awareness that we exist as bodies in contact
with other bodies, then there is no viable way to bridge the gap between
our thoughts about matter and matter itself. Neither God, nor Nature, nor
Causality, nor Chance, nor Being can mediate the primary relation of our
body with the world. Although Putnam's concerns are not exactly along
the lines of my reflection, he shows the ambiguity in a materialist world
filled with tendencies by the following example.

Imagine that Venusians land on Earth and observe a forest fire.
One of them says, "*I* know what caused that—the atmosphere of
the darned planet is saturated with oxygen." What this vignette
illustrates is that one man's (or extraterrestrial's) background
condition can easily be another man's "cause." What is and what
is not a "cause" or an "explanation" depends on background
knowledge and our reason for asking the question.[11]

Instead of a Venusian, who presumably has a body and in that crucial respect is like us, I will break with my general reluctance to use science-fiction examples and put forward for reflection an extraterrestrial intelligence whose body is a gaseous cloud composed of simple hydrogen. In its universe, the higher and more noble states of matter exist in the form of simple elements. In relation to such a being, *this* fire started because the *entire structure* of the laws of nature in our universe exists in this very magical way: namely, simple atoms seem to "degenerate" and become complex. Our mechanistic picture assumes that the intelligible structures in matter must lead to more complex unities as "higher" ones. There is no a priori reason why this should be the case. Complexity is "higher" only because, in the scientific picture of things, we exist as the successful evolution of complex matter from simple matter.

Furthermore, as I will show in the following chapter, David Lewis is right in his observation that modality is built into our perception of causality. This tree might *not* have been hit by lightening and may *not* have caught fire. Possibility is an essential part of the causal relations among things.[12] Lewis seems to edge toward an Aristotelian notion of causality as dependence rather than predictability,[13] but whether the notion of causality is predictability or dependence, it is clear that these notions require a healthy dose of reason and human intelligibility.[14]

The traditional picture of the world thus puts us in a bind in which we either accept a God's-eye view of matter or an idealistic union with matter: either we claim that matter of itself has the laws that our earth-bound science says it possesses—and, with Einstein, we simply admit our amazement about the fortuitous workability of our mathematics—or, we say that we project our scientific order onto matter—a matter that, of itself, has no intrinsic relation to our existence. I think that we can avoid this dilemma. All that is required is that we grant that the unities of things arise from their relations to our fleshy body. Thus, from a commonsense but nevertheless valid perspective, knowledge gives us the way the world is in its relation to a fleshy organism. This knowledge is, on a primary level, a bond of being between our bodies and matter: seeing blue is knowing blue because it is revealing matter to be bluelike. That you see blue differently than I see it or that what appears blue in this lighting appears green in another lighting is simply part of the relational aspect of being blue. On this ontological level, the significance of sensation is that if no organisms with sight existed, matter could not be discriminated as having a color like blue. A person born blind doesn't have the problem of seeing blue as green, but of perceiving the world as colored.

Secondarily, our historical practices also create systems to which matter can and does "respond" by allowing us to ask and receive meaningful questions and answers. From the perspective of our historical practices, the scientific picture of the world is both relative and absolute: colors, for example, are indeed wavelengths, and they are so essentially, but only in relation to our scientific instruments and theories. To repeat, there is no primordial goo, merely the differentiation of qualities by our senses and by our collectively constituted theories and instruments that extend these senses. But this ontology pushes Putnam's internal realism in a new direction, and I must back up to explain what is involved.

Putnam recognizes clearly that the contemporary scientific worldview mixes elements of our own consciousness with a mechanistic view of matter. It is important to keep this in mind before I note why I believe Putnam's internal realism should be ontologized. He states:

> The claim that a naturalistic relation *really is* synthetically identical with the relation of explanation is one that we cannot *understand* at all. It is as if someone, having built a certain mindlessness, a certain neutrality, (as we have done for centuries) into the notion of nature, then proceeded to tell us *without explanation* that nature has "built-in" epistemic properties. No intelligible philosophical claim is really being made.[15]

But if intentional structures do not exist in nature independently of a relation to our existence, what exactly do we mean by "nature"? For example, is there in nature a structure such as H_2O? Also, when I drink a glass of water to satisfy my thirst, am I drinking *water* or H_2O, or is there perhaps no difference between the two? The question brings us to the central theme of Putnam's internal realism.

Once we have discovered what water is in the actual world, we have discovered its *nature*: is this not essentialism?

It *is* a sort of essentialism, but not a sort which can help the materialist. For what I have said is that it has long been our *intention* that a liquid should *count* as "water" only if it has the same composition as the paradigm examples of water (or as the majority of them). I claim that this was our intention even before we *knew* the ultimate composition of water. If I am right then, *given those referential intentions*, it was always impossible for a liquid other than H_2O to be water, even if it took empirical investigation to find it out. But the "essence" of water in *this* sense is the product of our use of the word, the kinds of referential intentions we have: this sort of essence is not "built into the world" in the way required by an *essentialist theory of reference itself* to get off the ground.[16]

This is a statement of Putnam's internal realism, which claims that, given our interests and concerns, kinds of things do exist in relation to our projects. Putnam avoids both a weak relativism and historism because, *relative* to our present understanding of reality, there are facts of the matter. If we had no interest at all in finding out the internal composition of things, if we had no Greek philosophical tradition, then there would be no sense to the claim that water is H_2O. And if we had no more concern over gold than over different types of fingernail clippings, then there would be no meaningful distinction between fool's gold and true gold. Given our real concerns and linguistic practices, there are "kinds" to correspond to these concerns. Putnam thus summarizes his view: "the suggestion which constitutes the essence of 'internal realism' is that truth does not transcend use."[17]

In a similar way, our Western historical and philosophical concerns introduce a meaningful way of claiming that there is indeed a search for truth, even though our concepts and concerns are relative to our historical epoch.

Not only may we find out that statements we now regard as justified are false, but we may even find out that procedures we now regard as justificatory are not, and that different justification procedures are better. . . . Just as the objective nature of the environment contributes to fixing the reference of terms, so it also contributes to fixing the objective truth conditions for sentences, although not in the metaphysical realist way.[18]

For Putnam, given a particular disposition, language, and intention, it is true to say that H_2O *is* the essence of water and that there *is* a real distinction between fool's gold and real gold. On the other hand, neither water nor gold has any properties, intrinsic or otherwise, apart from our human intentions and usages. Once we are given a certain way of looking at things, what we then observe is *all* that is there *in relation to our perspective.* Putnam writes:

> Of course, the adoption of internal realism is the renunciation of the notion of the "thing in itself.". . . Internal realism says that we don't know what we are talking about when we talk about "things in themselves." And that means that the dichotomy between "intrinsic" properties and properties which are not intrinsic also collapses—collapses because the "intrinsic" properties were supposed to be just the properties things have "in themselves."[19]

Putnam comes very close to expounding the kind of relational realism with which I am concerned. However, there are two crucial differences. The first concerns a residual scientism in Putnam's views of natural kinds, and the second is that, for me, our explicit intentional concerns are not sufficient to ground a world.

Putnam's implicit scientism surfaces in his thought experiment involving "water" found on a "twin Earth." We are supposed to imagine that on Twin Earth everything is constituted the same as on this Earth, with one exception. On this Earth, it rains H_2O; rivers, lakes, and oceans are filled with H_2O; people and fish use H_2O for their pleasure and survival. On Twin Earth, the same functions are served by XYZ. It rains XYZ; fishes live in XYZ, and people drink and bathe in XYZ. For Putnam, the term "water" does not have the same reference in both Earths.

This example may seem to lead us back to intrinsic properties, but although I have serious problems with Putnam's claims, I do not think that he is trying to slip intrinsic natures into things of the sort that are supposed to exist independently of human intentions. Putnam notes that prior to Dalton chemistry, water was not understood to be H_2O. I would wish he said that, apart from the "invention" of Dalton chemistry, there would be no H_2O; but for the present, I will let that observation pass.[20]

There are, for me, two strange aspects to the twin Earth example of water: first, there is Putnam's claim that even before water was known to be H_2O it was still true that the term "water" referred to H_2O as *the* essence of water. Second, on Twin Earth, the term water could never refer to H_2O, that is, to water as it exists on Earth. Both claims are to be part of his internal realism, and there is to be no appeal to intrinsic properties. Let us see how this is supposed to work.

Putnam asks us to consider that prior to 1750 and the rise of Dalton chemistry there were different views about what constituted "pure" water. In ancient and medieval times, water was thought of as a pure substance. In fact, water was thought of as an element by many of the ancient and medieval thinkers.[21] Following this observation, Putnam would have us suppose that a believer in water as a pure substance is given a glass filled half with pure water and half with some other substance that looks and behaves like water. This combination quenches thirst and nourishes the body in the same way as real water. One now asks the believer in water as a pure substance, "Are you drinking water?" Putnam believes that the natural response would be, "No! I am drinking a *mixture* of pure water and some strange substance that acts like water."

Now this person of ancient or medieval times did not know that water is composed of H_2O; he erroneously believed it to be a pure substance. But the *reference* of the term "water" was still, according to Putnam, to the essential structure of that substance, whatever that might turn out to be. The enlightened medievalist should say: "I now believe water to be a pure substance, but if you could show me that water is composed of more basic elements, then I would want my term to refer to that composition, and not to my present false beliefs about water." In a similar way, Putnam claims that our present belief that water is H_2O must be understood in the sense that the term "water" refers to whatever is, in fact, the true essence of water here on Earth. If we should later discover that the basic structure of water lies in something more fundamental, we would want our term to refer to that more basic structure, whatever it might turn out to be.

The substance on Twin Earth that looks and behaves like water but which is really XYZ is not, for Putnam, water, even if our twins call it such. This may appear to be a backhanded emergence of intrinsic properties, but I do not think that this is the case, at least not in the usual sense of intrinsic properties that Putnam is denying. The point is that there is nothing really *hidden in principle* from human understanding. We know more about the essential structure of water today than people of two thousand years ago, and people in the future will continue to know more about what we now call water. We intend the term "water" to be part of a continuing process of human investigation. The reference to the essence of water is merely a shorthand way of referring to the continuing process of learning more and more about what really constitutes the structure of water.

Nevertheless, Putnam's realism is here on tenuous grounds. In the background of the twin Earth thought experiment is the conviction that, when all is said and done, there is a certain depth to the scientific way of looking at the world that is lacking in other ways of dealing with water. I suspect that this is not Putnam's intention, for he criticizes Quine on just that point. How then does this residual scientism slip into his internal realism?

I believe scientism slips into Putnam's thought because he cannot fully accept that water cannot have more than one essential relation. That is, Putnam's internal realism is not sufficiently relational. Putnam, in fact, has backed himself into a corner from which his own internal realism provides no exit. For suppose that Dalton chemistry had never arisen in human history, and suppose further that *it will never arise* in human history. Would the essence of water still be H_2O? And, if so, in relation to whose intentions?

Putnam gets himself in this embarrassing situation because, in the final analysis, the scientific essence of things is *the* essence. The relation that things have to our scientific concerns is thus, for him, privileged.[22] But if internal realism is true, why shouldn't other pragmatic considerations be just as "essential" to the nature of things? The relation of water to satisfying thirst is just as essential to the makeup of water as is its relation to our scientific formulas and instruments.

In focusing on the relations of water to bodily functions and sense perceptions, as well as to our scientific intentions and instruments, I modify Putnam's internal realism by ontologizing it. The only way to make internal realism both a relative realism and a realism constitutive of the world is to push it in the direction of an ontological relation of matter to the human organic body. In this way, the various relations that water has to the human body are constitutive of water as water, and each relation gives a true knowledge of water. Water *is*, essentially, just what it seems to be to a thirsty human: a healthy substance with its own fixed varieties of color and taste, capable of quenching thirst and nourishing the fleshy body. If the water on Twin Earth nourishes our bodies in the same way as H_2O, then in relation to the function of nourishing the human organism both waters are *essentially the same*. Further, I see no reason to suggest that the two waters could differ internally if *all* the external features were the same.

I believe the reason that Putnam does not make the move to relate natural kinds to the fleshy body is that he is too tied to a mechanistic view of the human body. If the body is nothing but a complex machine, then a natural kind, such as water, would be reducible to the scientific model of water as H_2O. Molding the known to the knower, if the body is mechanistic, the world is reducible to mere matter in motion. But in relation to the fleshy constitution of an organism, water is a wet substance falling in rain, lying in lakes, and flowing in rivers; and it is pure or impure, depending upon how it serves the health of the body.

Putnam needs to ontologize his internal realism if he is to avoid the ambiguity concerning natural kinds evident when he attempts to reply to the objection: ". . . some have objected, it seems that I am saying that we didn't know the meaning of the word 'water' until we developed modern chemistry." Putnam replies:

> This objection simply involves an equivocation on the phrase
> "know the meaning." To know the meaning of a word may mean
> (a) to know how to translate it, (b) to know what it refers to in

the sense of having the ability to state explicitly what the denotation is (other than by using the word itself), or (c) to have tacit knowledge of its meaning, in the sense of being able to use the word in discourse. The only sense in which the average speaker of the language "knows the meaning" of most of his words is (c). In that sense, it was true in 1750 that Earth English speakers knew the meaning of the word "water" and it was true in 1750 that Twin Earth English speakers knew the meaning of their word "water." "Knowing the meaning" in this sense isn't literally knowing some *fact*.[23]

This response is disastrous for Putnam's internal realism. If, to repeat, chemistry had never been invented, and if we further imagine a world in which chemistry will never be invented, then we would always be using words only in the sense of having a tacit knowledge of what we are talking about. Our so-called tacit use of language would never deliver to us knowledge of a *fact*. We would be indeed back to the Kantian thing-in-itself, or at least to something very similar, namely, to the Aristotelian essence that is more knowable in itself than it is in relation to us.[24]

RECIPES FOR STARMAKING

In approaching my relational realism, I seem to be traveling along the paths of what Israel Scheffler has called the "wonderful worlds of Goodman."[25] Goodman's voice is strong and clear when it is expounding on the need to avoid reducing things to their scientific structure. In *Ways of Worldmaking*, Goodman is also skeptical about the distinction between intrinsic and extrinsic qualities.[26] But Goodman pushes this insight to arrive at a more varied relational realism than the one offered by Putnam. If there are no privileged intrinsic properties, then there is no one realist view of the world; the worlds of common sense, science, and art give equally valid ways of interpreting our environment.

Is the seen table the same as the mess of molecules? To such questions discussed at length in the philosophical literature, I suspect that the answer is a firm *yes* and a firm *no*. The realist will resist the conclusion that there is no world; the idealist will resist the conclusion that all conflicting versions describe different worlds. As for me, I find these views equally delightful and equally deplorable—for after all, the difference between them is purely conventional![27]

Goodman's conventionalism, however, does not lead to a weak relativism: given a version of the world, there are criteria for constructing worlds in more or less meaningful ways. Goodman extends his worldmaking not only to the worlds of common sense and art, but to the world of science, but for my purpose of ontologizing internal realisms, the more relevant debate concerns our scientific picture of the world. In an interesting and continuing debate with Israel Scheffler, Goodman has steadfastly maintained that worlds are indeed "made" by us. We do indeed "make" stars.

> Now as we thus make constellations by picking out and putting together certain stars rather than others, so we make stars by drawing certain boundaries rather than others. Nothing dictates whether the skies shall be marked off into constellations or other objects. We have to make what we find, be it the Great Dipper, Sirus, food, fuel, or a stereo system.
>
> Still, if stars like constellations are made by versions, how can the stars have been there eons before all versions? Plainly, through being made by a version that puts the stars much earlier than itself in its own space-time.[28]

Goodman's answer to Scheffler's objection that our discovery of stars is not reducible to any whim we have about the heavens is to insist that worldmaking must fit proper criteria. Goodman writes:

> Scheffler also objects to the idea that we make worlds, and he is not alone in this. . . . We make chairs, computers, books, planes; and making any of these right takes skill, care, and hard work. . . . Scheffler contends that we cannot have made the stars. I ask him

which features of the stars we did not make, and challenge him to state how these differ from features clearly dependent on discourse. . . . The worldmaking mainly in question here is making not with hands but with minds, or rather with languages or other symbol systems. Yet when I say that worlds are made, I mean it literally.[29]

I agree with Goodman that we do indeed make stars. However, I find his recipe of discourse and symbols not sufficient to deliver the objectivity and materiality of the universe that seems evident to our commonsense intuitions. To be specific, I think that there is a *disanalogy* between the way we make constellations and the way we make stars. It is clear that the separation of the stars that we identify as the Big Dipper is a matter of convention. But is the unity of a star itself *that* conventional? I do not think so, and I suspect that reservations of this type bother Scheffler.

Goodman is right, however, in his general claim that stars would not exist without our existence, but he is wrong in claiming that stars are made by discourse alone. The issue is clearer when worldmaking is turned to the human body itself. There are clearly many versions of making the human body and many worlds in which to include it. Goodman is careful not to give us reasons to reduce the human body *essentially* to a mechanistic version of the body. Still, are we to go to the other extreme and accept that we could validly give a world-version that would eliminate our bodies? Could we be pure minds, and could matter be merely one of our thoughts? I think that Goodman wants to hold on to the reality of matter, but I think that he can only do so by accepting that, in some basic sense, the fleshy constitution of the human body cannot be interpreted away.

The only way that Goodman has of holding on to a starmaking that is humanly centered and objective is to root the relation in the human organic fleshy body. Stars are not made by language alone, but stars *are* "made." Stars come into being through the way matter arranges itself in relation to our organic existence, and through the way the world is filtered by our scientific instruments and theories.[30] Again, these relations give us different aspects of a star. In relation to a fleshy conscious body with eyes, the essence of a star is to be a far-away twinkling thing that appears in the heavens at dusk and night, and that has also proven to be useful in navigation. In relation to our scientific theories and instruments, a star is, among other things, the furnace that produces the heavy elements needed for life.

My recipe for starmaking is for hearty appetites. Goodman's talk about stars starves poor Scheffler. We can give Scheffler his real stars, and we don't have to worry about his additional caloric intake. It's ontological fat, not anthropocentric calories that Scheffler has to watch. Colors and sounds, atoms and stars feed hungry mouths before they satisfy linguistic criteria.

GAVAGAI, WHOLE OR IN PARTS

Of the analytic philosophies that I have considered, Willard V. O. Quine's thought is both closest and furthest from the anthropocentric realism that I am attempting to sketch in this book. Quine sees very clearly the central problem in the correspondence theory of truth: the only way to ground the correspondence theory of truth is to do so anthropocentrically. The background for Quine's views lies in his critique of classical linguistic philosophers. By turning our attention to the way language works, the "linguistic turn" was supposed to turn our concern away from the fruitless effort of fitting concepts to things.[31] But Quine's point is that this linguistic task is as mysterious as the former realist issue. We have no privileged access into language. The same metaphysical problems about the correspondence theory of truth reappear when we attempt to get hold of the essence of language.[32]

> If by some oracle the physicist could identify outright all the truths that can be said in commonsense terms about ordinary things, still his separation of statements about molecules into true and false would remain largely unsettled. We can imagine him partly settling that separation by what is vaguely called scientific method: by considerations of simplicity of the joint theory of ordinary things and molecules. But conceivable truths about molecules are only partially determined by any ideal organon of scientific method *plus* all the truth that can be said in commonsense terms about ordinary things; for in general the simplest possible theory to a given purpose need not be unique.[33]

A language is holistic, and thus one can always enter a language and readjust all the scientifically true statements to false ones. If the scientist tries to appeal to commonsense principles, these can also be given a new interpretation. A geologist may say that the earth evolved over billions of years; a creationist could say that God created the earth to make it appear that it was created over billions of years. But actually Quine is after more than just noting this type of ambiguity in language.

Quine's favorite example concerns the term *gavagai* in a tribal language. A visitor wants to discover whether this term refers to a rabbit, a stage of a rabbit's behavior, or a rabbit part. Quine shows that there is no hope for success. Quine will later bring his analysis to bear on the attempt to establish a univocal relation between one's home language and its objects, but, for the present, let us follow the translator's problems with *gavagai*.

No behavioral pattern can clarify the meaning of *gavagai* apart from the holism of the tribal language. There is no way to point to a whole rabbit without also pointing to a rabbit part or to a temporal stage of the rabbit. Further, it will always be possible to reinterpret both the sentences and the behavior of the native so that we think they refer to a whole rabbit, when in fact, they refer to part of a rabbit. The visitor may think communication has been achieved. He receives a whole, live, kicking rabbit, and he thinks that this is what the native means to give him. But the native's term *gavagai* points only to the kicking legs, and not the rest of the rabbit for which the native's language has no term.

> Insofar as the native sentences and the thus associated English ones seem to match up in respect of appropriate occasions of use, the linguist feels confirmed in these hypotheses of translation. . . . But it seems that this method, though laudable in practice and the best we can hope for, does not in principle settle the indeterminacy between "rabbit," undetached "rabbit part," and "rabbit stage."[34]

On reflection, the translator realizes that this same state of indeterminacy reappears in one's home language. We can now realize that our use of "rabbit" to mean whole rabbit could be understood by a Hegelian-minded speaker as referring to a temporal stage of a rabbit. No amount of behavior will clarify the issue. Thus, for Quine, reference in any language is indeterminate. Indeed, at the heart of both translation and reference, there exists a double indeterminacy.[35]

> Ontology is indeed doubly relative. Specifying the universe of a
> theory makes sense only relative to some background theory,
> and only relative to some choice of a manual of translation of
> the one theory into the other.[36]

Generally, when we try to understand another's language, we keep our own background language fixed. But this is just for our present convenience. Actually, our background language is itself in question; there is no way to map our entire language onto the world unequivocally.[37] Each sentence in our language takes its meaning relative to the whole of our background language, and the entire language itself is simply one way of mapping a holistic meaning structure onto the world. There is thus a twofold indeterminacy in translation: one that relates our sentences to those of others while keeping our background language fixed, and one that recognizes that our entire background language is itself not based upon the bedrock of any quasi-Aristotelian correspondence theory of truth. It is this second indeterminacy that leads to what Quine calls a fundamental inscrutability of reference.

The inscrutability of reference is the most controversial aspect of Quine's thought, from which even Donald Davidson attempts to rescue him.[38] Quine seems, at times, to give us a Kantian unknowable thing-in-itself that we can capture in any way we please according to our pragmatic intentions or language usages. But this is not Quine's intent. Quine's ontological relativity, the indeterminacy of what exactly is out there, is, as he puts it, not a question of not putting all our cards on the table, as there being no cards to put on the table. Inscrutability of reference does not refer to an unknowable fact, for "there is no fact of the matter."[39]

If Quine seems to slip into idealism, it is clear that this is not his intent. Our home language is intimately connected with observation sentences,

and these observation sentences report more or less directly the stimulations of our sense organs; or to use Quine's own language, observation
sentences report our surface irritations.[40] Theory begins as we move away
from observation sentences and attempt to give meaning to these surface
irritations.[41] Of course, our home language is not grounded in observation
sentences, since there is no unequivocal way of connecting observational
terms with sense data or surface irritations.

> In our own language, by the same token, the stimulus meaning
> of an observation sentence in no way settles whether any part of
> the sentence should be distinguished as a term for sense data, or
> as a term for physical objects, or as a term at all.[42]

For Quine, there is no fixed world behind language, and yet there is
more than just language. Quine is a behaviorist, and he talks in terms of
stimulus and response. Quine seems to hold out to us a form of realism
that seems close to my own intent to stay on the surface of things, or at
least to do so before we progress to our interior states: at least, the surfaces
of our bodies are real as well as the stimuli impinging upon them. But
unfortunately, the similarity does not hold. Unlike my own emphasis on
the fleshy nature of the body, Quine's bodies turn out to be intellectual
entities.

> When we want to check on existence, bodies have it over other
> objects on the score of their perceptibility. But we have moved
> now to the question of checking not on existence, but on impu-
> tations of existence: on what a theory says exists.[43]

Quine speaks of his robust realism. He is indeed a realist. But this is
a conviction, and it is a conviction born of the success of science. Science
works by adopting a realist perspective on the world, and science has
been successful in explaining our relation with our environment. It is up
to science to tell us what is real, but the language of science is nothing but
the language of common sense become self-conscious and critical. Here
the picture becomes a bit foggy, especially when we try to understand
how Quine's robust realism is related to common sense. The sentence

"This is red" is presumably an observation sentence; it reports a surface irritation on the retina of my eye. This sentence is minimally theory-laden. We would like to be able to say that it is not theory-laden at all, that it reports, if not redness itself in the world, at least a certain surface irritation on the eye.

And indeed, I suspect that Quine would allow us to say this. However, this claim would not imply that such irritations are, in fact, on the surface of the eye. Rather, all we would mean is that, in our present home language, with its present science, there is no other way to conceive of the world except as inhabited by human bodies that receive surface irritations. The entire structure, bodies-affected-with-surface-irritations, is, in Quine's term, a "posit."

> To call a posit a posit is not to patronize it. A posit can be unavoidable except at the cost of other no less artificial expedients. Everything to which we concede existence is a posit from the standpoint of a description of the theory-building process, and simultaneously real from the standpoint of the theory that is being built. Nor let us look down on the standpoint of the theory as make-believe; for we can never do better than occupy the standpoint of some theory or other, the best we can muster at the time.[44]

All this would be easy to grasp if we understood Quine to be advocating a belief in a Perceian limit to our knowledge: science gradually helps us to know the world more and more accurately, and we must thus live with the realization that our present knowledge of the world may not only be improved upon but may be radically altered. But this again is not Quine's position. For science is itself a posit. Indeed, the entire worldview that says that science is the ultimate posit is again a posit.

> [T]heory in physics is an ultimate parameter. There is no legitimate first philosophy, higher or firmer than physics. . . . Thus, adopt for now my fully realistic attitude toward electrons and neurons and curved space-time, thus falling in with the current theory of the world despite knowing that it is in principle

methodologically under-determined. Consider, from this realistic point of view, the totality of truths of nature, known and unknown, observable and unobservable, past and future. The point about indeterminacy of translation is that it withstands even all this truth, the whole truth about nature.[45]

But now we might want to ask Quine, "Yes, translation is indeterminate, but *are* there rabbits?" There is clearly a priority to bodies and perhaps to organic bodies in Quine's world.[46] However, the priority seems to mean nothing more than that everything seems to make more sense and be more pragmatically justifiable, if we *posit* bodies. Quine himself could *in principle* be something other than a body. But how is Quine to separate himself from the idealism of Bishop Berkeley? He can and does claim that behaviorism gives us the posits that make science workable; or, to be more precise, that science is more workable if there are bodies that can be subject to the investigation of evolution and behavioristic practices. But it is difficult to see how this would answer an idealist, who would claim that the entire complex is a posit made, not by a material thing, but by a spiritual mind conceiving the *idea* of bodies. And, from another perspective, it is difficult to see how Quine can escape Barry Stroud's observation that, if physics provides us with the ultimate parameter, then mathematical formulas and not bodies should be the ultimate posits.[47]

Quine seems aware of this charge of idealism to his philosophy. When he considers the notion of induction, he must claim that the very notion of a body is a posit. His answer is, "Yes," but that his *attitude* is naturalistic.

> At this point let me say that I shall not be impressed by protests that I am using inductive generalizations, Darwin's and others', to justify induction, and thus reasoning in a circle. The reason I shall not be impressed by this is that my position is a naturalistic one; I see philosophy not as an *a priori* propaedeutic or groundwork for science, but as a continuous with science. I see philosophy as in the same boat—a boat which, to revert to Neurath's figure as I so often do, we can rebuild only at sea while staying

afloat in it. . . . Darwin's natural selection is a plausible partial explanation.[48]

Quine finds it as natural to posit the existence of universal classes needed to base the foundations of mathematics as he posits the bodies needed to interpret our commonsense intuitions about the world. This is perhaps an exaggeration. It seems that Quine would like to eliminate the need for positing the existence of mathematical classes, but since they seem to be needed at present both for the functioning of mathematics and science, he is as willing to accept them in his ontology with the same right of existence as bodies. "The reason for admitting numbers as objects is precisely their efficacy in organizing and expediting the sciences. The reason of admitting classes is much the same."[49]

Quine thus attempts to avoid the mystique of naturalism by substituting for a correspondence theory of truth, the human enterprise of positing the entire universe as well as our efforts at interpreting it. There is an integrity in Quine's position. But the price of this integrity is the loss of the very materiality of the world. The world evaporates into a *solution* of an intellectual enterprise. Quine cannot reply that this is the philosophical game. This is true; but it is also true that, if we are to avoid idealism, our primary intuitions about the ontological status of organisms must be acknowledged. I think that we can acknowledge this status without resurrecting the notion of a glassy essence, or appealing to mysterious links of language with the world.

Kant taught us that the question to ask about knowledge is not how our notions correspond with the world, but how the world enters our knowing apparatus. This Kantian insight must be pushed to reveal a bond between the human body and the world. We must thus substitute for the Kantian categories our organic existence with its various sense organs. Prior to our acting in the world, prior to our conceptualizations about the world, prior to our speaking about the world, there is a bond of being between the unity of things and the organic differentiation of our bodies. This bond of being is not mysterious. On the contrary, it reveals that color is just the way matter has to be, if there are fleshy eyes in the world. And because, with our technology, with our theoretical language and with our books, we can view the eye as a sophisticated camera, this bond of being also reveals color to be a certain part of the electromagnetic spectrum.

We can't *feel* Quinean surface irritations. Or, if we do feel the irritations, they must first be baptized by theory before we can admit the feelings to be knowledge. Quine sees our everyday perceptions to be in need of scientific validation, because he accepts a continuity between science and common sense. However, every continuity between science and common sense is established from a particular perspective. Quine chooses to relate common sense to science, while working within a scientific perspective. There is nothing wrong with this, but it is not philosophically privileged.

Language is holistic, but it is not so in any one sense, and this is my basic internal critique of Quine's holism. English, for example, works within several holisms, and in this respect, Goodman's way of worldmaking has a proper place. From my own perspective, I here recall my three distinctions of the given, each of which gives rise to distinct holisms. These holisms are related, but only ambiguously so. To repeat, the givens of common sense are based upon the organic differentiation of the body, and from this perspective, a holistic language of common sense arises. We thus speak of the world in terms of colors, sounds, textures, odors, etc. I have already noted that these givens are not part of a "myth." I here note that the linguistic holism engendered by these givens has an anthropocentric but nevertheless true bond with the world.

The two other states of the givens, those that supposedly found our culture and those that supposedly form the base of our science, are indeed "myths." These holisms are consequently underdetermined. If these holisms were completely separate from the commonsense linguistic holism that arises from the organic differentiation of the body, I might be willing to grant Quine's indeterminacy on the levels of history and science. But in fact, they are intertwined, at least to the extent that they all refer to the same world, and to the extent that we frequently use the same terms— such as "water" to mean that which is composed of H_2O and that which feels wet to the touch.

I am willing to grant that these holisms to which I refer are part of a larger holism: for example, English language. But I insist that there is no privileged point from which to reflect upon this larger, ambiguous linguistic structure. In the concrete, our reflections arise either from the vantage point of common sense or from that of science or from that of culture. Given a vantage point as a perspective, we then attempt to relate the other two perspectives and their consequent holisms. Quine can thus do it all from the vantage point of science. I just wish to add that we can also relate science and culture from the vantage point of common sense. We have no neutral perspective, except one that we forge, and I will examine that in the last two chapters.

Still, I see a certain priority in returning to the way language is rooted in our organic fleshy body. If one stays within the framework of history or science, the givens of common sense tend to appear as interpreted, and we then approach idealism. It is only by shifting perspective, returning to that of common sense, that we are able to keep our fleshy feet on mother Earth. With our feet on Earth, we can then begin the task of understanding the relation of common sense to history and to science.

We do make worlds, and the most important world that we make is the world revealed by our common sense. Our common sense gets us in touch with the essential aspects of the things of its world. Given this relational realism, we can now return to a correspondence theory of truth. The meshing of mind and matter now work anthropocentrically. A star is a star because that is the way that part of matter arranges itself in relation to a fleshy body differentiated with organs of perceptions. There is still mystery. However, it is through our bodies that the mystery is one about stars and not about some other possible arrangement of matter.

Chapter 4

Matters and
Modalities

Our common sense delivers to us a world filled with diverse kinds of matter. In relation to our perceptions and our practical usages, matter never appears to us as a purely quantitative thing. We don't drink H_2O. How could we? We can't see H_2O; we can't feel it or taste it. We drink water; we drink that which quenches thirst and nourishes and refreshes. The point of relational realism is that, given the fleshy constitution of the body, water is essentially just that wet, nourishing, refreshing thing that we encounter in our experience.

True, water is also H_2O; that is, in relation to the intentions, formulas, and instruments of chemistry, wetness resolves itself into a molecular structure. We can go further in our attempt to find out what things have in common and reduce water to its subatomic parts. Water could be reduced to the equations that explain the movements of its subatomic particles. In each reduction water manifests itself as a different reality. We are not, therefore, merely concerned with different meanings of the term "water," but with diverse facets of the thing we designate as "water." If we should feel uncomfortable with such diversity and demand a transcendental view that unites all facets of water, we will no doubt be able to produce such a perspective. We could put forward a neuroscientific or a Husserlean reduction, or my own version of a relational realism as a transcendental perspective. (I would not do so, but I can imagine someone else interpreting my perspective in that way.) In relation to such a perspective, all other reduction might seem to be "explained"; but the explanation is relative to the transcendental perspective itself. A "transcendental" outlook is simply another relational perspective on the world, constituted by a special set of human practices that I will examine in the last two chapters.

One could question whether this relational realism implies a Kantian, unknowable thing-in-itself that can now appear to be this and now that, but whose fundamental nature eludes us. Such a view, however, arises only by taking a transcendental perspective as privileged a priori. For Kant, this privileged perspective arose from God, who, although explicitly on the scene only in ethics, was always there. But if we accept the anthropocentric view that I am advocating, then things, precisely *as* they are things, with an intrinsic but relational continuity over time, arise from their relation to our organic bodies and the practices instituted by these bodies.[1] There are no divisions apart from relational ones, for the very notion of a division is relational. Even Aquinas, who held to a strict correspondence theory of truth, saw that truth is ultimately relational: the divisions among things—that is to say, the truth of things—arose from their relations to the Divine Mind. In a sense, I am merely substituting the human, conscious, fleshy body for the Divine Mind.

I want to emphasize once again that the relation to which I refer is one of matter to matter—the specific matter of the human body with the matter of the world. This is a kind of a dualism, but I see it as philosophically harmless since it remains within the physical realm. It is difficult, indeed impossible, to describe the so-called matter from which the things of the world arise, but this impossibility has nothing to do with a lack on our part. Given our own creation of transcendental philosophies and religions, we imaginatively wonder about how things might be if we did not exit. We then reconstruct this wonder into a claim that a relational realism implies that some world-goo preexisted our own existence. All that a relational realism implies, however, is that matter is almost infinitely rich, and that what we call "things" are matter differentiated in relation to the human fleshy body and, of course, the practices that we establish through our bodies.

My main point here, however, is that, in relation to the organic body, qualities such as color, sound, and wetness truly exist in the world as do the differences among minerals, plants, and animals. In what follows, I attempt to give some substance to this claim by examining David Lewis's notion of supervenience and Sartre's notion of negation.

MODALITY AND PLURALITY

The impetus of David Lewis's *On the Plurality of Worlds* is to get us to see that linguistic formulations cannot account for modalities; that is to say, language as such cannot be the foundation for the "cans" and "might have beens" that are so much a part of our language. For Lewis, the truths of modal statements, such as "I might not have written this sentence" or "That house might have been painted green instead of white," demand that other worlds exist in which these possibilities are realized. This one, actual world of ours is not expansive enough to ground the modalities that are reflected in our linguistic practices.

In a similar way, Jean-Paul Sartre's *Being and Nothingness* aims at showing that negative statements, such as "Pierre is absent," need a more than linguistic foundation. Sartre claims that there are real "absences" in things that he calls *négatités*. Further, he claims that these *négatités* arise from the human reality which is itself an option on being. Sartre expresses this aspect of nonreductive materialism through the expression that the human reality is what-it-is-not and is not what-it-is. Thus, in place of Lewis's plural worlds, Sartre gives us one world in which possibilities arise from the presence of a unique kind of material being, the human reality.

Both Sartre and Lewis see that our one actual world could be composed of other "thises" and "thats" than the ones that actually exist in it now. Although Sartre expressed his views prior to Lewis, I will start with

Lewis. In any case it is clear that there was no influence of Sartre on Lewis. Lewis begins his *On the Plurality of Worlds* by inviting us to marvel at this seemingly innocent complex that we call a world:

> The world we live in is a very inclusive thing. Every stick and every stone you have ever seen is part of it. And so are you and I. And so are the planet Earth, the solar system, the entire Milky Way, the remote galaxies we see through telescopes. . . . There is nothing so far away from us as not to be part of our world. . . . Likewise the world is inclusive in time. No long-gone ancient Romans, no long-gone pterodactyls, no long-gone primordial clouds of plasma are too far in the past, nor are the dark dead stars too far in the future, to be part of this same world. . . . The way things are, at its most inclusive, means the way this entire world is. But things might have been different, in ever so many ways. This book of mine might have been finished on schedule.[2]

Modality concerns possibility and necessity, which are expressed by verbs such as "can," "might," "may," "must," and "could." It seems that we are involved in a question of a linguistic interpretation of the world. But what allows us to speak this way about the world? If a completely scientific view of the universe were correct, all these modal ways of speaking about matter would be forms of a folk psychology that should be displaced by a single quasi-mechanistic view that gives us not only the way the world is, but the way it has to be. My point throughout, however, has been that such a scientific view is merely one stance on matter, a stance that is itself a complex of theory and instruments. As a web of theories wedded to instruments, the scientific ideal of the internal constitution of a thing truly enters into the world. The essence of water can thus be said to be an essential intrinsic structure of which the chemical structure H_2O is a present-day approximation.

However, this scientific stance, this scientific materialism, cannot provide a basis in reality for modality. To give Putnam's more general point, if all our primary intuitions about the world are to be explained in terms of folk psychology, then why should science not be explained in terms of a folk logic? But now I am straying somewhat from Lewis's own development. What is clear is that, for Lewis, the plurality of worlds is needed for reasons beyond those provided by a semantical analysis of language.

> When I say that possible worlds help with the analysis of modal-
> ity, I do not mean that they help with the metalogical "semanti-
> cal analysis of modal logic." Recent interest in possible worlds
> began there, to be sure. But wrongly. For that job, we need no
> possible worlds. . . . Where we need possible worlds, rather, is in
> applying the results of these metalogical investigations . . . and
> then we are doing metaphysics, not mathematics.[3]

Lewis sees that counterfactuals point to real possibilities. To repeat his own example, if it is true that Humphrey might have won the election, then either this claim points to a real possibility or it is a mere linguistic expression. But if the linguistic expression is not more than a mere fiction, then the possibility has to be real. For Lewis, this means that another world must exist in which Humphrey does win the election. To give an even more concrete example:

> If counterfactuals were no good for anything but idle fantasies
> about unfortunate kangaroos, then it might be faint praise to say
> that possible worlds can help us with counterfactuals. But, in
> fact, counterfactuals are by no means peripheral or dispensable
> to our serious thought. They are as central as causation itself. As
> I touch these keys, luminous green letters appear before my eyes,
> and afterward black printed letters will appear before yours; and
> if I had touched different keys—a counterfactual supposition—
> then correspondingly different letters would have appeared.[4]

But why do counterfactuals have to point to the existence of other worlds? Perhaps counterfactuals merely indicate possible worlds of our own construction, or they reflexively refer to the linguistic expressions them-selves. For Lewis, this is a quest for "paradise on the cheap." It attempts to provide human-made objects of counterfactuals, either in abstract entities or in sets of linguistic expressions. "Linguistic ersatzism typically constructs its ersatz worlds as maximal consistent sets of sentences."[5] Lewis correctly sees that all such constructions presuppose the very possibility of counter-factuals that they attempt to explain; they do not provide us with the reality of different possibilities. Speaking about a linguistic ersatzer, whose position, for him, is the strongest of all alternate positions, Lewis states:

> It sounds as if he is meeting me half way: when I demand many possibilities he does not offer me that, but at least he offers me many *possible* possibilities. Then I could very well say: call them what you will, at least we have many of something. Not so. There is no such thing in his ontology as an unactualized possible pos-sibility. He has gone no part of the way toward granting what I took to be plainly true. I say there are many ways that something might have happened. He denies that there are many of anything relevant, though he grants that there might have been.[6]

The ersatzer can deliver only actuality, and as Aristotle would say, act cannot explain potency. Potentiality was one of the great "discoveries" of Aristotle, but it required seeing form as act and matter as potency. Unfortunately, as we have seen, this matter-form distinction concedes too much to Plato; the form consumes matter, and the Prime Mover consumes all earthly actuality by being its own actuality. Clearly Lewis does not want to head in this direction.

Before we turn to Lewis's solution, it is important to be aware that counterfactuals not only give rise to questions about possibilities, but also to issues about the distinction of one thing from another. It happens that things are constituted thus in our world, but they could be constituted dif-ferently in another world; or more simply, there could be other universes.

I interpret Lewis's notion of "supervenience" to imply not merely that human actions could be different, but that the very distinction of one thing from another has its basis in modality. "Supervenience means that there *could* be no differences of one sort without differences of the other sort."[7] Lewis's notion of what constitutes a thing is very open-ended: A "thing" is any combination that language can unite for a purpose.

> We have no name for the mereological sum of the right half of my left shoe plus the Moon plus the sum of all her Majesty's ear-

rings, except for the long and clumsy name I just gave it. . . . It is very sensible to ignore such a thing in our every day thought and language. But ignoring it won't make it go away.[8]

In a similar way Lewis approves of all sorts of properties, "gruesome" or otherwise.[9] I prefer, however, to highlight his simple but profound intuition that differences among things and their modal qualities need more than either a Kantian or a linguistic basis. With this fundamental insight in mind, I think that we can see why Lewis is forced to turn to the existence of plural worlds for the basis of modality.

Lewis seems to be a reductionist. At least, he seems to believe that whatever explanation we have of the world and consciousness will be provided by science, especially physics.[10] I hope it is clear that I am here concerned only with that aspect of Lewis's thought that helps me make my point about the viability of a noneducative, relational realism. I thus see Lewis's claim about plural worlds to be the result of a dilemma: like Kripke, whose views I will examine in the next chapter, Lewis recognizes that language should not merely slide over things; he sees that our behavior indicates that we are in contact with things as they are in themselves. Nevertheless, Lewis also sees that no ordinary scientific interpretation of matter can explain the fortuitous correspondence of language and thing that we experience to occur in our world. Particularly, a mechanistic view of matter cannot explain our modal and counterfactual claims about the world. Still, for Lewis, matter is the way science describes it; it is quantitative and devoid of qualities. Thus he logically concludes that the basis for our modal judgments and counterfactual claims must point to other worlds in which these claims are true. Further, since the same reasoning holds in regard to the particular differentiation of matter into things that characterize our world, for Lewis other worlds must exist in which other combinations of matter exist. The reasoning throughout is, to repeat, that modality, counterfactuals, and worldhood must have a basis other than our concepts and our linguistic expressions.[11]

I agree with Lewis's premises, but not with his conclusion. A more expansive view of matter and a proper emphasis on the unique role of the human fleshy body can provide a less inflationary foundation for modality and worldhood than the postulation of plural worlds.

Lewis's search for an ontological foundation for counterfactuals is similar to Sartre's pursuit of the basis of our ability to make negative judgments about the world. Just as Lewis claims that the existence of plural worlds provides the ontological foundation for counterfactuals, Sartre insists that the distinctive existence of human reality creates both our ability to make negative judgments about the world as well as the negative and modal aspects of the world itself.

In the early part of *Being and Nothingness*, Sartre introduces us to both a realistic and anthropocentric view of negation:

> One will perhaps be tempted not to believe in the objective existence of a non-being; one will say that in this case the fact simply refers me to my subjectivity; . . . [But] to destroy the reality of the negation is to cause the reality of the reply to disappear. . . . There exists then for the questioner the permanent objective possibility of a negative reply. In relation to this possibility the questioner by the very fact that he is questioning, posits himself as in a state of indetermination; he *does not know* whether the reply will be affirmative or negative. The question is a bridge set up between two non-beings: the non-being of knowing in man, the possibility of non-being in transcendent being.[12]

Sartre's claims about negation are related to Lewis's concerns about modality. Both insist that language itself cannot account for either negation or modality. We ask questions and make negative judgments about the world, but somehow the world must be open to allow such questions and judgments to be made. Sartre puts the matter in these words:

> . . . we must consider the question in dialogue to be only a particular species of the genus "question". . . . If my car breaks down, it is the *carburetor* or the *spark plugs*, etc., that I question. . . . What I expect from the carburetor. . . is a disclosure of being on the basis of which we can make a judgment. And if I *expect* a disclo-

sure of being, I am prepared at the same time for the eventuality of a disclosure of a non-being.[13]

The carburetor that actually breaks down might not have broken down. Lewis refers to this as a counterfactual situation, but Sartre focuses on the possibility *in* the carburetor to either break or continue its function. This state of affairs implies, for Sartre, that "lacks" are not merely mental projections but real aspects of matter, or what we might term "nothings."

These terms referring to a state of nonbeing do not signify an empty space or void. Such a conception would imply a tacit acceptance of a mechanistic view of the world, in which a void or empty space (another mechanistic view) was supposed to account for modality. Such a notion of nonbeing would not explain our ability to question the world, ourselves, or one another.[14] On the contrary, the source of negation arises from the distinctive materiality of the human reality itself.

> It is essential therefore that the questioner have the permanent possibility of disassociating himself from the causal series which constitutes being and which can produce only being. If we admitted that the question is determined in the questioner by universal determination, the question would thereby become unintelligible and even inconceivable . . . the questioner must be able to effect in relation to the questioned a kind of nihilating withdrawal. . . . Thus in posing a question, a certain negative element is introduced into the world.[15]

These remarks would be easy to understand if Sartre were maintaining a traditional dualist distinction between matter and mind. The break from a causal series could then be assigned to the presence of mind in matter. But this is not Sartre's point. This nihilation is somehow within the human body itself; it is that which makes the human body *human*. I take this distinctive quality of the human body to be its flesh; but admittedly, this requires a bit of interpretation of Sartre's texts. Still, Sartre is clear about the unique role that the human reality provides for the origin of the negations and nonbeing that enter into the world.

Man is the being through whom nothingness comes to the world. But this question immediately provokes another: what must man be in his being in order that through him nothingness may come to being?[16]

From this perspective, Sartre is close to Lewis's concerns: just as the negations expressed in sentences and judgments require an ontological basis, so too with possibles. The origin of negation and modality is not a plurality of worlds, but a novel view of the human reality.

But it is true that the possible is—so to speak—an option on being, and if it is true that the possible can come into the world only through a being which is its own possibility, this implies for human reality the necessity of being its being in the form of an option on its being.[17]

Both Sartre and Lewis ask why it is that our language allows us to speak about things being other than they are. For Lewis, this capacity of ours implies that there must be worlds in which the other options on reality are realized. For Sartre, the ontological basis consists in seeing that human reality is not like other beings in the world; human reality is itself an option on being. *It is because we can be other than we are that things can be other than they are.*

Indeed, Lewis is forced to introduce the human element into the explanation of plural worlds. True, he frequently speaks of alien properties of matter being realized in other worlds, but even here he is forced to introduce a consciousness in relation to which they are alien.[18] Lewis would probably claim that this is merely our way of referring to things as if they had witnesses. But I think that Sartre is right. The human element is present not merely as an observer or tabulator of possibilities, but as the origin of possibilities.

All of Lewis's possible worlds are versions of our one world. The point is very clearly made if we recall Putnam's insistence that intentionality is over all things. To speak of things as having other possibilities or alien properties is a meaningful claim. To call something "a property" is already to see it as imbued with intentionality, and supporting this intentionality is the presence of human consciousness.

There is only one way to understand how the world and its possibilities mesh with the human body, and that is to see them related intrinsically to each other. We have the world we have only because we have the bodies we have. Lewis's multiple worlds (and, as I will show, Kripke's essences) remain too remarkably related to human fleshy consciousness not to have originated from a relation to that consciousness.

On the other hand, Lewis correctly ontologizes Goodman's wondrous worlds and Putnam's internal realism to the extent that he recognizes that language alone cannot unite matter into things nor account for the possibilities we discover in things. Putnam's internal realism and Goodman's ways of worldmaking do not give us the essences and the possibilities that Kripke and Lewis rightly claim are the foundation of our ordinary intuitions about the world. By continuing with Sartre, I believe we can nudge Putnam and Goodman to be more in line with the intuitions of Lewis (and of Kripke), while still keeping us within the human realm of our one world.

NEGATION AND FLESH

A being that is its own possibilities may be a more economical postulate than plural worlds, but can we recognize this being as us? Do possibilities enter into the human constitution only at the price of a dualist view of human reality? I have always read Sartre as a materialist, albeit a nonreductive one. Recently, it has occurred to me that one can concertize his claims about negation and modality by putting the emphasis on the fleshy aspect of the human body. The existence on Earth of any organism is probably sufficient to establish an internal relation with matter that accounts for most of the universe as we see it. But this relation cannot account for all possibilities. Many counterfactuals demand that we look at the distinct character of the human body, and I note three of these: first, the fleshy unity of the organic differentiation of our body makes it "meaningful" in itself as a conscious organism. Not only the gestures, but the entire movement of the body is an intentional structure that is one with the body. The body is that through which things are distinguished as things, and reciprocally, this organic revealing of matter as things reunites the body as the archetype of matter as thing. Second, our body is the source of language. This does not mean that one can deduce language from gestures. Rather, as I will indicate in the last chapter, our body, in its toolmaking function, is the origin of language in the sense that we have slowly, collectively forged worlds of artifacts and webs of meaning from a world of nature. (Of course, from another perspective, the world of "nature" is itself anthropocentrically related to the body.) Third, our body is our freedom; it is that which is now this way and which can be now differently than it is. The body in its fleshy nature is thus the source of possibility and modality. There is no single quote from *Being and Nothingness* that captures all these aspects of the body, but the following is a sample of Sartre's remarks that I take to be leading in this direction.

> Being-for-itself must be wholly body and it must be wholly con-
> sciousness; it can not be *united* with a body. Similarly, being-for-
> itself is wholly body; there are no "psychic phenomena" there to
> be united with the body. There is nothing *behind* the body. But
> the body is wholly "psychic."[19]

But what precisely does this mean? Obviously, Sartre expects us to connect the fact that the body is wholly conscious with the fact that it is itself an option on being and the source of both negative statements and real lacks within the world. Can this claim be made more concrete? To begin with, I think it is important to backtrack somewhat in order to see why Sartre does not begin his work with a study of the body:

> Perhaps some may be surprised that we have treated the prob-
> lem of knowing without raising the question of the body and the
> senses or even once referring to it. It is not my purpose to mis-
> understand or to ignore the role of the body. But what is impor-
> tant above all else, in ontology as elsewhere, is to observe strict
> order in discussion. Now the body, whatever may be its function,
> appears first as the known.[20]

This is an interesting and, I believe, a true observation. The child does not first know its own body; it learns about its own body as it learns about others. *Its* feet are as remarkable to it as its mother's breast. It is a simple but profound observation that we do not see ourselves seeing or hear ourselves hearing. We cannot even touch ourselves touching. Indeed, when we perceive things, we pass through our bodies: we see the glass of water and not ourselves seeing the glass of water. The intentionality of consciousness is fundamentally nothing but the fact that we pass through the body as we get to know the world.

> . . . consciousness (of) the body is lateral and retrospective; the body is the *neglected*, the *passed by in silence*. And yet the body is what this consciousness is; it is not even anything except body. The rest is nothingness and silence.[21]

We have to speak as if our awareness of our body is a consciousness *of* our body, but for Sartre, consciousness *is* the body. To perceive a glass is to pass through our body as eyes toward the glass. In our perception of the glass, the body itself is not known as an object of knowledge. Rather, we get to know about our own bodies as we observe the bodies of others. The other's body is also a consciousness; it thus does not appear to us in the same way as tables and chairs or stars appear.

The human body is fleshy, but again we don't easily perceive this fleshiness. At first, we pass through the fleshy constitution of the other's body, and what is revealed to us is the way things are related to each other *through* the flesh of the other.

> . . . we cannot perceive the Other's body as *flesh*, as if it were an isolated object having purely external relations with other thises. This is true only for a *corpse*. The Other's body as flesh is immediately given as the center of reference in a situation which is synthetically organized around it, and it is inseparable from this situation.[22]

Negation now starts to become a little more concrete. I take Sartre to be hinting that things are the way they are because consciousness is fleshy.

We would like to say that things are the way they are because consciousness *happens* to be fleshy, except that we do not have a concrete idea what nonfleshy consciousness would be like. Here, I might note that a partial explanation of why we began to think of our minds as immaterial is that, in perception, we *pass through* our fleshy sense organs: we are aware of the red apple and not that we are perceiving the apple through our fleshy eyes. For my purposes, however, I want to consider further how the fleshy constitution of the body can account for modality. Sartre continues:

> Similarly here the Other's body as flesh can not be *inserted* into a situation preliminarily defined. The Other's body is precisely that in terms of which there is a situation. . . . Far from the relation of the body to objects being a problem, we never apprehend the body outside this relation. . . . A body is a body as this mass of flesh which it is defined by the table which the body looks at, the chair in which it sits, the pavement on which it walks, etc. . . . The body is the totality of meaningful relations to the world. In this sense it is defined also by reference to the air which it breathes, to the water which it drinks, to the food which it eats.[23]

This quote can be taken as a springboard for my nonreductive, anthropocentric realism: the world is the way it is because our body is the way it is, and the body itself is fleshy only in relation to the rest of the world's matter. Thus, the texture of the organic body is fleshy in relation to the texture and density of, for example, the wood of a tree; on the contrary, this same flesh is dense like wood in many of its relations to fluids. Further, the unity of things arises precisely in relation to the human organic body: we can regard the movement of air as a hurricane only when we it acts as a hurricane on our body or on things related to our body. Could not other qualities and graduations exist without the presence of the human body? It is in this context that I think that Lewis is right about his claim that all sorts of mereological sums are possible. This seeming nonhuman possibility is, however, the result of the way matter relates to our theories, instruments, or images; or to be more exact, these nonhuman mereological sums result from projecting consciousness on to matter, and then denying that we have done just that. However, in general, what restricts matter to the unities that de facto constitute what we call "nature" is matter's relation to the organic unity of our body—to the fact that matter is related to consciousness as seeing, hearing, feeling, smelling, tasting, remembering, imagining, conceptualizing, reflecting, verbalizing, and acting in all sorts of fleshy bodily ways. To repeat, this relation is not a conceptual enterprise. Given the human body as this fleshy thing, then trees and stars are the things that they are. And the converse is also true; that is, the body is fleshy because stars and trees are not fleshy. But this converse relation exists only if we are given the existence of the body. To look for some *need* on the part of matter for consciousness is to call into being either Aristotle's Prime Mover or some more mystical Heidegerian *Being*. On the other hand, chance cannot account for life, for chance is also a meaningful structure; chance implies rather than explains consciousness. The existence of the conscious, fleshy body is the *given* from which all our speculations about the world arise.

That we may, for example, in our evolutionary theories, be inclined to explain the contingency of the human body is understandable. However, all such explanations must be rooted in and return to the ultimate contingency of human existence. It may be possible to construct theories that explain our contingency, but at present, all our theories are mystified by passing over the fact that we constitute the theories themselves. Thus, as I interpret Sartre's notion of contingency, it should be viewed as a demystifying notion, perhaps a reinterpretation of Edmund Husserl's notion of "bracketing." The import of the notion of contingency is that, at present, we do not have the tools to forge a dialectical view that retains both the uniqueness of our own existence and the relation of matter to the origin of this existence.

The point of this immediate reflection, however, is that different textures of matter truly exist, once we see them in relation to the flesh of the body. The hand feels the cool hardness of the glass of ice water. What is this feeling? In relation to the flesh of the hand, it is the negation that flesh *is* this cool hardness. Or to be more precise, *we* feel the cool hardness of the glass through our fleshy hands. We hear the sound of the tenor voice, and this hearing is the fleshy ear *not being* a tenorlike sound.

The senses do not receive impressions, as Aristotle said, nor do they impose order, as Kant would have it. Rather, they really divide and organize matter into a world, and this organization is also our nonthetic knowing of the world. That, for example, we respond to a rock as dense and air as easy to pass through is a differentiation of matter that is real, but real only in relation to our fleshy bodies. This relational existence of things retains objectivity while eliminating the need to root this objectivity in some inner hidden nature. To repeat an earlier example: that my voice can be heard by me, by others, or through a telephone creates the possibility of other relations; for example, that it could be heard in a recording. There is no need to speak of an infinite series; the other possibilities are simply other relations that *might* exist for the human voice. If we should ask "What is the true sound of my voice?" we see that the question is meaningless. In relation to my own hearing of my voice, there is a normal way it sounds to me as opposed to the way it sounds when I have a cold. In relation to others, my voice sounds different. In a recording, I can approach the way my voice sounds to others, but not perfectly. Even if I could make my voice sound the way it sounds to others, that relation would not be more privileged than the way my voice sounds to me. None of this implies relativity of meanings; rather, it is a question of making explicit different relations.

In a similar way, something like virtual presences and their corresponding negations enter into reality through the existence of the fleshy human organism. Given that our perspective on things arises *from* our organic fleshy constitution, we can notice a *downward* hierarchy. In relation to us, animals have life but not reason; plants grow but do not feel, and minerals endure but do not grow. It is not necessary to add "insofar as we know," since the notion of feeling and growth that I am referring to is precisely one that arises from a relation to the human fleshy organism. It is perfectly possible to take a more mechanistic conception of "life" and see quasi minerals as things that grow; but now growth is seen not in relation to our fleshy body but in relation to our scientific concepts and apparatuses. This new relation in no way demotes the more commonsense relation of things to the fleshy organism.

The hierarchical view of the world, which attempts to see a *natural* evolution from the bottom up, implies a bird's-eye view of reality, which science mystifies by introducing the notion of "nature." It is not necessary to attack this view here, for at present, my only purpose is to show that a downward hierarchy is sufficient to account for the objective relations that we observe in things, and to merely suggest that much of the rest—for example, the belief in natural laws—is excess baggage, unnecessary beliefs that really deliver no fruit edible by mortal humans.

Although it arises from a relation to the human fleshy body, the downward hierarchy is real and objective. The "thises" and "thats" of the world are ordered by their relation to the flesh of organisms: there are stars *because* there are fleshy organisms. For example, the stars are the furnaces that produce complex molecules such as carbon only because life needs complexity; that is to say, we regard complexity of molecular structure as something praiseworthy only because of its relation to human organic existence. Indeed, molecular complexity would be lost among a million other relations if it were not for our existence, an existence that highlights it as that which leads to life

Given our present scientific cosmological and anthropological views, an "upward" evolution requires us to start with a big bang theory of the universe as its true initial state, a state that happened to lead to us. This "happening," however, is retrospective; it is a view of things from the vantage point of our existence as organisms. For example, *given* that Melville wrote *Moby Dick*, the earlier works *Typee* and *Omoo*, are now revealed as preparatory for the writing of the more difficult and subtle latter work. In a similar way, we see the initial stage of the big bang as a beginning, because complexity of organization rather than density of homogenous matter is *our* criteria for evolution. To give, reluctantly, a science-fiction example, if consciousness required simple stable subatomic elements separated by vast differences, then the so-called death of the universe as predicted by the second law of thermodynamics would be the "birth" of life. Thus the direction of "time's arrow" arises from a relation to our organic existence.

Of course, the Aristotelian-Thomistic univocal notion of body has to be abandoned, and something like the nominalism advocated by the analogy of inequality, which is explained in appendix II, has to be put in its place. Or to be more exact, a univocal notion of body that applies to all bodies is indeed valid, but only in relation to a scientific conception of body. Such a notion of body is not privileged, and it cannot account for modality. On the other hand, our reflective judgments about our qualitatively rich world, a world filled with minerals, plants, and animals, a world containing true possibilities and true laws of nature—our philosophical reflections return this world to us at the noninflationary cost of seeing it related to our organically differentiated, free, fleshy body.

PART TWO

On Things
and
Names

Chapter 5

Names and Things

If we limit ourselves to a commonsense view of things, then it is my claim that we know their essences by knowing their surface characteristics; we know what water is by feeling its wetness and making judgements based upon this experience. The statement "Water is wet" is an eternally true claim, for it denotes a necessary relation of water to flesh. Also, we know who Socrates is by reading about Plato's description of his looks and behavior and in making claims based on this information.

We can begin with this kind of essential knowledge to ask other, seemingly deeper questions about a thing, but this new knowledge will not displace the old. Discovering that water is H_2O does not eliminate that it is also essentially wet, and discovering more about Socrates's parents and his genetic structure, or about his neurological makeup, if that knowledge could be accessible to us, would not alter our knowledge of him as the ugly ancient Greek who taught Plato, and whose questions aimed at getting at the definition of things. In a sense, Saul Kripke takes this commonsense view of things.

In *Naming and Necessity*, Saul Kripke is concerned with justifying our commonsense intuitions. He does this by inviting us to take a new look at proper and common names. "My main remark then, is that we have a direct intuition of the rigidity of names, exhibited in our understanding of the truth conditions of particular sentences."[1] For Kripke, names are "rigid designators," because they indicate a quality that would remain true of something even if many conditions were altered: whether water is solid ice, a running stream, or scalding steam, it still has the quality denoted by the term "water."[2] To see what this intuition entails, it helps to see that Kripke is objecting against the theory that claims names fix a definite property of things.

> The picture associated with the theory is that only by giving some unique properties can you know who someone is and thus know what the reference of your name is. Well, I won't go into the question of knowing who someone is. It's really very puzzling. I think you *do* know who Cicero is if you just can answer that he's a famous Roman orator.[3]

I am in favor of these and other remarks that Kripke makes in *Naming and Necessity* that seem to aim at justifying our commonsense intuitions.[4] Indeed, Kripke is not after giving us a new theory of reference, but a new context in which to understand how our proper names and general terms hook onto both individuals and kinds of things. Certain aspects of the picture that Kripke wishes to present are clear, and I think they correctly sketch our use of terms. In particular, Kripke is right to note that the attempt to explain how language works by claiming that names hook onto intrinsic properties fails to do justice to our use of words. For example, when we found out that we were wrong to believe that heat is constituted by the flow of phlogistons, we still retained the name "heat" to designate whatever it was that caused us to feel warm.

> First, although we can try to describe the world in terms of molecules, there is no impropriety in describing it in terms of

grosser entities. . . . Unless we assume that some particulars are "ultimate," "basic" particulars, no type of description need be regarded as privileged.[5]

This seems to be just the relational realism that I have been attempting to describe, and it seems to give us the proper emphasis on the surface aspects of things that accord, in general, with our commonsense intuitions about things. So do remarks such as:

> . . . are these objects *behind* the bundle of qualities, or is the object *nothing* but *the bundle*? Neither is the case; this table is wooden, brown, in the room, etc. . . . Don't ask: how can I identify this table in another possible world, except by its properties? I have the table in my hands, I can point to it, and when I ask whether *it* might have been in another room, I am talking, by definition, about *it*.[6]

Here Kripke seems to side with Putnam and Goodman, and he seems to be advocating a kind of internal realism. That is, names as rigid designators are also contextual; they are relative to the different ways we have of referring to a thing. However, we should recall the title of Kripke's book, which is not simply *Naming*, but *Naming and Necessity*. Kripke is concerned with names that refer to the necessary aspects of objects. Necessity is also the issue of modality; that is, the identity of a thing as revealed in counterfactuals: "I think that Nixon is a Republican, not merely that he lies in back of Republicanism, whatever that means; I also think that he might have been a Democrat."[7] For Kripke, there is no Aristotelian essence behind the appearance of Nixon and no common substantial substratum that underlies his changes; still, Nixon might have been other than he was. In some way, then, we must explain how names work, how they can refer to the same entity, even when our understanding is false and even when the thing might have had other qualities than it has.

What both complicates and enriches Kripke's view is that names refer to the essential aspect of an object in two ways: one that indicates its temporal qualities, and another that refers to an object's so-called transhistorical and eternal aspects. The true modal question arises only in this later, transhistorical use of words.[8] If I understand Kripke's distinction correctly, it appears similar to the one I refer to in appendix I, namely between the being of a thing and its essence: the being of Socrates includes his particular flesh and bones and all his distinct qualities, whereas the essence is what makes Socrates human. This, of course, cannot be exactly Kripke's position; he would reject Aristotelian essences because they are hidden and because we supposedly get to them by knowing a distinct property of a thing.

Nevertheless, Kripke's view of names as rigid designators has interesting Aristotelian aspects. For example, Kripke seems to naturalize the notion of what is "eternally true" by viewing a thing in relation to its origin, and, further, he pushes the Aristotelian notion of essence to include artifacts. While neither of these aspects are, strictly speaking, Aristotelian, they invite the kind of comparison with Aristotle given by Charlotte Witt. Witt, from whom I took the idea but not the substance of my own comparison of Aristotle with Kripke, notes that:

> [Aristotle] does not derive his essences from reflecting upon the identity of individual substances... but is tied to his notion of definition... and there is no obvious link between that question... and the object's source or origin.... For Kripke, but not for Aristotle, objects such as artifacts have essential, or necessary, material properties."[9]

Kripke's attempt to tie the necessary essence of a thing to its unique origin is one with his need to explain our modal judgements. Indeed, what interests me most about Kripke's analysis of names is the way he handles contingency. Kripke takes it as part of our intuition connected with Socrates that he might have become a merchant rather than a philosopher; also, Nixon might have been a Democrat rather than a Republican. If this is true, then there must be more to Socrates than the fleshy thing that greeted Plato's eyes and more to Nixon than appeared to the American public, but what can this more be? Kripke has ruled out hidden substances.

For Kripke, the necessary aspects of a thing are connected with its unique coming-to-be. "How could a person originating from different parents, from a totally different sperm and egg, be *this very woman*?" [10] If we are after the eternally true nature of Socrates, we must seek it, according to Kripke, not in Socrates's visible flesh, but in the quantitative relation that his body has to its origin. In general, for Kripke, the essential and necessary aspects of a thing are the quantitative ones, and these are related to a thing's origin.

At the risk of misunderstanding Kripke, I will attempt to explicate the difference between the eternal quantitative and the temporal qualitative aspects of an object. In both cases there can be change, and questions can arise about what has remained common throughout the change. For example, from a qualitative perspective, Socrates was essentially an ugly Greek philosopher who taught Plato and who drank hemlock. He would remain such whether he took the hemlock with his right or left hand, but would he have remained such if he recanted his views and refused to accept the death penalty? From a temporal perspective, perhaps not. Still, his body would be the same. Thus, from a quantitative view, Socrates is eternally that unique individual who was one with his body, and this unity arises from the relation that Socrates's body retains to his unique origin. This quantitative view of Socrates gives us the basis for true counterfactuals. Socrates would be himself not only if he refused to accept the death penalty, but even if had lived his life as a merchant rather than as a philosopher. [11]

If Kripke's distinction between the temporal qualitative and the eternal quantitative aspects of things can be taken as more or less synonymous with the distinction between a commonsense and a scientific understanding, and if, further, the eternal quantitative is taken as merely another interesting but not privileged way of referring to things, then Kripke is close to advocating a relational realism. But these are big "ifs."

To align the quantitatively genetic origin with the eternal and to bring both over into the realm of the necessary is to imply that names fundamentally signify the quantitative aspects of things. The qualitative aspects of things become secondary, and we do not, in fact, have a true relational realism. Further, I do not understand how all the qualities of a thing can change while the thing still retains a unique relation to its origin. I do not see how such a view can be supported, unless one is claiming that things do have a hidden essence. "This table is composed of molecules. Might it not have been composed of molecules? Certainly it was a scientific discovery of great moment that it was composed of molecules (or atoms). But could anything be this very object and not be composed of molecules?"[12] If this perspective and the quandary to which Kripke's question gives rise are merely other ways of stating the scientific project, then I have no objection to them. But Kripke does seem to want to privilege the quantitative in relation to the temporal qualitative view.

I would want to ask, "Can this table look and feel like this very table and not be it, essentially and necessarily?" Of course, the "essentially and necessarily" here means "in relation to what can be discriminated by our sense of sight and touch." If someone substituted another table for this one, and no human could distinguish the difference by sight and touch, then the tables would be identical. If essences are relational, this presents no problem, but, I suspect Kripke would not be pleased with this conclusion.

More to the point, I do not think that the distinction between temporal qualitative and eternal quantitative aspects works in regard to people. (I do not think it works in respect to natural kinds, but I will not press that issue here.) Could Nixon have been a Kennedylike Democrat? Kripke thinks that, to the extent that our names imply necessity, the answer must be yes, since obviously we can imagine the bodily thing that we call Nixon to have made other political choices. While this may be true in the abstract, I do not think that it is true in the concrete.

I can accept the general framework of Kripke's distinction between the temporal and the eternal in the sense that I agree that there are certain qualities that a person can alter and still remain, as it were, true to herself. Or, to put it more strongly, still remain the same person. And, on the contrary, I think that there are other qualities that, if changed, alter one's personality and thus alter our eternally true judgements about the person. But I think that the distinction remains along qualitative lines, or, at least, I claim that it can remain such and still deliver to us necessary aspects of things and persons. Thus, I claim that there is a legitimate and necessary perspective from which we can say that Nixon was a Republican in the sense that this political choice indicated the basic structure of his personality, and that his name necessarily referred to the personality formed by just that political choice made at that time.

Although there are no a priori ways of determining whether such choices are determinative of a personality, I think that we must grant that such exist. Otherwise, we have to accept Kripke's counterintuitive view of Hitler. "If Hitler had never come to power, Hitler would not have had the property which I am supposing we use to fix the reference of his name."[13] From the quantitative perspective of his genetic origin, true. But I think, more properly, that the name "Hitler" refers rigidly to his choice of attempting to eliminate the Jews. There is no a priori reason why the property of attempting to rule the world with Aryan supremacy should be less essential than having a particular body that arose from this ovum rather than some other. Indeed, both are contingent in the sense that there is no necessary reason why they had to be; they are both special contingencies that, once in existence, define a thing.

Kripke does not go in this direction because he is concerned about certain aspects of counterfactual possibilities. Suppose it were found out that Hitler did not do the things attributed to him? Kripke would now have us claim that the name "Hitler" would still refer to the same physical organism. But would it? My answer is yes and no. Part of what we mean by "Hitler" is the person who aimed to exterminate the Jews. In this context, when I speak of Hitler, I imagine myself to be present witnessing the concentration camps. I can, to paraphrase Kripke, say: "I do not have to worry about criteria; I know what I mean when I say that this very person is the killer of Jews." What about the possibility of error? I think that I follow Kripke's intention when I say that we get nowhere by trying to solve *that* problem first. Thus, we can say that it is eternally true that Hitler was a killer of Jews. The question about counterfactuals should be handled by claiming that, while *abstractly* Hitler could have been another person than he really was, *concretely* his flesh and bones were essentially related to his decision to exterminate the Jews.

I want to repeat that, from one perspective, I do not think that Kripke would object to any of the above reasoning, but he would probably claim that it concerns the temporal aspects of things. Hitler's body was a particular quantitative arrangement of cells, precisely as these had a necessary relation to his parents, and it is to this necessary relation that, for Kripke, the name "Hitler" refers, so as to give us necessary judgments about Hitler.

I agree that it is legitimate to view things from the aspect of their origin. However, there seems to me to be an important ambiguity in claiming that Socrates could have been a merchant and still be Socrates or that Hitler could have been a lover of the Jews and still have been Hitler. Hitler may have decided not to invade Russia just when he did invade it, but his consuming hatred of the Jews was essential and necessary to the concrete flesh-and-blood person who bore that name, and I think that the same was true of Socrates's decision to be a philosopher. In brief, I think that, particularly in regard to people, the perspective of origin is abstract. Here, it does not seem to be a case of shifting from one legitimate perspective to another, but of competing perspectives, the one abstract, the other concrete. In the concrete, it is eternally true that Socrates is Socrates through the important choices that he made in his life, and in this sense he could not have been a merchant. What I mean by the views being competing is brought out in Kripke's analysis of gold, an analysis that is similar but not identical to Putnam's twin Earth example of water as H_2O. Kripke writes:

> Let us suppose the scientists have investigated the nature of gold and have found that it is part of the very nature of this substance, so to speak, that it have the atomic number 79. Suppose we now find some other yellow metal, or some other yellow thing, with all the properties by which we originally identified gold, and many of the additional ones that we have discovered later. . . . We would instead describe this as a situation in which a substance, say iron pyrites, which is not gold, would have been found in the very mountains which actually contain gold and have had the very properties by which we commonly identify gold. But it would not be gold; it would be something else.[14]

As with Putnam's twin Earth example, Kripke here helps me clarify my claim that there can be multiple essential views of a thing, views that sometimes, but not always, compete. I take it that Kripke is claiming that we could discover that a metal, like iron pyrite, had all the qualities that we now think gold to have, and yet it would not be gold. This state of affairs could arise because we might discover gold to have the atomic weight of 79 rather than the 76 of our present conception. Still, regardless of the fact that it appears similar to another substance and regardless of the fact that we are wrong about its intrinsic makeup, we would still refer to this substance as "gold." However, our essential knowledge about gold would have been wrong.

If this counterfactual situation was merely a statement about the indefinite character of the scientific pursuit of the nature of things, there could be no quarrel with Kripke's remarks. What is bothersome, however, is Kripke's willingness to grant that our essential knowledge would change if we discovered that we were wrong about the atomic weight. The *Third Webster's Third International Dictionary* does not give the atomic weight of gold, and I think that the dictionary is right in not doing so. From a commonsense perspective, gold is essentially and necessarily a distinctly yellow and malleable substance, and it is easily recognized as true gold, by those who handle it with some frequency. Many jewelers and miners can tell the difference between fool's gold and true gold; one does not need to be a chemist. We may, of course, be mistaken in our present understanding of the internal structure of gold, but that does not affect the necessary and eternal relation that gold has to our commonsense understanding of it and to our nonscientific practices surrounding it, for example, our monetary practices. The monetary value of gold is based upon its scarcity and social value. If physics changed its mind about the inner nature of gold, and if gold was socially just as scarce and desirable, it would still have the same "nature" in relation to these social practices. Indeed, long before the development of chemistry, the ancient Egyptians and the Aztecs properly identified gold as a "precious" metal, and even when it did not have direct monetary value, its possession frequently pointed to wealth and royalty.

The same issue arises when Kripke asks us to consider what occurred when science discovered that whales are mammals. For Kripke, this discovery did not change the essential meaning of our term "whale." Like Putnam, Kripke holds that ". . . the possibility of such discoveries was part of the original enterprise."[15] But to what enterprise is Kripke referring? Whalers knew the behavior of whales before this discovery. They knew that whales "sounded" and "blew," and this knowledge was independent of any discovery that whales were really mammals. Nor did this discovery alter their practice. It makes no difference to a whaler whether a whale breaches because it is a mammal living in the water or because it is a strange fish. From the perspective of our commonsense perceptions and practices, the *essential* features of a whale, the ones that a whaler needs to know to succeed in fishing for whales, are acquired by practices that are valid in their own right.

Of course, there may be relations between our science and fishing practices, but this is only to say that the practices of catching whales may change. But if science had never arisen, whales would eternally be just the beings that appear to our commonsense perceptions and to our everyday successful practices that engage whales. The eternal, dramatic contest that brought Ahab to destruction was not with a mammal accurately placed within its proper taxonomical category but with the largest living creature whose playgrounds are the oceans of the world.

Partly, I think that the tension in Kripke's views arises from the question of just how to handle materialism:

> I suspect, however, that the present considerations tell heavily against the usual forms of materialism. Materialism, I think, must hold that a physical description of the world is a *complete* description of it, that any mental facts are "ontologically dependent" on physical facts in the straightforward sense of following them by necessity.[16]

The ambiguity in this passage stems, I believe, from the difficulty in formulating a nonreductive materialism. A nonreductive materialism maintains that we can give a complete description of the world in physical terms while denying that these descriptions need be mechanistic. Mental states are reducible to physical states but not to a mechanistic picture, such as the firing of C-fibers. There are times when Kripke seems to be aiming at such a distinction, although he never actually makes it. Thus it is not clear what Kripke means by "usual forms of materialism" in the above quote. If the usual forms of materialism are those captured in the scientific picture of the world, then Kripke might be hinting at a nonreductive approach to matter; for me, this is the more fruitful way to understand his thought.

Most importantly, I approve of the general way Kripke leads us to understand how a so-called contingent quality can become an essential and necessary characteristic of a thing; the temporal origin, when properly viewed, can be seen to be the foundation of our necessary predicates about a thing. However, I do not think that we have to limit ourselves to the purely quantitative perspective of the body. After all, an ovum is a qualitative whole, and, more to the point, our free choices can mold us in such a way that we become eternally and necessarily just this being of flesh and bones and no other. From this perspective, the judgment "Socrates is Socrates" is a necessary but synthetic statement that indicates the uniqueness of the flesh and bones that were Socrates's body, a distinctiveness that arose not only from his parents, but from his basic choices.

Thus we make ourselves essentially who and what we are. This simple claim breaks not only from the Aristotelian matter-form view of human nature but with the entire Cartesian-Lockean-Humean view of the body. The point is to push Kripke's insight so that qualities can have a role as essential in the makeup of an individual as do the cells of a body. I see Sartre as one of the few philosophers who develops his view of human nature in this way. I will expand upon Sartre's views in the following chapter, but here I want to introduce his emphasis on the qualitative determination of personality.

ON PERSONS

In *Being and Nothingness*, Sartre writes:

> I start out on a hike with friends. At the end of several hours of walking my fatigue increases and finally becomes very painful. At first I resist and then suddenly I let myself go, I give up. . . .

Someone will reproach me for my act and will mean thereby that I was free. . . . I shall defend myself by saying that I was *too tired*. Who is right? Or rather is the debate not based on incorrect premises? . . . It ought to be formulated rather like this: could I have done otherwise without perceptibly modifying the organic totality of the projects which I am; or is the fact of resisting my fatigue such that instead of remaining a purely local and acciden- tal modification of my behavior, it could be effected only by means of a radical transformation of my being-in-the-world—a transformation, moreover, which is *possible*? In other words: I could have done otherwise. Agreed. But *at what a price?*[17]

Sartre's point is that there are some contingent qualities that become de facto essential to who and what we are. A person who habitually strolls leisurely, who eats slowly enjoying every bite, who cannot wait to come home and sink into the large cushy chair which snuggles his flesh like a mother's hands fondle a baby, could be more energetic. But would this more energetic person be this very person? Would the flesh be the same? Kripke would say that, in regard to our eternal and necessary claims about the person, from the perspective of the relation of the cells constituting the body to the origin of the body, the person would be the same. And he would no doubt comment that Sartre himself agrees that the change is possible, even at a price.

But Sartre's true point is that the person is a fundamental choice of living one's body, a choice that is no doubt influenced by childhood expe- riences and which fixes itself over time, differently with each person. The child "Hitler" might not have become the adult "Hitler"; once the mature Hitler kept to his personality as a vow, he was, essentially and eternally, just the person who was the author of his deeds. His pervading misan- thropy was the way he related his body to the world; it revealed itself in his gestures, in his speech, and in his friends, as well as in the decisions that he inflicted upon the world. The true counterfactual situation in regard to Hitler is that the child may not have become the adult. Another "Hitler" might have arisen from the same parents and the same child- hood, one that might not have established concentration camps nor even tried to do so. But once the child grew into the adult, once, to use Sartre's term, the fundamental project was fixed and kept to, the flesh-and-blood adult body was itself its own essence. And when Hitler died, his essence became fixed in a special way, so that the name "Hitler" eternally and necessarily means, among other things, "the killer of Jews." I here condense and interpret a good deal of Sartre's thought, but I have commented upon it elsewhere.[18] Still, the above analysis does not adequately sketch how a relational realism can provide a basis for our universal notions and names. In the last two chapters, I wish to frame the discussion of universality within the broader issue of an anthropocentric perspective on structure and meaning.

Chapter 6

The Transcendence of Mind

In the preceding chapters, I have worked within the context of thinkers such as Aristotle, Sartre, and Putnam, attempting to sketch an anthropocentric realism. There are two distinctive features to this realism: first, there is the claim that, in relation to the organic constitution of the body, the qualities and natures that we perceive in a commonsense way truly exist as essential features of our world, even when we are not actually perceiving them. That is, there is a relational bond between the qualities and things of the world and the human body. Second, this anthropocentric realism affirms that this bond is knowledge of these very qualities and things. In relation to our fleshy eyes, red is *essentially* just the quality of the particular shade of color that we see, and further, this seeing of red is knowing red. I am not concerned here with distinctions between comprehension and knowledge or related distinctions. Rather, I am attempting to encourage the realization that, on the basic level of worldmaking, our sense perceptions immediately get us in contact with aspects of the world, and this contact is a true form of knowing the world. Simply, in distinction to those who are blind, those of us who are fortunate enough to have sight know what colors are by seeing them.

Of course, terms like "color" and "red" also have explicit general meanings. Here, a reductionist perspective would advise us to turn to science to find the basis for these universals, and a mentalist view would have us look for proper epistemic condition. As a general quality, color then becomes a certain type of photon or wave, and red an even more specific form of quantitative matter. As I have repeatedly stated, I have no objection to scientific reductions of qualities; I simply do not see them as privileged. We produce scientific theories and instruments in relation to which color then becomes essentially a part of the electromagnetic spectrum. Also, with proper qualifications, I can even accept a connection between flashes of neurons in our brain and general meanings; but I would not consider these connections primary.

Still, if one remains, as it were, on the surface of things, how does one explain universality? My answer is again a relational and a realistic one: we forge the surface of things to be universal; for example, we make a fork to be both this fork and a fork. I realize that this brief allusion does not seem to account for the universality we encounter in language or in scientific laws. Nevertheless, I believe that the basis of our universal claims about the world lies in this direction. My anthropocentric and relational point will be that, from a legitimate explanatory perspective of remaining on the surface of things, what we call our "mind" has a status analogous to an artifact: mind is a structure that arises from the relation of matter to our historical practices. This relation presupposes matter already differentiated by its relation to the conscious organic body, if not temporally, at least ontologically. Thus, it is abstractly possible to separate the way matter is related to the organic body from the way matter is related to our historical practices. The first relation gives us Nature, the second history. In the concrete, however, the two are difficult to separate, since any particular understanding of Nature is imbued with cultural interpretations. Nevertheless, I return to my three senses of the given, and I claim that, in principle, we can separate the level of worldmaking from that of interpretation. There are colors in the world because there are eyes to see colors. True, each perception of color will be laden with particular interpretations. Still, a person who can see is bonded to the world as colored in a way that a person who is blind is not. Further, if we all lacked sight, then blindness as a privation of sight would not exist, and, reciprocally, the world would not be colored.

INTRODUCING MIND

In *The Twin Earth Chronicles: Twenty Years of Reflection on Hilary Putnam's "The Meaning of 'Meaning'"*, Putnam notes that much of of his later thought can be viewed as moving in the direction of putting the mind in the world:

> I was not sure when I wrote "The Meaning of 'Meanings,'" whether the moral of that essay should be that we shouldn't think of the meanings of words as lying in the mind at all, or whether (like John Dewey and William James) we should stop thinking of the mind as something "in the head" and think of it rather as a system of environment-involving capacities and interactions. In the end I equivocated [between the view of narrow mental states in the mind, and broad mental states in the world]. Subsequently, under the influence of Tyler Burge and of John McDowell as well, I have come to think that this conceded too much to the idea that the mind *can* be thought of as a private theater (situated in the head).[1]

I agree with Putnam's attempt to objectify the mind. In a sense, my own efforts follow more in line with those of James and Dewey than with Putnam's own "division of linguistic labor." However, my own attempt to empty our minds of meanings has been more influenced by the thoughts of Karl Popper and Jean-Paul Sartre, and I will here use their thought to make my point. I should also note that, unlike Putnam, I think, at least now, that a certain amount of ambiguity in regard to the notion of the mind is healthy. In particular, I would more or less follow Søren Kierkegaard, and later Jean-Paul Sartre, in their notion of subjectivity as something that we slowly constitute by our actions. Still, like Putnam, I am beginning to have doubts about even this qualified use of mind. After twenty-five years of reflecting upon Kierkegaard's thought, I am coming to the conclusion that

THE TRANSCENDENCE OF MIND   **131** he, Kierkegaard, had no subjectivity whatsoever. Kierkegaard's subjectivity was all on paper, in his endless and constant writing about subjectivity. From a different perspective, I think Sartre also had no subjectivity, nor did Picasso. However, Paul Klee did indeed have an interior life. Perhaps the interior life is something that characterizes only certain types of people, more in line with the old distinction between introverts and extroverts. It is, I think, interesting to note that Sartre himself was very interested in people who could be said to have had an interior life of the mind, for example, Jean Genet and Gustave Flaubert. Although Sartre never puts it this strongly, I would say that one has an interior life of the mind to the extent that one attempts to give one's actions a "deeper" meaning than these actions appear to have. One thus creates one's own unconscious life. However, I do not wish to pursue this line of thought here, except to note that I agree with what I take to be Sartre's implicit claim that our efforts to create an interior life in which the true meanings of our actions are stored end in failure: in the final analysis, one's true "self" and one's true "mind" are in the world. Sartre's massive study of Gustave Flaubert, *The Family Idiot,* is directed to showing that, in the final analysis, the true meaning of Flaubert's life is visible, if we know where to look for it.[2] The length and detail of Sartre's work is directed to showing that the constitution of a human nature is a complex affair, arising partly from the way parents, friends, and even strangers mold a child's body and from the way the child asserts against, yields to, or interprets the affect of this molding; from the way the parents themselves are conditioned by the times and then freely interpret and live this historical conditioning, interacting with the child's body; from the way the child sees its own body in the eyes of others and then interiorizes and interprets its body as seen; and from the general dialectical relation between the child's view of itself and its world and the world's view of it; and, finally, to the degree to which the adult growing from the child interacts with the "spirit" of its age. Genetic influences, biologically inherited conditions of the body, are important, and they should be considered where they are known; but I agree with Sartre that there are no a priori reasons for considering them primary. Or, to be more precise and to keep to my relational realism, I agree that there are indeed a priori reasons for considering genetic characteristics as primary, but I think that these reasons are of a piece with genetics itself. We constitute science to have the appearance of disinterested and a priori knowledge, and then we are tempted to yield to it as a nonhuman source of our human nature.

I think that the truths of mathematics are also constituted. Quine is right: the workability of mathematics implies the existence of universal classes. However, I think that we have forged these universal classes over a long time and with great effort, and I believe that a similar situation exists in regard to the workability and universality of language in general. This anthropocentric point is the thrust of these last two chapters.

To refer to the world or nature as "mind" may seem idealistic or anthropomorphic, but my anthropocentric point is that we collectively mold matter into a web of meanings. As we gradually interiorize this web of humanly constituted meanings, we discover upon reflection that it escapes us, precisely because we cannot interiorize it all and because the roots of its human causes are hidden. What escapes us becomes the "unconscious," "nature," or the "world." Indeed, I understand Sartre, in the *Family Idiot*, to naturalize the notion of the unconscious in this way. I think that this would be the direction to naturalize our notions about myth.[3]

I am indebted to Sartre for my use of the term "transcendence" in relation to mind, and to those familiar with Sartre's thought it will become clear that I owe to him some of the content of the term as I use it, namely that transcendence is consciousness as found in the world. I also find it useful to develop the view that mind is something that exists outside in the world within the context of Karl Popper's notion of a "third world." It will be clear, however, that I naturalize his views. My own views are most clearly evident in the next chapter, where I offer the phenomenon of writing as a partial basis for our universal notions.

I have reached the most controversial aspect of my anthropocentrism, but I look upon it basically as a movement toward demystifying our notions of mind, consciousness, and unconsciousness, and, in general, our relation to language. I thus conceive that Plato was right in his claim that universality cannot exist merely in our thoughts and in our language, but

I conceive him to be wrong to think that we need another world to house these entities. We have made room for universality here on Earth. The embedded meanings that permeate our cultured life, our cities, our books, our notions, and our language are all of one fabric, and that fabric is the durability and malleability of matter, the wondrous quality that permits matter to receive and retain the centuries of efforts of our craftsmanship.

Implied in this view of the mind's transcendence is a certain notion of abstraction. I will expand upon this in the next and last chapter, but here I simply note that what we call "abstract" is first and foremost an aspect of our artifacts. One of the interesting aspects of modern art is its recognition that by properly isolating an everyday object, a drinking glass or a stone, the distinctive quality of the object is highlighted. In a similar way, the mere act of placing a log felled by lightning under an object to be moved is an act of abstraction that may have been the beginning of the invention of the wheel. Thus, before the abstract is in our minds, it is in our actions and in the way matter receives our actions. However, I begin with a few remarks about Karl Popper, whose views help locate my discussion.

POPPER'S THIRD WORLD

Popper distinguishes three worlds: the world of physical objects, the world of conscious experiences, and the world of theoretical truths.

> We can call the physical world "world 1," the world of our conscious experiences "world 2," and the world of the logical *contents* of books, libraries, computer memories, and suchlike "world 3."[4]

Popper here approaches what I want to say about the transcendence of mind. Popper indeed sees his third world to take the place of Plato's World of Ideas.[5] Unlike Plato's World of Ideas, Popper's third world is produced by us, although once produced, it has a life of its own. Popper seldom puts his solution in the form of finding objects for our universal notions, but the implication is there. Further, he correctly sees that the world of written language and books can explain our inclination to believe that there is a sense in which a "statement in-itself" or a "theorem-in-itself" has an objective meaning. Specifically, he places the objects of mathematics in the third world.

> For the objects of mathematics can now become citizens of an
> objective third world: though originally constructed by us—the
> third world originates as our product—the thought contents
> carry with them their own unintended consequences. The series
> of natural numbers which we construct create problems of
> which we never dreamt.[6]

Nevertheless, Popper does not seem to follow through with this healthy anthropocentric insight. His "evolutionary approach," as cautious as it is, implies a reliance on meaningful relations in nature that preexist human existence. Popper, of course, recognizes that his approach to evolution is a conjecture; but, as such, it is difficult to see how it can be refuted according to his own principles. "Survival" must mean "survival" for us. That is to say, the existence of the human species is already taken to be the archetype of existence, for the dinosaurs did not survive. Further, as has so often been pointed out, if we destroy the earth through our science, then the survival benefits of our present evolution would be short-lived.[7]

To put the matter somewhat differently, Popper's distinction between first, second, and third worlds implies an "upward" hierarchy that seems to presuppose that we have a bird's-eye view of reality, and it is thus in opposition to my own "downward" hierarchy that begins with the human organism. Some of this may be a matter of emphasis, but I suspect that there is a core of essential difference. For example, I agree with Popper's opposition to reductionism and his emphasis on the priority of biology when trying to understand the specificity of the human organism. Still, Popper *seems* to arrive at his three worlds by arguing from inanimate matter up to consciousness and from consciousness to the world of conjectures and refutations as embodied in inscriptions and books. That is to say, Popper does not seem to recognize the way that distinctions and modality enter into the matter through organic flesh and its operations. More generally, I am not sure that Popper would agree that the entire world of science and the world it reveals have only relational validity, that their truth is only in relation to the contingent happening of science in human history.

The ontological status of Popper's second and third worlds is not clear. The ambiguity arises because Popper concedes to scientific realism the world of physical objects. In this way, the distinction between consciousness and physical object becomes mystified, for if consciousness is not a physical object, it is difficult to see what it is. Popper seems to be working with a reductionist view of matter, even if his view of reality is not reductionist.

The ambiguous status of Popper's second and third worlds come into focus when Popper attempts to identify consciousness with the human body and meanings with written inscriptions and books. Language, Popper claims, *embodies* meaning. Language, either written or spoken, however, is *not* an embodiment of a meaning. Embodiment implies something embodied. Meaning, for Popper, seems to be a "something" prior to its embodiment in the spoken or written word. Popper seems to be trying to hold onto a viable sense of meaning-in-itself *apart from language in all its concrete forms.*[8]

But if I am a little hard on Popper here for not being sufficiently anthropocentric, I want to conclude my brief remarks on a more positive note. To the extent that Popper's second and third worlds seem to be products of human actions, he is indeed on the right track to seeing how universality and matter are one. Before I put forward my own views of the transcendent world of constituted meanings, I again turn to Sartre, who, more than any other thinker, comes closest to sharing my own anthropocentric views.

SARTRE: TRANSCENDENCE OF THE EGO AND BEYOND

As early as 1937, in *The Transcendence of the Ego*, Sartre made the striking claim that what we call our *I* is not an a priori structure of consciousness, but rather a constituted object.[9] "Our character," "our intimate self," and "our mind" are facets of our life produced by our own actions. Once created, we subsequently interiorize these aspects of our objective existence as our own. In Sartre's terminology, we produce our intimate self by our prereflective actions, that is by our conscious, knowing spontaneous actions. Spontaneous does not mean blind, rather, Sartre is referring to the way we can become absorbed in an activity, such as reading or playing tennis. We do not first conceptualize our prereflective involvement in the world. On the contrary, although our interior life is produced by us, our conceptualization of this activity occurs relatively late in life, and it is a difficult conceptualization to achieve. It is in this sense that we become surprised by the meaning of our own actions, particularly as these are reported by others. "Hence the classic surprises: '*I*, I could do that! — *I*, I could hate my father!'"[10]

Sartre thus rejects the traditionally interpreted Cartesian *I Think*. "Let us note that the *I Think* does not appear to reflection as the reflected consciousness: it is given *through* reflected consciousness."[11] And, most strikingly, Sartre concludes, "My *I*, in effect, is *no more certain for consciousness than the I of other men*. It is only more intimate."[12]

Sartre is making a distinction between the *I* and the *me*, and his point is that what we normally call the *I* is, in fact, the *me*. We could partially rehabilitate the privileged status of the *I*, as the intimate aspect of consciousness in the sense that it is a mode of our unreflected, spontaneous actions: the particular way I am absorbed in a book, the special way I respond "naturally" to people and to arguments—these are aspects of my true personality. Here, however, we would encounter the complexities of Sartre's later qualifications, as given in *Genet: Saint and Martyr* and especially in *The Family Idiot*—qualifications that take into account the degree to which the quality of our spontaneous actions are conditioned by other people and society in general.

Nevertheless, for Sartre, there is always freedom, the freedom to react to what is being done to us, and we could take this freedom as the *I*. But it would not be the Cartesian *I*, for it is empty of content and has no independent existence apart from the way it qualifies our actions and thoughts. But I don't wish to press this point here. For our present purpose, what is significant is that, for Sartre, the meaning of our self exists first in the world as an objective structure for us and others to study. We then interiorize this objectivity, and we give it the quality of being "mine." For example, I might insist that *I* am not angry, but others may see that my behavior clearly indicates anger. I then may either reconsider my view of myself, or I might continue to insist that *I* am not angry.

Sartre extended the notion of the transcendence of the ego toward the end of *Being and Nothingness,* in the last section of part 4, "Quality as a Revelation of Being,"[13] where I see him trying to extend transcendence to such qualities of the world as the "slimy." Here Sartre attempts to establish that seemingly anthropomorphic judgements about the world are frequently based upon the way the world arranges itself anthropocentrically about the body. Although Sartre's early efforts are in the right direction, I do not think that they are successful: the "slimy" may very well be only a Western, male-oriented view of matter.

However, I think that Sartre was more successful in extending this notion of transcendence in 1960, in the *Critique of Dialectical Reason.* In that work, he developed the notion of group action, or praxis, as something that is more than the union of individuals happening to act together, and he showed how matter can receive a distinct unity from this praxis. Specifically, matter, for Sartre, becomes totalized in an open-ended way; we are always in what we are totalizing, and thus every totality is a detotalized one. As a detotalized totality, matter reacts on the individual with "forces" that are genuinely unexpected and that frequently act against the original intentions of the individuals who organized the matter for a particular purpose. From this perspective, the matter thus totalized, or what Sartre calls the *practico-inert,* is said to be capable of "inverted praxis," that is, authorless actions that act against our present intentions. (Sartre uses three examples to make his point: (1) that of Chinese peasants cultivating land, (2) the role of precious metals during the Spanish hegemony of the sixteenth century, and (3) an examination of the iron and coal complex during the eighteenth and early nineteenth centuries.) Group praxes can coalesce the environment into quasi-unities, and in this respect, Sartre distinguishes historical unities from natural unities.[14] Nevertheless, even so-called natural facts are brought about by human existence:

> From this point of view, it is possible to accept both Durkheim's maxim "treat social facts as things," and the response of Weber

and many contemporaries, that "social facts are not things." That is to say, social facts are things in so far as *all things* are, directly or indirectly, social facts.[15]

Sartre never develops his position on the ontological status of things, nor does he develop his views of the abstract and universal as a separate tract. With admittedly some interpretation, I have framed the thesis of my own anthropocentric views: we distinguish the world into thises and thats because of matter's internal relations to the human fleshy organic body and to the historical practices of that organism. Consistent with this anthropocentric perspective, I claim that the ontological basis for abstractions are to be found by paying attention both to the differentiation of the senses and to the way we have forged our language to be universal. There is a sense in which our senses perform a basic abstraction. Through sight, knowledge takes the form of knowing the yellow of the lemon as distinct from the texture and taste of the lemon. That is, insofar as our consciousness appears in the form of sight, the yellow of a lemon is not the texture of the lemon, although both are aspects of the lemon.

At this level of sense knowledge, abstraction is a special bond of being; the lemon *is* a lemon because matter is unified here as a yellow thing with this texture, with this odor, and with this taste. The import of referring to the relation of the lemon to the senses as a bond of being is that both the differentiation of the qualities—yellow and texture—and their union in this lemon truly exist in the world, although their existence is relational, that is, in relation to the differentiation of the senses.

Because knowledge is in the form of differentiated senses, both texture and yellow can be considered apart from the lemon, and more explicit abstractions can now arise. For example, yellowness can become the yellow of the lemon in relation to knowledge, precisely as this knowledge is both sensual and free, that is, precisely as it arises from a fleshy organism with the intention and need to consider yellow in this way. Although I here become far more explicit than Sartre, I understand him to imply that there is yellow in the world because knowledge can exist as fleshy sight, but that yellowness as an explicit abstraction is an historical interpretation of yellow. That is to say, yellowness as a concrete abstraction exists because we have molded a social structure in which concrete universals have a place: we live in a world in which *this* chair is also *a* chair.[16]

The issue of the kind of universals that we find in predications of the type "Socrates is human" is more complex. Still, the guiding thread is that of historical constitution that gives us both a relation to human praxes and, nevertheless, objectivity. Universality is an aspect of actions of civilized people, that is, they are actions of people precisely as they have historical relations among each other and with the world. More explicitly, I would want to say that the universality that we encounter in science and in much of our Western culture is the special product of that culture, and, as Michel Foucault notes in *The Order of Things*, we could be living in a world that would accept a much different ordering of things. However, I do not intend to develop these asides, nor do I intend to follow Sartre's own analysis in the *Critique* very closely here. Rather, I think it more fruitful to illustrate how action brings about universals by using an example. The example is related to what Sartre, sometimes in passing, refers to as his dialectical nominalism. My example concerns a sport and thus clearly a human artifact. Nevertheless, my point is that something analogous occurs in science and in mathematics.

Playing tennis is a purely physical phenomenon. There is nothing in the game that is not matter: there are fleshy human bodies moving about courts, holding rackets with which they attempt to put a ball over a net so that it stays within the court, and so that an opponent cannot return the ball with the same restrictions. Precisely as a game, playing tennis has an historically constituted universality. Thus, tennis games are unified not merely because a group of people happen to think that they are unified. Rather, these games are played in accordance with rules that are codified in books as well as in the trained bodies of those who play the game. A practiced eye can tell how good one player is in relation to other players, and a trained coach can tell a promising player prior to any formal competition.

Thus, whether one is aware of it or not, the moment one begins to play tennis a practical hierarchy of tennis playing exists throughout the world. Even if no one is actually playing tennis, as long as the game is a viable and active sport there are plans and discussions about it, and books and magazines are being written and read about the game. All of these activities and efforts keep the practical hierarchy that is tennis in existence. The moment one begins to play tennis one enters into this hierarchy: one plays as having "promise" or not, and this is true even if one is determined merely to enjoy the sport, with no or little desire to compete. Competition, in fact, is part of the sport, and as one continues to improve, regardless of one's personal intentions, one moves up the hierarchy, acquiring a certain ranking.

Indeed, there exists a practical sense in which *this* stroke of hitting the ball during a tennis match is ranked the moment it takes place. A practical feedback takes place between tennis playing throughout the world and this particular stroke of the game. A good computer could, in principle, compare this stroke with every other stroke that is now taking place throughout the world and that has ever taken place. This ranking actually does not have to be performed for a "universal" meaning of tennis to exist within the world: the web of material structures provides the condition for the possibility of such ranking and thus the basis for universality.

I thus understand Sartre's dialectal nominalism to imply both: that only individual games of tennis exist in the world, and that, nevertheless, these games share in a worldwide meaning of tennis playing. If tennis ceases to be a lived sport, then the universality exists in retrospect as part of history.

I believe that this example of tennis helps to illustrate how both novelty and causality enter into the world. For example, given the game of tennis, certain shoes and material for courts are "better" than others; different sizes and shapes of rackets become possible. On the other hand, there are certain limits to what can be done. Some of these possibilities and limits arise from the rules of the game, but there are also "surds" that come from matter itself. These surds, or irreducible and surprising aspects of matter, are not the Kantian thing-in-itself. Far from being unknowable, they are part of the "stuff" of which the game of tennis is constituted. The precise difference between grass and clay arises from matter; but a grass court and a clay court come into existence as part of the game of tennis, and this player now wins because she can play on a grass court better than her opponent. Far from being an unknowable, the novel aspects of matter arise as novel only in relation to a human intention and from the fact that human intentions concretely take the form of some activity of the fleshy body. Indeed, the game of tennis is meaningless apart from a relation to an organism that has legs, arms, eyes, ears, as well as a brain, and it is also meaningless apart from the way collective actions have historically forged matter to have the ambiguous but real unity of the universal game of tennis.[17]

The universality of the game is referred to as "nominalistic," only in the sense that this universality is rooted in and arises from individual human organic actions acting collectively and as groups. The "dialectical" aspect refers to the feedback between the way the matter is unified (into courts and books of rules) and the way the players keep this unity in existence, transcending it for their own purposes, such as by playing the game to relax or to make money. From a broader historical perspective, one could make a case that a more complex dialectic exists in the interaction between the game and other social unities, such as dress and codes of behavior, that, from one perspective, tend to level class distinctions, but that, from another, may bring these very distinctions back into the game in the difference between the teachers and courts available to the rich and to the poor. Indeed, in his study of Gustave Flaubert's *The Family Idiot*, Sartre does extend the notion of dialectical nominalism and the practico-inert to that of the "spirit of an age."

I further suggest that this dialectical universality provides sufficient foundation for our general mathematical and scientific claims. As soon as a scientist begins an experiment or attempts to formulate a theory, there exists throughout the world a milieu of scientific practices and writings that either adumbrates the theory or makes it appear radically "new." Similarly, mathematicians work within the practical hierarchy of the work of other mathematicians—although with mathematics, I suspect that writing, and particularly the world of books, play crucial roles, and I will return to this in the next chapter. Here I simply wish to note that, if we put the emphasis on pure mathematics as a craft, then the debate between formalism and intuitionism seems less extreme: the formalist view that mathematical truths can be reduced to "scratches" on paper is untenable if these scratches are seen divorced from their historical formation. However, within an historical context that would relate the mathematical symbols to their historical formation, these symbols are seen to be not arbitrary but conventional. I thus suggest that mathematical symbols embody meanings in a way that is not too dissimilar from the manner in which tennis dialectically embodies the meaning and the universality of the game itself. Further, insofar as any artifact retains the history of human efforts in a way that does not require us to know this history in order to use or understand the artifact, one can also be said to "intuit" a mathematical truth. That is, insofar as one now sees the meaning of the symbol apart from the historical practices that have won this meaning for us, the meaning has the appearance of being a priori true.

Again, I hope that it is clear that my references to historical practices does not mean that I am historicizing or psychologizing our relation to the world. Such "relative" relations exist; but they are not my concern. To give an example: a can of Diet Coke can be viewed as resulting from our interest (some would say obsession) with our weight, and it could be considered a sign of our culture.[18] But that does not interest me. I would want to point to the existence of the can and its fluid as an artifact that can be reproduced relatively easily, and which, as such, is the objective foundation of our universal notion of "Diet Coke." For the most part, everyone who purchases Diet Coke gets Diet Coke; that is, until the format of the can is altered or unless there is tampering, the can and its content are, for the practical purposes of drinking Diet Coke, identical. Each can of Diet Coke is also the archetype, Diet Coke. This repeatability is both objective and remarkable: it is obviously objective, because we made it to be that way, and it is remarkable, for although it took a great deal of effort on the part of thousands of people to make it work, the effort is hidden in the workability of the artifact.

A can of Coke is not a star, but relational objectivity is in both. Aside from our psychological and historical interests, a can of Coke is objective because it is an artifact. In a similar way, a star is objectively in space because that is how matter is arranged about our fleshy organic body and in relation to our fleshy astronomical practices—theorems and instruments designed by fleshy hands. True, we don't mold stars, and it is also true that there is more mystery to the nature of a star than in a can of Coke. Nevertheless, a star is a star because of matter's relation to our organic body, and whatever mysteries about the nature of stars arise do so only because we have eyes to seem them and because we have localized, through our instruments and our language, that part of matter to study rather than some other. A star, nevertheless, is not dissolved into these relations. It is a "star" that is revealed by these particular relations, and not a tree. Thus, through its relations to our fleshy body and its practices, matter is thereby differentiated into things, things which we examine and about which we wonder.

Thus, while the mind is, to some extent, our mental life and even our brain states, primarily the mind is the web of structures in the world. These structures arise either from matter's relations to our fleshy body with its senses, or from matter's relations to our collective historical practices. These latter produce the cultural web of artifacts that, for better or worse, characterize an age.

Like a city, nature and mind are each beyond the creative power of any one individual, and yet, to the extent that, in their own ways, each embed the structures that give rise to meanings, Mind and Nature have, in Putnam's words, a Human Face.

Chapter 7

The Written Word

The contemporary approach to consciousness considers the external activities as mere passageways to meanings, which are then found within us either in concepts, silent speech, deep-rooted structures of language, or flashes and connections among neurons. It is indeed true that thinking sometimes takes the form of rummaging about the notions in our mind by whatever form, and here I admit that we find meanings within us rather than on the surface of things. Still, if Rodin's *The Thinker* is not the archetype of the posture of thinking, there is always some posture connected with this internal form of consciousness. But I do not wish to press the point. More importantly, these internal activities are secondary; our thoughts are primarily associated with our fleshy activities such as speaking, listening, writing, and reading, and indeed, with the entire external movements of our body, for example in dance, acting, or just walking.

Universality is also first found on the surface of things because we have molded the surface to be just that way. Although we frequently forget the history of our efforts, we collectively craft matter into universals, and then we individually confront this universality as a gift, a gift of Nature, of

Chance, or of God. Universality is a gift, but we and our ancestors are the givers; it is we who crafted language into sounds and into letters. Our relation to universal notions and terms, to scientific laws, to mathematical truths, and to the entire workability of language is similar to entering a room in which the furniture and fixtures are all comfortably there, and we usually forget their origin. In general, our relation to the world is frequently interpreted in a way that is similar to those science-fiction examples in which, after some nuclear disaster, sophisticated computers and machines remain working while people gradually forget their human origin. I think that this is, in fact, the case in regard to the workability of spoken language, but since this history is lost to us in prehistory, I want to begin with what we do know—the history of writing and the manufacturing of books. This history affords an insight into the way we craft matter into meanings and ultimately into that web of meanings: the transcendent mind. We thus craft the world as a set of meaningful relations that we then interiorize, giving our personal stamp to it, and thus gradually forge our individual minds.

Crafting universals would be a mysterious process if it were not merely a particular aspect of the collective making of artifacts. It took a great deal of effort and dedication of purpose to make *this* fork *a* fork. Indeed, in retrospect, it seems that an aspect of our crafting was always directed to making the unique common. The history of how a throne became a chair is probably similar to the history of how a noblewoman's knife and fork became everyone's knife and fork. At first, a fork was so unique that noble persons carried their own to a feast, and they were distinguished as noble partly by their possession and use of a fork. In general, much of this history is in our books. But the history of how grunts and gestures that signified "come here" slowly became the elegant, meaning sounds "come here" are lost to us in prehistory. Fortunately, however, through the dedication of many scholars, the history of crafting marks into meaning is available, although as I will indicate, its significance is misunderstood.

Again, I regard my procedure here as an attempt to demystify our relations with the world. In particular, this demystification takes the form of challenging the necessity of appealing to a deep structure within the brain or consciousness to explain the workability of language in general and of writing in particular. Language may indeed have deep structures, but they are to be traced to the history of our own collective actions. At least, I think that this is a more sensible solution than appealing to some mystic guidance of Nature that supposedly gave us the ability to think and speak as means of survival. Further, my notion of seeking meaning on the surface of both the spoken and written word also calls into question the attempt to explain language as a mere sign of our behavior. Language does signify behavior and other things, but this sign-signified relation is constituted by our actions, and, more to my point, it presupposes language as the workability of the sign as a thing. In so-called natural signs, such as smoke being a sign of combustion, smoke must be smoke and be recognized as such. In a similar way, a hammer must be workable as a hammer before it can be used as a tool. I suggest that the same is true in regard to sounds that work as language, and here I explicitly make the case that the workability of the written work presupposes its use as a sign.

Thus, insofar as it is given as the only explanation for our competent use of language, deep-rooted and behavioristic explanations mystify rather than demystify our experience. When someone speaks, I understand the words directly, and when I read, I understand the written words directly. For example, fluently reading "A rose is a rose is a rose" with fleshy eyes or in braille with fleshy fingers, we understand just the surface meaning of that expression, whatever wonder may follow about the "true" meaning of it. To claim that we should not or cannot be doing just what we seem to be doing is similar to claiming that we cannot be certain that the back of the room exists because we are not perceiving it. One of my philosophy teachers tried to convince me of that nonsense thirty-odd years ago. I did not accept it then, and I do not accept it now. Nothing can be more certain than my commonsense experience of the world, and my implied thesis throughout this work has been that arguments that attempt to dismantle common sense undermine themselves in the process.

For all that, it is useful to repeat that I do not propose a philosophy of common sense (which would be to propose another bird's-eye view of the world), but, rather, a relational realism in which common sense has a valid place. We experience the sun to rise, and my point throughout this manuscript is that this experience is valid precisely as it is a relation to a fleshy substance that can feel warmth, see light, and is situated on Earth. The error of the Ptolemaic system was to turn the centrality of the human body into a theoretically privileged view of the universe. The error of the science that dismantled (by way of the Copernican principle) the Ptolemaic epicycles was to disembody our fleshy organism, thereby placing our mind as a neutral spectator of the universe. Indeed, the Copernican principle gave us a new privileged position in the universe, for our neutral perspective on the laws of the universe arose from the fact that our place in the universe was not a special place. But this supposed neutrality is an achieved phenomenon. We project ourselves throughout the universe and then deny the projection. Further, the neutrality of the traditional scientific perspective masks its reliance on the correspondence theory of truth, the magic meshing of mind to matter, that is itself lifted from the very Aristotelian system that it supposedly dismantles.

Neurophilosophy and the appeal to deep-rooted structures in language resurrect this scientific Copernican and philosophic Cartesian perspective on the world. The contemporary neurophilosophical approach to consciousness and the linguistic approach to language attempt to describe both consciousness and language from some privileged position outside both systems. In place of human actions collectively forging structures, we are supposed to "discover" what Nature has given us. Following Sartre, however, I take human action to be the source of all structures, not by making them out of some goo, but either by highlighting these rather than other aspects of matter, or, as with artifacts, by crafting structures. Here I want to make this later claim more specific by examining writing. My relational realist point is that, in relation to the educated fleshy fingers and eyes that write and read, the written word is meaningful in itself, as it appears on the page. In brief, the written word works as language because we crafted it that way.

I am not putting forward a picture view of language, and I do not claim that the word "chair," whether spoken or written, looks in any way like a chair. Rather, my understanding of the crafting of meanings in language and in mathematics is part of a particular view of abstraction. Our written language embodies a history of practical abstractions that is not much different from that contained in the evolution of the electric lightbulb. The inventions that took us from the torch to the candle to the gaslight and then to the electric lightbulb emerged from our practical need to separate light from heat and from the ability of matter to be molded to these needs. Every artifact results from the wonder of a matter durable enough to sustain our human efforts over time and yet malleable enough to receive our impressions. Writing is one with the history of these abstractions, and it arises from our need to separate meaning from speech, or at least this is my claim.

CRAFTING MARKS INTO MEANINGS

Philosophical and critical reflection seem to require that we see that the sounds or marks of a language are merely arbitrary carriers of meaning. In regard to writing, the marks are supposed to trigger in us a meaningful response. In *Quiddities*, in the section "A" for "Alphabet," W. V. O. Quine neatly summarizes some aspects of the remarkable feat of discovering how alphabetic marks came to represent sounds.

> . . . the full power of writing awaited the convergence of writing with speech, and this reached its early stages five thousand years ago. Depictions of visible objects came to be pressed into phonetic duty on the rebus principle, as if in English we were to write *melancholy* by depicting a melon and a collie. This expedient was rendered more flexible and powerful, if less picturesque, by devoting the phonetic representations to brief sounds—single consonants or syllables. The sound was represented by a hieroglyph depicting something whose name merely began with that sound. The rebus principle thus gave way to an acrophonic one. It was a notable step of abstraction. Finding a melon and collie in melancholy is a matter of punning with familiar words; extracting a meaningless *me-*, on the other hand, and meaningless *-lan-*, and so on, calls for appreciating fugitive sounds that are not words and name nothing.[1]

From the perspective of relating the written word to the spoken one, Quine is right about the move from the rebus principle to syllabic representation of sounds as being an advance in abstraction, but he bypasses another feat of abstraction. I do not blame him, however, for it is not his concern, but it is mine. Assuming, for the present, that writing began by attempting to associate written symbols with sounds, is that the way writing works now? From the perspective of competent reading, I do not think that is the case, and as already noted, I am moving to the claim that, when we read fluently, we find the meanings on the written page itself.[2]

In *Reading*, Frank Smith seems to make just such a case. He notes: "How is it possible to recognize written words without sounding them out? The answer is that we recognize words in the same way that we recognize all other familiar objects in our visual world—trees and animals, cars and houses, cutlery, crockery, furniture, and faces—'on sight.'"[3] This perspective on writing requires that we see the movement of the eyes (or fingers) over the written (or embossed) page as finding meanings on the page itself. I want to preserve this insight while attempting to explain how we made it possible.

Although I seek meanings on the surface of the text, I repeat that I have no intention of resurrecting the picture view of writing. Our ability to read marks as meanings is *not* due to some strange, primordial connection that meanings may have with marks. Prior to the discovery of the Rosetta Stone, this was one of the popular views about ancient Egyptian hieroglyphics: the glyphs were supposed to connect naturally but mysteriously with meanings, somewhat as a cross connects naturally and yet mysteriously with Christianity. Learning how to "read" the connection between a cross and Christian beliefs has nothing to do with spoken language, but it has a great deal to do with knowing the history of Christianity. I am *not* making a similar case about alphabetic writing. On the contrary, my point is that we live in a world of convention, and that crafting marks into meaning is one of the more "immaterial" forms of convention, with its own specific qualities.

The view I urge is thus based upon a distinction between what is arbitrary and what is conventional. Writing is conventional but not arbitrary. I thus see only a degree of difference between the convention that teaches us to "read" a wooden artifact as a chair to sit upon and the one that instructs us to read the word "chair" as the meaning chair. In a society in which everyone squats on the ground, a chair would not naturally signify something in which one arranges one's body in such a way that a sitting posture can be attained. Writing simply raises this convention to a higher level of abstraction, except that none of this was simple.

Since our English writing is alphabetic, I want to approach writing with some observations about its history. Among others, David Diringer in *The Alphabet* provides a good introductory survey to the history of the formation of alphabetic writing. The characteristic of alphabetic writing is that it reproduces the sounds of speech by using a small number of marks, called letters, and, in its strictest form, the alphabet seems to have been invented only once.[4] Other writing systems, such as ancient Egyptian or Chinese, may use figures to represent either sound or notions, but a pure alphabet is completely divorced from picture writing.

Or is it? Certainly the resemblance is gone. To emphasize, I am not attempting to resurrect any mystic tie of writing to meaning. Rather, I want to show that, as far removed as alphabet writing is from pictures, its origin is one with the general social convention whereby marks can be read as meanings, and this frequently first appears in pictures and in pictograms. Later, I will suggest that the history of writing may have had a different origin, but the principle of social abstraction is the same, and the movement from pictogram to alphabet is the more usual interpretation.

As a beginning, it is important to note that abstraction is present even in "reading" pictograms. For example, the use of a circle to represent the sun is a feat of abstraction. As Diringer notes, by itself, a circle could represent the sun, and such representation would be a form of art. What makes the circle a pictogram is that it is strung together with other pictures as a narrative. It is in this way that pictograms become a form of writing.

> However, picture writing even in its more elementary stage is
> more than a picture. It differs from picturing, which is the
> beginning of pure pictorial representation or art, in the fact that
> it is the utilitarian beginning of written language, aiming to con-
> vey to the mind not the pure representation of an event, but a

narrative of the event, each notion or idea being expressed by a little picture or sketch, which we term a *pictograph*. The distinction is important, for the change from embryo-writing to picture-writing implies an immense progress in the art of transmitting and also (quite incidentally) perpetuating thought.[5]

I would put the emphasis in this quote on the "feat of abstraction," and I would note that it had to be a social process. Further, there had to be some need on our part to separate meaning from sound. Moving from pictogram to ideogram, we encounter another long history of successful abstractions, with their corresponding acts of social learnings. In an ideogram, "a circle, for example, might represent not only the sun but also heat or light or a god associated with the sun, or the word 'day.'"[6] But as with pictograms, ideograms are not ideographic writing, which once again requires a leap to recognize the stringing of the ideograms together as something to be read as a narrative.

The further jump to phonetic writing required that attention be paid to the sounds of the words. Phonetic writing, however, is not necessarily alphabetic. If you listen to the sounds of a conversation with an eye to representing them by written symbols, the more natural course would probably be to focus on the syllables. Syllabic writing requires that some symbol be used to represent the syllables in a word. This can be cumbersome. As Diringer notes, "it would be easy in a syllabary system to form a word like *fa-mi-ly*, but the word "strength" would have to be written *se-te-re-ne-ge-the* or the like, and such a representation of sounds would be far from satisfactory."[7] In alphabetic writing, the sounds are broken down to more ultimate unities, phonemes and letters are chosen to represent these. The result is that a handful of letters can represent the sounds of a language, and memory can connect the letters with the phonemes.

I do not deny the plausibility of any of this history, but I do question whether it is primary and whether such an explanation can explain the fluency with which we read. In crafting the marks of the alphabet, did we not go beyond our original intentions and fashion the marks themselves into the meanings of our language?

Florian Coulmas in his *The Writing Systems of the World* helps us focus on the abstractions that lead to writing. Coulmas sees the origins of writing to be earlier than pictograms, but he also stresses the leap in abstraction needed to reach the conventional marks used in writing. "The step from simple mnemonic devices such as tally sticks to the first conventional system of writing capable of recording information on clay tablets was immeasurably greater than all subsequent steps combined."[8]

I think it useful to press Coulmas's point about the leap from mnemonic devices to writing. First, however, I want to observe that, granting his point about the great leap in abstraction from mnemonic devices to marks used for writing to be generally valid, this claim has to be put in proper perspective. The move from mnemonic devices to numbers and from pictures to pictograms established a distinctive kind of convention, but not convention itself. The world of artifacts had already made things exist "by convention." No matter how natural their function may appear, all artifacts, even a wheel, are conventional. They involve a use of matter arising from human intentions: matter itself gives no motivation for the coming-to-be of a wheel precisely as it is a means for moving things. In itself, a rounded piece of wood could be an art form, an object whose use is to provoke wonder. Once the connection between that rounded shape and the task of moving something has been socially fixed, it seems natural.

D. Schmandt-Besserat's account of tokens helps us to be even more specific in grasping the specific kinds of abstractions that must have preceded the invention of writing.[9] I understand her discovery to consist of two parts, each indicating a distinctive leap in our abstractive abilities. First, we find tokens or counters in use about ten thousand years ago, and then the tokens give way to written marks. A token is a shaped marker that designated an object; for example, this shape signifies a garment. I interpret the significance of this use of tokens, as well as the way they gave way to written marks, to point to different degrees of practical abstractions, each of which were preceded by earlier stages of practical abstractions.

Thus, in comparison to using an animal skin, a garment itself is a practical abstraction; that is, a garment is an abstract animal skin. One has to learn to "read" a robe as something that can be worn to cover the body. The creation of tokens is the beginning of a new kind of abstract covering for the body; if a garment is an abstract animal skin or abstract plant leaf, the token is an abstract garment and requires a new kind of reading to use it. This reading of the token is its use. Thus, by handling tokens, one handles garments, that is, abstract garments.

Like the more concrete garments that we wear, these more abstract garments needed to be stored. Tokens were thus placed in a container; but just as the more concrete garments could be lost or stolen, so too could one add to or subtract from these abstract ones. To prevent them from being manipulated, they were later sealed in a container. However, to get to the abstract garments, one had to break the seal. Another great leap in abstraction occurred. The form and number of the tokens were impressed on the seal before it hardened. The tokens were still considered the true representations of the garments, that is, the tokens were still handled as the true abstract garments. Gradually, one learned to "read" the impressions themselves as an even more abstract form of the garment, and it became clear that the tokens themselves were not needed.

While obviously none of these feats of abstraction were explicitly known as such, they were effectively created as concrete abstractions, and they were read as such. My further suggestion is that the written alphabetic word "garment" is simply a more recent and more abstract stage in the gradual making of matter to be more and more immaterial that was the progression from animal skin to garment to token to impression. (True, the sound "garment" was there first, but this merely means that the sounds were surely cultivated through an earlier history of abstractions.)

In *Language: The Unknown,* Julia Kristeva helps us to consider the specific abstraction that led to alphabetic writing, and she takes us to the door (which she herself does not enter) of understanding the ultimate break from the spoken word made by the slow process of forming the written word. She notes that the Sumerian symbol for water was related to the Sumerian sound for water. However, when the Akkadians appropriated the

Sumerian symbol, they used it to stand for the sound but not the signified, since water in Akkadian was pronounced differently than in Sumerian. The Akkadian abstraction separated the original sign/signified relation. The result was that the script gained a new priority. True, the script was still related to sound, but since the sound was not the sign of the original signified, the path was laid for the eventual separation of the orthography itself from speech. This path, if I am not mistaken, was completed with the invention of cuneiform. Although Kristiva does not give to this history the full weight that I think it deserves, she nevertheless writes: "This hypothesis explains the change to phonetic if not alphabetic writing as being the result of a process of mentalization and breakup of the intimate relation referent/signifier/signified, proper to the pictogram and ideogram."[10]

Still, neither Kristeva nor Coulmas accepts writing as a legitimate form of language, and, to the best of my knowledge, their opinion is shared by other linguists and historians of language. However, I interpret not only many of Kristeva's comments, but those of other historians such as Diringer and Coulmas, to imply that the gradual break from the signified of the spoken word allows the written sign to be read on its own level, that is, to be read *not* as a sign, but as a meaning. Of course, the relation of the written word to both spoken language and to the object signified are implicitly present. We can and do treat the written word as a mere sign, or to be more exact, we treat the written sentence as a movement from sign to sign. But we do not do this in our fluent reading, precisely as this is a comprehension of meanings. On this level, we find meanings on the page itself, and thus the movement is not from sign to sign but from meaning to meaning.

The abstractive leap to alphabetic writing was not made by many civilized peoples. Abstraction, however, always comes at a price. A road sign picturing a knife and a fork can be "read" by almost anyone, speaking any language. (Although even here I would note that the individuals are in a culture in which writing exists, and that they have thus been instructed how to interpret these signs.) For example, in alphabetic writing, the beauty apparent in Chinese calligraphy is compromised. But if one is willing to live with such disadvantages, the result is that a handful of alphabetic symbols can represent a great diversity of sounds, meanings, and things.

I suspect that we can trace a history similar to that which led to writing in regard to the so-called natural numbers, but here my account will be even more of a sketch than the above account of writing. Nevertheless, my general points about practical and social abstractions have been made, and I see the history of our formation of numbers in the same light, regardless of the problem of transfinite numbers, which I think can be handled dialectically as classes sustained by the interplay between the activities of mathematicians and their embodiment in books.

As Tobias Dantzig puts it in *Number: The Language of Science*, it seems clear that numbers were first a practical matter concerned with counting and weighing. In its early history, counting was as cumbersome as writing. The simplicity of the numbers 0, 1, 2, 3, 4, . . . is again the result of a history of human practices. This history of the number system gradually produced the abstractions that we now receive as if they were handed to us by "nature."

> The greatly increased facility with which the average man today manipulates numbers has often been taken as proof of the growth of the human intellect. The truth of the matter is that the difficulties then experienced were inherent in the numeration in use, a numeration not susceptible to simple, clear-cut rules. The discovery of the modern positional numeration did away with these obstacles and made arithmetic accessible even to the dullest mind.[11]

In the development of the history of numbers, perhaps the greatest achievement, and the one that proved the most difficult to make, was the invention of zero. The use and the understanding of zero allowed us to give numbers a position. "Thus, the same digit 2 has different meanings in the three numbers 342, 725, 269: in the first case it stands for two; in the second for twenty, in the third for two hundred."[12] This positional notation meant that one could conceive of an empty set or class: "The concrete mind of the ancient Greeks could not conceive the void as a number, let alone endow the void with a symbol."[13]

The Hindu expression for zero did not really mean "nothing"; rather it signified a "blank." The actual way the Indian term *sunya* became the mathematical zero seems to be as much an accident as the result of planning, but it was recognized for what it was, because people were trying to do things with numbers that required *seeing* zero as an empty set.[14] The empty set was not there waiting to be "found," and it might never have been invented. The need to see zero as the empty set merely provided the necessary but not the sufficient condition for its invention. We certainly waited long enough to invent zero, and we could still be waiting. (In such a history, "we" would not be "we.")

Through the historical refinement of the alphabet and the number system, we have slowly constructed a system of meaningful symbols that objectify consciousness. The claim that these symbols are arbitrary in relation to our thought about them or in relation to the things they represent is itself the result of yet another practical abstraction: we abstract from the efforts that went into the formation of languages, and *then* we point to the fact that different sounds and symbols can represent the same thing.[15]

THE WORLD OF BOOKS

I recall passing a laundromat on Second Avenue in Manhattan on whose steps a young girl of nine or ten sat reading. Her mother was inside using the washers and dryers. More affluent or lazier people like myself could leave their laundry and have it cleaned and folded for a fee—not ironed and pressed as in a "real" laundry, but good enough to pass casual inspection. What struck me was the commonplace phenomenon of the young girl totally absorbed in reading her book while hundreds of people were walking by, while cars were honking and sirens sounding. The girl noticed none of these. She was not sitting there impatiently waiting for her mother to finish the wash; she was living *in* her book. I thought that if an alien consciousness were walking the same street it would be amazed that an organic, thinking, fleshy substance could be absorbed in this strange object made of paper and ink. But why speak of alien consciousness? To the illiterate, the world of writing must seem as strange as colors to the blind. Melville's Queequeg was fascinated by the strange things called "words" that were on the page of his book about whaling.

It is easy to understand how someone can be absorbed in the great spectacles of nature, the rising mountains and the vast expanses of ocean. It is even easy to understand how someone can be absorbed in watching television or in listening to recordings of music, for in these cases we reproduce qualities that exist in the observable world. But writing, and books in particular, allow us to do something far more extraordinary: these strange marks become, in the turning of pages, the secret lives of people, the vast beauty of nature, the history of the world, and the grasping at the universe. We take the magic of books for granted, but no fairy tale could invent a wand as magical as a book nor wizards as powerful as writers and readers.

It may help to locate my efforts in interpreting the role of books in our thinking by returning to the discussion in the previous chapter concerning Popper's three worlds. To repeat, the first world is the world of natural things, the second world that of subjectivity, and the third provides the objects of our universal notions. I have already noted that, once we adopt a more expansive view of matter, the first two worlds become part of our one world. The world of natural kinds arise from matter's relation to the fleshy human conscious organism. And while the human body is material and thus part of our world, it is irreducible to a mechanistic view of matter. I here carry through my suggestion that Popper's third world can be identified, in general, with our web of artifacts, and more specifically, with the networks of our books. We are each immersed in this world; the world acts upon us, and we act upon it.

My suggestion here is that there is a special feedback between the world of books and our search for the foundation of our scientific and mathematical claims.[16] The basis for this suggestion is in the unique way books establish the basis for the repeatability of notions. This repeatability needs readers, but in these concluding remarks, I want to point to the unique way structure, and thus the possibility of interiorizing structure as meaning, is reproduced in books. (For convenience, in what follows I refer interchangeably to meaning and structure.) I wish to suggest that, because books are easily and accurately repeatable, they can serve as a dialectical basis for some of our general notions.

Of course, the spoken word can be repeated; the early Greeks, for example, memorized Homer. But the identity of text achieved by writing is formally different from that of the memorized spoken word.[17] The repeatability of the spoken word requires the accuracy of an individual's memory, and this can never be guaranteed. More importantly, in listening to one recite, the personality and interpretation of the one reciting is always evident. In acting, the personality of the actor is as important as the words recited: we can read the words of Shakespeare, but we attend the theater to hear these words interpreted for us.

Just as the personality of the reciter was consciously meant to be attended to in the recitation of a poem, so too the earlier manuscripts were admired as much for the beauty of their calligraphy as for their content. Also, just as writing was initially seen to be merely an aid to memory, the printed book was first seen to be merely a cheaply reproduced manuscript. Thus the quantum leap in the repeatability of language achieved by the book was initially passed over. Indeed, Johann Guttenburg and Peter Schoeffer saw their achievement primarily to consist in making relatively cheap forms of manuscripts available to the public. The early printing was made to imitate the manuscript. The initials of at least the opening paragraphs of each section were left blank so that they could be drawn in by hand. In this way, the person possessing the book would have something approaching a manuscript.

Aldus Manutius, however, recognized the printing was distinctly different from writing. His books were printed with a new, legible type that made no attempt to imitate written script. The initials were left unadorned and simply printed in as part of the entire text. The modern book was invented, and its initial independence from the manuscript was gradually acknowledged.[18]

The remarkableness of modern printing is that, from the viewpoint of *meaning*, it perfectly abstracts from the personalities of the printers, publishers, binders, and graphic designers. This is not to say that the choice of type and formation of the page is unimportant, but in relation to the content of the modern book, these choices do not carry additional semantic value. True, beauty is (sometimes) reintroduced in artistic dust jackets and in special editions that allow a reader to enjoy the book artistically,[19] but the fact remains that today's average reader can, for the most part, read a text as accurate as that available to any scholar.

One way of understanding what we have accomplished in producing books is to view them as demystifying Plato's World of Forms. Insofar as each book is indefinitely repeatable, it is a universal idea. Even if we consider Quine's reservations about translation, we have repeatability at least in one's home language. But with science and mathematics, the repeatability is more universal because the language is initially more abstract. Thus, perfect repeatability among languages is, perhaps, achieved only in mathematics and in physical theory.

But the practical efforts of translators are not in vain. Aside from the fact that a translation may only approximate what is said in another language, a translation may be a better literary work than the original. From another perspective, these qualifications are nothing more than a specification of the kind of universality that exits in the meaning itself. No one expects Shakespeare to mean exactly the same in French as in English; the language of a Shakespearean play or sonnet does not require the kind of universality that mathematics possesses, for there is a sense in which each person has his or her own Shakespeare. The issue of individuality and subjectivity that arises in the milieu of the printed book, however, is of a different order than that which would occur without the printed book. An English text is capable of being indefinitely repeated, and it can be made available to any person who wishes to examine it. Whatever problems exist in constructing an accurate text, each effort becomes present in another text capable of being examined by succeeding scholars.

We take printed books for granted, but we must recall that they are the product of a specific kind of historical consciousness. The Chinese, in their system of moving blocks, seemed to have hit upon the nature of a book prior to the printing press, but for them, writing by using moving blocks in no way challenged the accepted forms of writing. Perhaps the Chinese were not willing to make the exchange required—trading beauty and individuality for universality. Printing from blocks, like fireworks, may have seemed to them an interesting phenomenon, something to be admired and not something to be developed for general use. Also, the nonalphabetic form of the Chinese language and the hierarchical division between the scholar and the nonreader may have discouraged any thought of mass production.

There is no one process of abstraction. In general, however, I think that my notion of forging matter to be abstract, together with a dialectical nominalism that expresses these abstractions (suggested in the previous chapter and in appendix II), can handle many of our questions about the basis of our universal notions. Thus, the universal chair and the universal five are both crafted. We make this chair to be every chair: you can purchase a chair; it may not be comfortable and it may not be beautiful, but, if it is a chair, it will function as something you can sit upon. We also crafted five things to be seen as five things. We might have been trained to see only two and more than two, with no notions of three, four, and beyond. With a great deal of effort, we also forged both the sound "five" to mean five, and the marks f-i-v-e to mean five. Of course, the full range of mathematical truths needs a more sophisticated basis, and I suggest that it is to be found in the special way that mathematical theorems are stated in books and in the way these books can have dialectical relations to potential readers.

Today, the question of whether language has achieved a new quantum leap with the invention of the computer is an open question. Anyone adept at writing with a computer notes that, for better or for worse, one seems able to say things through a computer that are different than what emerges from the act of typing. Whether this difference distills to mere loquaciousness remains to be seen, but apart from so-called word processing, the computer does seem to achieve a new quantum leap in the existence of what I call the transcendence of mind. I completely agree with Putnam that it makes no sense to attempt to reduce human consciousness to that of a sophisticated computer. To Putnam's arguments, I would add the necessity that human consciousness be flesh, for it is only through flesh that the world can be seen to have those not-fleshy qualities such as color, heat, or sound.

However, I repeat: we forge matter to be immaterial in the sense that we craft instances of things that can also be archetypes of them. *This* chair, *this* fork, *this* five is every chair, every fork, every five, because we make them to be that way. After countless centuries of effort, and with the contribution of millions of people, we have constructed a world in which we are surrounded by tokens that are also types. From another perspective, this forging gives us matter as immaterial, for the immateriality is simply that, with little effort, each token is potentially repeatable. This history of forging structures and meanings is one with our history of making artifacts, but it is nonetheless remarkable.

From this perspective, the computer may be a new form of our efforts to separate meaning from flesh, efforts that arise from and are reducible to our fleshy consciousness and its activities. Indeed, to the extent that computers are considered a form of artificial intelligence, I would note that writing, and especially books, can be viewed as the first form of artificial intelligence. In writing and in books, intelligence is already objectified so that it achieves both a permanence and a degree of complexity not available to conversation.

If we can use books to rehabilitate Plato's World of Ideas, we may be able to do the same with Aristotle's matter-form theory. Each book is an individual book, in its own time and space, with its own accidental features. Nevertheless, each book is an instance of a book: my copy of Melville's *Moby Dick* is *Moby Dick*, and if the text be found later to be somewhat different from Melville's manuscript, this text at this time represents a perfect embodiment of the meaning that is the text; or to be more accurate, the text *is* the meaning as this meaning is here rather than there.

Focusing on books, we can thus make the good Aristotelian point that there is no *Moby Dick* as such. It appears as if *Moby Dick* is embodied in many instances, but this is merely a question of craftsmanship: the one text is made so that it can be indefinitely repeated. We made *this* fork to be *a* fork, and now we have made *this* meaning to be *a* meaning. I can refer, as I am doing now, to *Moby Dick* as if it were an archetype, existing independently from its concrete existences. Then, concentrating on the archetype, I can consider the individual instances to be "embodiments" of the one meaning. In effect, the situation is the opposite. The archetype is merely the abstraction from the instances, an abstraction based on the fact the each copy of *Moby Dick* is equally *Moby Dick*.

We can find, if we wish, the basis for Aristotle's knowledge-in-itself and Kant's a priori categories in books. In the closed books dealing with historical studies, philosophical views, physical theorems, and mathematical formulas, we find, prior to any individual act of opening the book, the "potential existence" of what can be called "knowledge-in-itself." This potential existence, of course, is itself the product of the actual production of the writing and publishing of books by other people. Thus, at the source of every network, every a priori form, and every structure, we find the historical activities of our fleshy human organisms.

My strong claim then is that, even as unread, even with their covers closed, even as they lie dormant side by side on library shelves, books provide the justification for the pure objectivity of mathematics, science, and all our other universal claims about the world, precisely as these are taken to be static and fixed. Writing in general and books in particular—and perhaps now the computer—are the culmination of the efforts of our fleshy organic consciousness to transcend itself by producing mind. In retrospect, our crafting of matter into meanings all began with the flintstone and with our first grunts, and the world in which we now live carries the weight of those efforts.

Thus the world of natural kinds, the world of water, trees, and stars, arises as differentiated into these rather than other things from matter's relation to the human fleshy organic body and its practices. As I have stated throughout this work, an anthropocentric relational realism can help to demystify our relations to the world: in relation to our fleshy eyes, there is color in the world, and the color exists in the world because of the way our consciousness as sight differentiates matter as colored. Regardless of how you and I see this or that colored object, regardless of whether or not we are actually seeing anything at all, color is an essential aspect of things, because of the way the sense of sight makes matter potentially visible. Although I have not spelled it out, and must leave the discussion for a subsequent work, I have also suggested the unity of natural kinds arises from the relation of matter to the unity of the organic fleshy body.

In a broad sense, we craft both the world of natural kinds and the world of meanings that, more or less, correspond to them. The world of natural kinds we craft through our senses, not out of a primoridal goo, but by highlighting certain aspects of matter rather than other. The world of meanings we craft through the slow forgings of the elegant sounds of speech and inscriptions used in writing. Between the two, between the world of natural kinds and the world of language, binding them, as it were, together, there is the world of artifacts. Thus, making fire by rubbing two sticks connects, as it were, the natural kind "fire" with the word "fire."

In these last two chapters, I have outlined an anthropocentric perspective on abstraction, on meanings, and on universality. The world of meanings arises from the history of our individual actions. Even the most abstract mathematical expressions must be expressed in some way, and this way always reflects the human body in its fleshy nature. The mouth forming words, the hand writing, and even the postured body thinking all reveal that our most abstract thoughts arise from and are tailored to our fleshy organism. The attempt to make the organic nature of the body and its fleshy nature incidental to the world is like attempting to make the fleshy sweat, toil, and labor of our individual and collective efforts incidental to our farming, our cities, indeed, our civilization and culture. We may forge our mathematics and our mental concepts as if they might fit any conceivable intelligence, but here we mystify ourselves and create and worship false gods, gods of nature, gods of being, gods of language, gods of system, gods of chance, gods of myth, gods of the unconscious, gods of God. Because the prehistory and history of human efforts have created a web of meanings that surpasses any one of our minds, we stand in wonder at and at times in shame of our own efforts, and indeed we should. The wonder and the shame, however, must be placed where they belong, in us.

The Anthropocentric Universe

Aristotle and Ptolemy place us comfortably in the center of things. From this privileged position, the goings and comings of the planets yield their secrets to our mathematics; the movements, mixtures, and compositions of the elements reveal their inner natures to our science.

Snugly reassuring, this anthropomorphic world still masks enough ambiguity to engender that wonder that Aristotle says is the beginning of philosophy: although we are mortal flesh, we delve into things, grasping hold of their essences, and our reach goes to the stars, laying at our feet the eternal movements of the heavenly spheres. Aristotle would have us see that all things shed the spotlight of their existence on Earth in general and on us humans in particular; nevertheless, their functions serve their own ends. We admire the mountains, oceans, and forests of the Earth; we bend to our needs the warmth of the Sun, the pull of the Moon, and the movements of the planets and stars; but our use, wonder, and knowledge do not constitute the existence of things. We use wood to make houses, but trees are given to us by that strange entity, force, or happenstance that we call "Nature." And beyond Earth, this Nature appears even more mysterious and even less localized to the needs of Earth: in an attempt to escape an anthropomorphic view of the world, Aristotelian naturalism begins to reach for transcendence by raising the "matter" of the Sun and planets above mortal flesh. Such "matter" is incorruptible, unchanging, and under the guidance of intelligences that transcend the human psyche. Thus, if for Aristotle and Ptolemy we are at the privileged center of all things, we are so as mere spectators of a universe whose nature transcends us.

True, Aristotle weds spirit to matter. He grants to us the reality of the tree we climbed as a child as well as the essential reality of the plant life we read about in our college textbooks on botany, or he tries to. But how can that cherished oak, perhaps, felled, sawed, and axed into firewood, hold its own alongside the essential oak that endures now and forever in each newly generated oak? If Aristotle's matter-form distinction accounted for the presence of essences in Nature, he would not have had recourse to those strange spiritual substances that guide and sustain the complex of natures on earth and the movements of the spheres in the heavens. And if his notion of abstraction accounted for our knowledge of essences, he would not have attempted to wean Socrates's soul from his body.

Aristotelian anthropocentrism is really an anthropomorphism rightly uncomfortable with itself; it is shot through with essences that are more at home in Plato's World of Forms than here on earth. Aristotelian-Ptolemaic geocentrism shoots its roots upward, finding fertile ground in the spiritual substances that guide the development of species on Earth and direct the perfect movement of the spheres that encircled the heavens. Copernican heliocentrism and the expanded big-bang theory of the universe, affected with Cartesian philosophy, follow this move to ground meaning in some Beyond. We are, in the scientific picture of human nature, thinking matter, localized in time and space, and yet we still know essences transcending time and space: here, at this time in history, on this sheet of paper I draw a triangle, using this fleshy hand, holding this pencil, writing with this shade of black. But then, I make a strange Platonic claim about truth: I insist that the sum of the interior angles of every triangle that ever was and ever will be is one hundred and eighty degrees, and to guarantee this claim, to justify its truth, I must allow that somehow this mortal flesh has contact with meanings that are eternal.

The Copernican revolution dethroned the Earth as the center of the universe. The tough-mindedness of scientific truth forced us to accept that our great Sun, upon which all our life depends, is just an average, middle-class star, neither a red giant nor a white dwarf. As if this were not enough to humble our spirits and send us adrift, astronomy placed our Sun itself in an innocuous position, about two-thirds out on the arm of our spiral galaxy, which itself was merely one member of a cluster of galaxies moving together away from countless other clusters of galaxies. From an anthropomorphism that placed the Earth as the objective center of the universe, we were taught by science to see ourselves as part of a vast universe that has a history of four or five billion years, and is also about four or five billion light years in its dimension.

A curious god speculating on how this Copernican revolution might influence philosophy might have placed a bet that philosophy would continue Aristotle's efforts to naturalize Plato. Of course, the Copernican revolution made us homeless; we no longer had a special place in the universe. Yet, if our feet were not on privileged property, science at least seemed to place them on firm ground. And so, one might expect that a philosophy offering its consciousness to be raised by science would take the human body seriously. If she were speculating thus, our curious god would have lost her bet. Ironically, the historically important philosophy arising within the context of the Copernican revolution breathed new life into the shade of Plato.

Descartes did not desire to begin a new Platonism, and it is not clear that he had any great understanding of Plato's works. On the contrary, Descartes initiated the modern attempt to think philosophically in a way that was independent from historical influences. If he ended with a dualism that seems similar to Plato's, it is because, like Plato, Descartes was also enamored with the apparent clarity and certainty of mathematics.

Descartes's razor-sharp criterion of truth is to heed only clear and distinct ideas. Since ideas such as color, temperature, texture, and flesh appear to be relative, it meant, for Descartes, that matter does not exist with these qualities. When we are taking a bath, we may think that a liquid, warm substance is soothing the cramped tautness of our flesh. For Descartes, this pragmatic way of looking at things is useful but not true. What is actually happening to us is that the machinery of our bodies is being cared for the way an engine is cared for when it is properly oiled. Our "feeling" of contentment as we luxuriate in our bath is only a message sent to our spiritual mind that we are doing well by the wheels and pulleys of that complex machine that is our body.

Descartes's criterion of clear and distinct ideas sharply divides reality into matter and spirit; his dualism is neater, indeed nastier than Plato's. Plato merely asks us to pass beyond the appearances of things to a deeper reality, the spiritual nature of the self and the eternal essence of each thing. Once we recognize the things of this material world to be images and shadows of stronger, more permanent realities, Plato allows us to accept these images for what they are: the image of ourselves reflected in a clear, still pond is not of flesh and bones; nevertheless this image exists in the pond, visible to others. Thus, for Plato, the real Socrates is his soul, and although his body is, in a way, a mere reflection of his soul, this body is flesh. And this fleshy body is in contact with things, albeit the shadows of true things.

Descartes, however, splits Socrates into a mind that thinks its own thoughts and a denuded matter that moves like a machine: pure thought without eyes, ears, lips, or limbs and pure extension without heat, textures, odors, sounds, or colors. Unlike Plato's dualism, Cartesian dualism confronts us with the task of uniting our ideas and perceptions of matter with matter itself. Descartes thus asks more of us than Plato ever dreamed of asking. Descartes wants us to interpret our perceptions of qualities such as colors and sounds to be our subjective responses to matter in motion. Neither Plato nor, indeed, Aristotle would see a need to pursue philosophy in this way. When Aristotle explains how we get at the essence of a material thing through the perception of its qualities, he does not have to pause to show that qualities such as heat and color have objective existence, for Plato had not denied their shadowy but earthy realities.

Indeed, the Copernican revolution, guided by the spirit of Descartes's dualism, rendered the malleability of the universe to mathematics and physical theory more mysterious than it was when Aristotle claimed that the human soul is the highest principle of organic life, and thus capable of knowing all lower material things. The Aristotelian perspective relies on a tenuous contact with the divine originator of the essences and meanings that we discover in the world. This contact with the divine puts in question the status of our organic nature; but at least it recognizes that there is a problem with the meshing of a fleshy being with seemingly eternal essences.

Descartes's mechanistic picture of matter is tailor-made for mathematics, and in considering mind as pure thought, his dualism also provides a safe haven for what William James calls the tender-minded, spiritual types. The tough-minded and the tender-minded need not have any serious conflict, and it would be civilized if the two now and then converse. The tender-minded philosopher will suggest that science is merely one way thought or language has of viewing matter. Courtesy demands that the scientist not totally disregard the worlds of literature, history, and philosophy. The conversation, however, falters when the tough-minded insists that only science yields true insights into the natures of things.

Unfortunately, if we allow the scientist to set the standard for what we should accept as essential knowledge of things, the worlds of common sense and culture lose their own secure footing in the world. Gradually, the neurologically constituted brain takes the place of Descartes's mind: the firings of fibers become thoughts, feelings, moral views, the beliefs of cultures, and the wisdom of common sense.

And what is wrong with that? Nothing, as long as this neurophilosophy is understood to be one of many historically constituted programs of study directed toward a limited but useful understanding of human nature. When, however, this scientific materialism pretends to emerge from philosophically neutral ground, when it sees itself to be above and not within culture, then this seeming materialism is Plato's spiritual World of Forms in a new guise.

Of course, when contemporary mainstream scientists or philosophers examine our knowledge about the universe, they explain it in different ways. Some, like Einstein, accept the meshing of our mathematics with the universe to be a mystery. Some become pragmatic and interpret our knowledge to be merely our way of coping with the world. Some give a linguistic twist to this pragmatism and focus their attention on our ability to speak meaningfully about things. Some adopt the religion of Chance and Mechanism: there are billions of suns with billions upon billions of planets and the law of probability together with the blind, mechanical workings of matter were bound to produce intelligence somewhere in the universe.

My objection to scientific materialism is that it masks an unjustifiable transcendent perspective on the world. My objection to pragmatism, linguistic or otherwise, is that it gives the impression that essences are always inaccessible, stately things that condescend to serve but withhold intimacy. But essences can be modest, earthy things. If looked at in relation to our commonsense practices, they are no more mysterious than our linguistic usage or pragmatic dealings with the world. Thus essences are not absolute; they are always in relation to something: the flesh of the organism, the elegance of an equation, or the structures of experiments.

Thus, the anthropocentric and relational realism sketched in the preceding chapters gives a modest, ontological answer to the question of how we can have true knowledge of things. My answer is more ontological than pragmatists would allow, because I claim that we know the essential features of things: the knowledge that water quenches thirst and is healthy for the body *is* knowledge of the essence of water.

The relational aspect of my realism is also evident in my insistence that we have no privileged, no neutral, no absolute perspective from which to judge the connections of science to common sense or common sense to science. We can, of course, adopt a privileged, neutral, or absolute perspective for a purpose: for the sake of simplicity and for the sake of testing a program connecting thought to the movement of neurons, neurology and neurophilosophy can choose to forget their history. I speak of this neutral attitude as a choice; it would be more accurate to say that the choice of putting history in the background is part of the program of science itself.

Writing makes it particularly easy to forget the history of our crafting. Even when writing is about history, it must use the crafted workability of the script in such a way that one passes through this history. But this is part of the mystery of every artifact. We use a hammer only by passing through the historical efforts that brought us the hammer. However, the case with writing is, I suggest, unique. As a particular instance, the passage through the alphabet is unique, because the alphabet forms written words that deliver meanings to us. These meanings are not the meaning of the alphabet itself. What makes the alphabet work is that, in isolation, its letters do not have meanings of their own. But this is itself a feat of practical abstraction, a feat of forging elegant conventional marks that, when properly arranged, are then meaningful structures. Writing thus allows us easily to pass through the historical efforts of our craftsmanship, even when it relates the history of this craftsmanship.

Indeed, I suspect that writing also makes it easy to pass through the history that formed our notions about things. Our notions seem to be *there* on the written page, and it is easy to deceive ourselves that we have a neutral and an ahistorical outlook on the nature of things. We seem to encounter the abstract clarity of a triangle; but a Euclidian triangle is as weighted with history as an Egyptian pyramid.

Writing may contribute to our notion that we have a disinterested, bird's-eye view of things. Perhaps it is our writing that allows us to think that we can hold a neutral perspective from which to connect common sense to science or science to common sense: the scientist or philosopher who pretends to judge common sense or science from a neutral vantage point will be tempted to show us *the* way that the liquid feel of water is connected to the chemical composition of water. Reflection, however, shows that every attempt to connect common sense with science arises either from within science or from within the realm of common sense. I do not deny that we may not in the future be able to adopt a more "disinterested" perspective, one that retains and connects the essential insights of both common sense and science. At present I do not know how to do this or even how to begin to do it. Before such a perspective can be achieved, the essential insights of science and common sense have to be given their due equally, and we will have to learn how to give heed to the historical weight of the crafted word.

My own attempt to connect science with common sense arises from within common sense itself: from a commonsense perspective, clarified by philosophical reflection and with some attention to the history of writing, I claim that sound, for example, is an irreducible quality existing in the world, a wavelength and a word, both spoken and written. From my commonsense perspective, I claim that these different essential structures arise because phenomena such as color can exist both in relation to scientific equipment and explanations, and in relation to well-functioning fleshy organs such as eyes. I also claim that we have historically forged immaterial things such as the spoken and written words "color." Different languages and questions of translation are secondary issues; in each case sound and script were made to work.

When, working from the perspective of common sense, I attempt to connect the different aspects of a phenomenom such as color, the quantitative aspects, the red as a wave, take second seating to the qualitative aspects, the red of an apple as it is in the apple, and as it is perceived in the apple. But this is my project, namely, to restore the ontological place of our commonsense world. The restoration is relative both to our body and to the collective history of the practices of our bodies. Nevertheless, this relational anthropocentric realism gives us a world that exists independently of our private conceptions and linguistic expressions about it. And this same anthropocentric realism turns our attention to the way we forge abstractions and mind itself, as well as the web of abstractions that is Nature. Thus, through the differentiated organic structure of our fleshy organism, through the prehistory and history of the collective efforts of our fleshy organism, through the wonder of matter that is sufficiently malleable to yield to those efforts and sufficiently durable to carry their weight throughout our history, we connect everything to ourselves.

APPENDICES

| Appendix | I |

The Snub and the
Population Question

In the *Metaphysics*, Aristotle seems to give us the emphasis on the concrete that we need, and he seems here to suggest that we begin our philosophical reflections by focusing on individuals rather than on clarifying definitions.

> Substance is thought to belong most obviously to bodies; and so
> we say that not only animals and plants and their parts are sub-
> stances, and so are natural bodies such as fire and water and
> earth and everything of the sort. . . .[1]

This statement is not far from my own claim that the most obvious examples of substances are organisms, primarily the human organism in its fleshy constitution. Is Aristotle inviting us to begin our philosophical reflections by focusing on concrete organisms as such? Yes and No. As L.A. Kosman notes:

> Animals, in Aristotle's view, are paradigm instances of substances-
> being. We may wonder whether Aristotle began with that
> conviction and shaped his ontology in the light of it, or arrived

at it as a result of what his ontology revealed the nature of substance to be. . . . On the whole, Aristotle was less concerned with the correct identification of a class of entities which are substances than with the proper understanding of the principles and modes of being by virtue of which those entities which we commonly understood to be substantial beings are substantial. He was, we might say, less interested in substances than in substance-being, less concerned with the question of what beings are substances than with the question of what it is to be a substance.[2]

Do we begin with things or do we begin with the definition of what should be a thing? We could, for example, take substance to denote animals in general and humans in particular: I am a substance and a thing, you are a substance and a thing, a goat is a substance and a thing, etc. On the other hand, height and weight are aspects of substances. This would mean settling what Charlotte Witt and Mary Louis Gill refer to as the "population question" before the "definitional question."[3] Of course, any reference to substance already brings us into a philosophical discourse, but this could be merely by way of a nominal definition of the term, some vague notion that merely guides us in a very general way. Such a nominal definition, however, is not the substantive use of definition in the present discussion. Rather, it is my point that, if we began with a nominal definition of substance, and if we attempted to answer the question of what a substance is by focusing on particular substances, such as Socrates, we would be attempting to solve the population question before the substantive definitional one. If Aristotle had been able to adopt this approach, we would have completely reversed Plato's thought, and we would have received a different history of philosophy.

Indeed, ambiguity about the starting point for our philosophical reflections can be traced back to Aristotle. Soon after the passage in the *Metaphysics* quoted above, Aristotle qualifies his acceptance of the primacy of individuality by clarifying the meaning of substance in a way that goes beyond a mere nominal definition of the term. Thus, he notes that when we examine the notion of substance, it appears to be concerned equally with issues of predication as with individuality. Substance is that which is not predicated of anything else, "but of which all else is predicated."[4]

In itself, this recognition of the way we predicate words could be the simple extension of a nominal definition: "Look, I want to use the term 'substance' in such a way that I can say 'Socrates is a substance and fire is a substance.'" Such a nominal definition would not itself commit us to clarifying first what Socrates and fire have in common. We could be claiming, "I think that 'substance' should apply to Socrates and fire, but let me first clarify what it means to predicate substance of Socrates, and then, *if possible*, I will move on to see if I can make a similar claim about fire." Aristotle does not do this. He aims first to clarify the meaning of substance in general in some detail, and when he does this, it is no longer clear that matter is a substance. With this in mind, the usual Cartesian break with Aristotle, while radical, is not as drastic as it is usually presented.

For example, Richard Rorty in *Philosophy and the Mirror of Nature* sees a radical break from the Aristotelian-Thomistic tradition of the West to arise with Descartes's *cogito*.[5] Rorty notes that the usual historiography of J. H. Randall and Etienne Gilson, and I would also include Jacques Maritain, is that by making ideas the immediate object of knowledge, Descartes broke the natural bond between the human organism and the world. But *if the definitional question of substance must be settled first, then Aristotle has already mediated the bond between perception and the world.* If the philosophical task of comprehending the substance of Peter is to wonder whether the fleshy thing before me *is* Peter, if I must dig deeper than the appearances to obtain a clarified notion of substance, if I must wonder how to justify predicating substance both of Peter and of fire before deciding whether Peter is a substance, then my formal conceptual understanding of substance mediates my perception. This is not to claim that perception is of some brute given, divorced from understanding; rather, perception is an understanding. The issue at hand, however, concerns the degree to which formal clarifications must mediate our perceptions.[6]

There are fortunately more naturalistic strains in Aristotle's thought to follow, and I will come to those shortly. Now, however, I want to show how, by beginning with the attempt to clarify the notion of substance, Aristotle finesses flesh from Socrates.

SUBSTANCE AND FORM

Substance, for Aristotle, is loosely both that which can exist independently of a relation to something else and that which is also the subject of alterations. If we focus on the first aspect of substance, the one that draws our attention to the fact that a substance can exist by itself in a way that shape cannot, then it seems to make perfect sense to claim that Socrates is a substance. If we focus on the second aspect of substance, the one that would have us heed the fact that we call the individual "Socrates" by the same name throughout his life, then we have to make the sticky distinction between what is essential to Socrates and what is accidental.

On closer inspection, however, both aspects of substance present us with a problem of identifying Socrates with his body. We might imagine ourselves to be looking at Socrates's youthful body and saying, "Why yes, this *is* Socrates." The substance of Socrates is nothing else than what is facing us here and now. We now imagine ten years to have passed, and once again we are face to face with the flesh of Socrates. But now the flesh is older; the body more mature. Is it the same Socrates? If we quickly answer yes, then we are claiming that there is something that remains the same during aging that enables us to identify Socrates as Socrates. But this answer seems to invite us to look deeper within Socrates to something not obvious to perception, to something that remains the same throughout Socrates's life.

Thus Aristotle aims at understanding substance by describing what remains the same in change. From this respect, he frequently compares the constitution of natural things with those of art. Consider ten bronze castings of a Degas dancer and ten people. Aristotle wants us to see that just as the "form" of the dancer was received in bronze to make ten dancers, so too a more basic form, what he terms a "substantial form," is received in a more fundamentally potential matter that he terms "prime matter," matter that results in the natural differences among things. The reason why a tree can change into coal and then into a diamond is that the primary matter remains the same while the forms differ.

But such matter is pure potency; it is nothing but a substratum. This substratum cannot exist by itself any more than clay can exist without a particular shape. However, just as clay does not have a natural shape—if it did, this shape would inhibit it from becoming other shapes—so too primary matter has no natural form, that is, no actuality, and thus it can become the substratum for all natural things. This view set the basis for the ancient dream of changing base metals into gold, a dream that the magic of science has realized. However, the only point I wish to make is that all the actuality of a natural thing arises from the form. True, Aristotle would have us note that matter must be put in the definition of a thing. But the matter seems to be there merely to bring Plato's forms into the world, and one wonders how "natural" such things are.

Indeed, Aristotle's view of matter as potency and form as act causes him to hesitate to identify substance with the composite of matter and form. Aristotle thus compromises his naturalization of Plato. True, in the *Physics* and *On the Soul*, and in the biological works, Aristotle does indeed refer to the composite as the material thing. But, when the question of substance is explicitly raised, as it is in the *Metaphysics*, he hedges. Or worse; for when the dust begins to settle, it is clear that form alone is primarily substance. The tension between the claim that form is substance and the requirement that matter be essential to natural things is noted by almost all the commentators, and I will return to some of their observations. In general, however, the issue of how essential matter is to substance arises most clearly in what is called the problem of individuation.

Contemporary Aristotelian scholars seek a solution to the problem of individuation by attempting to tighten the relation between matter and form. The point is to emphasize that at the moment of actualization the matter and the form are one. That is, since all the actuality comes from the form and all the receptivity from the matter, the form is actually just what the matter is potentially. ". . . the proximate matter and the form are one and the same thing, the one potentially, and the other actually."[7] Perhaps the most caustic comment on this solution to the problem of individuation is given by G. E. M. Anscombe.

> All this is supposed to be resolved by the consideration that the
> form and the matter are the same, but one *dunamei* (in poten-
> tiality) and the other *energeia* (in actualization). But this is
> Greek to me.[8]

What I suspect that Anscombe is getting at is that if Aristotle really means that matter and form are merely two different aspects of one reality, one potential and the other actual, then it appears that here he no longer holds matter and form to be real principles of being. Is Aristotle merely claiming that the bronze and its shape are only conceptually different? If this is true, then we have to accept that Aristotle is now rejecting the view of matter and form that he put forward in the *Physics*. Anscombe appears to want to push Aristotle in this direction. I suspect, however, that this push nudges Aristotle outside the framework of his entire physical system. That would be alright with me, although I am not sure it would sit well with Anscombe. However, the problems connecting matter to form are more clearly evident, I believe, in Aristotle's analogy with the snub nose.

THE SNUB NOSE

In his attempt to understand the nature of physical things, Aristotle frequently forsakes the loose analogy with art and asks us to understand physical things as we understand snubness. In the second book of the *Physics* he writes:

> Since two sorts of things are called nature, the form and the
> matter, we must investigate its objects as we would the essence of
> snubness, that is, neither independently of matter nor in terms
> of matter only.[9]

What distinguishes snubness from curvature is that snubness must be a quality of a nose. It is not simply the question of putting any form in any matter. Snubness implies flesh and bones ". . . of concavity flesh . . . is not a part, but of snubness it is a part . . ."[10] On reflection it becomes evident that the same situation is true in the analogy of art with natural things: a Degas statue could not be made out of a liquid. But the requirement that form needs a certain kind of matter in order to be a composite is clearer in the analogy of natural things with snubness. Or is it? D. W. Hamlyn observes:

> It follows that for Aristotle matter and form are not merely correlatives, or rather it is inaccurate to say that they are merely that. They are correlative in relation to an actualizable substance. . . . This is summed up in Aristotle's notorious example of the snub—or would be if both we and Aristotle were clear about it.[11]

If we could develop the analogy with snubness correctly, we might be able to see how an Aristotelian perspective could help us understand our intuition that Socrates is both a unique individual and a fellow human; and, most importantly, we would be able to understand how both his individuality and common nature follow from his distinct fleshy appearance. Putting aside any logical problems about hidden tautologies, we would like to be able to say that just as snubness has to be in flesh and bones, so too the form of Socrates is uniquely tailored to this flesh and these bones.[12] Unfortunately, it is not clear that Aristotle intends to claim this, or if he intends it, that it can be maintained within his matter-form perception of the world.

The tension arises because the form of Socrates is both that which makes Socrates to be Socrates and that which is itself determined by Socrates having this flesh and these bones. Prior to the union of form and matter, the matter that is to become Socrates is only equivocally "Socrates." Aristotle is very clear that a detached arm of Socrates or the corpse of Socrates is only equivocally called "arm" or "Socrates." Likewise, the matter that is about to be Socrates is not Socrates, and cannot be Socrates until the matter is one with the form of Socrates.

If individuality is to mean anything, Aristotle must inform us that Socrates is essentially and substantially himself and himself alone. D. M. Balme brings Aristotle about as close in this direction as anyone can and still keep the matter-form distinction. The following comments, while not a systematic exegesis of Balme's text, keep, I believe, close to its spirit.[13]

If Socrates is like the snub, then the specific fleshy substance of Socrates would have to be included in his essence. But such a view of essence would require a closer bond of form to matter than is ordinarily understood to be possible in the Aristotelian understanding of things. The issue to be considered can be brought into focus if, before turning to Balme's comments, we reflect once again upon the rather extreme case of a functionalist interpretation of the union of matter and form. Thus, although Nussbaum stresses the empirical aspect of Aristotle's thought, she interprets the behavior of animals functionally. To repeat and expand upon the quote given in the first chapter of her study of *De Motu*, Nussbaum has Aristotle respond to Democritus in an imaginary conversation:

> But living beings are necessarily enmattered. Although the account of what it is to be a man or animal should not make the mistake of supposing that the flesh and bones in which such creatures always, in our experience, turn up are necessary parts of their essence (for if we found tomorrow a creature made of string and wood who performed all the functions mentioned in our formal account of what it is to be human, we could not rule him out simply on material grounds), it should at the same time be recognized that *some* sort of matter is necessary for the performance of these functions. . . . The snub, unlike concavity, is inseparable from, and inexplicable without reference to, its realization in some material stuff of a suitable kind, so with beings in nature. . . . Soul is the first actuality of a natural body potentially having life . . . soul and body are as much one as the wax and its shape.[14]

If the soul and body are one the way wax and its shape are one, then how can Nussbaum claim that we can abstract the essence of Socrates from his flesh and bones? She can make this claim only because, like Descartes and Armstrong, she is also working with an historically constituted neutral conception of mind of the sort discussed in chapter 1. But if Aristotle is leading us in this direction, then he has failed to naturalize Plato. If the essence of Socrates merely requires some kind of union with matter, then Descartes's notion that our spiritual soul guides a mechanical body by working through the pineal gland is no less a union of soul and body than Aristotle's matter-form union.

If Balme is to succeed in bringing us closer to a Socrates whose essence requires this flesh and these bones, then we had best first follow him and take another look at that strange section in the *Metaphysics* that seems to justify Nussbaum's functional interpretation. It may be useful to repeat here the text in question:

> In the case of things which are found to occur in specifically dif-
> ferent materials, as a circle may exist in bronze or stone or wood,
> it seems plain that these, the bronze or the stone, are no part of
> the essence of the circle, since it is found apart from them. Of
> things which are *not* seen to exist apart, there is no reason why
> the same may not be true, e.g. even if all circles that had ever
> been seen were of bronze (for none the less the bronze would be
> no part of the form); but it is hard to effect this severance in
> thought. E.g. the form of man is always found in flesh and bones
> and parts of this kind; are these then also parts of the form and
> the formula? No, they are matter; but because man is not found
> in other matters we are unable to perform the severance.[15]

If this quote states more than a problem to be resolved, then Aristotle is indeed close to functionalism. However, if this is the case it is hard to understand the entire movement of the books of the *Physics* that aim at explaining substantial change through the tight union of a matter that is pure potency with a form that is act. In particular, it leaves unexplained both Aristotle's frequent use of the example of snubness to explain the relation of form to matter. Balme, however, sees the passage in the *Metaphysics* to be a mere query.

> In *Meta.*, Z.10 he says that the matter (flesh) is part of snubness,
> in a way that the matter is not part of concavity (*Meta.*, 1035a4).
> In Z.11 he considers whether we could mentally isolate man
> from flesh if man were also embodied in other materials; for a

circle can be in bronze or in stone, and this helps us to separate its form from its matter in thought (1036a31). But it would not help in the case of man, for that is different, he says: man is a this-in-this or these things in this state (1036b23).[16]

I am not primarily interested in making a textual point, but I do want to use Balme's quote to steer us toward another way of looking at Aristotle's matter-form distinction. The issue is whether Aristotle's form must be seen primarily as that which gives a thing its species-being. Balme is directing us to see not only that flesh and bones are essential to humanity, but that this flesh and these bones are essential to Socrates qua Socrates. In this interpretation, the issue of explaining and justifying our predications becomes secondary. Presumably, for Balme, we might be able to accept the subject-predicate logic as a human construct.

> So the problem is not created by the logical method of subject-attribute predication but by the ontological analysis of things into form and matter. To solve it Aristotle re-examines this analysis and produces a solution in *Meta.*, H.6 which is of radical importance, for it shows that the formal description of Socrates can—indeed must—logically include all material details and accidents.[17]

If we are to exorcize the ghost of Plato's Forms, we must indeed include "all material details and accidents" in the definition of Socrates. But, as Balme notes, it is impossible to avoid the all-too-numerous references of Aristotle that matter qua matter is indeterminate and unknowable and that definition denotes primarily the composite of form and the matter *only through the form*. Balme's solution is to interpret the crucial passage in the *Metaphysics*, where Aristotle claims that at the *moment* of actualization matter and form are one thing (1045b18), to mean that there Aristotle is considering material things as static. Balme wants us to read the text, putting the emphasis on the word "moment."

I must confess that I am not clear what either Balme or, as I noted in chapter 5, Kripke, means by considering things from a static perspective. Every definition, by being a definition, indeed, every use of language as such, considers things statically. Even if we are referring to the lived aspect of things, we do so statically; that is, we temporarily freeze things in order to consider them. If the difference between the static and the lived aspect of things is to be more than a question of degrees, than the distinction hides a subtle identification of the static with an eternal, neutral perspective on things, a perspective that I have rejected throughout this work as one suited more to angels than to humans. However, it is instructive to see just what Balme is aiming at by his distinction.

To get a handle on Balme's perspective it may be useful to recall that, for Aristotle, a separated substance is its essence. Still, separated substances are not Plato's Forms, but, rather, individuals. Nevertheless, since they do not include matter in their essence, each is a distinct kind of thing. Aquinas will use this notion to define angels.[18] If we follow Balme's lead, the distinctive feature of a physical thing is that its substantive constitution necessarily goes "beyond" its essences. "Beyond" here means that the being of material substances always includes matter and motion.[19] For Balme, the difficulty in analyzing the snub in relation to natural things is that the analogy attempts to hint at a definition of the being of material things and not just their essence. If I understand Balme correctly, the snub aims at the being rather than the essence, because it attempts to show how the eternal essence arises from the particular temporal movement that brings the thing into existence. The fact that at the moment of actualization form and matter are one means that *the* snub refers to nose flesh placed *so*.[20]

Let us temporarily accept Balme's distinction between the being of something and its essence. Let us grant that the analogy with the snub seems to invite us to look beyond the essence of a natural thing to its being. In Balme's own words, this means that:

> ... whereas the definition of Socrates which is now legitimized
> will state that he is animal with two legs *so*, with blue eyes and
> arms thirty inches long ... flesh of such constituents, blood *so* ... ,
> a definition of the human class will be stated in approximations
> and disjunctive (man is animal, biped, eyes blue or brown.) ...[21]

If we keep our eye on the *being* of Socrates, it is clear that "... *nous* in Socrates must be formally distinguishable from the quality of *nous* in

Callias. . . ."[22] Thus the definition of Socrates as a member of the human class does not get at the being of Socrates, but merely gives us an approximate estimate of his common essential qualities. I think that claim to be just about right; but is it Aristotle? Certainly it is not the Aristotle that has influenced the tradition, the Aristotle for whom the definition of a thing in some way hits the substance of a thing. Indeed, in Balme's view, the matter-form distinction now appears to be functioning only to give us quasi-pragmatic universal definitions. But when Balme considers his own distinction between essence and being, he retracts from this implication.

> But this universal remains important to Aristotle for other reasons which only really become clear in his biology. The different classes of animal—man, horse—are primarily distinguished by essence (*To Ti en enai*). Those with the same essence are in a way "one" and indivisible (*Metaph.* Delta. 1016a32). . . although *nous* in Socrates must be formally distinct from *nous* in Callias, *the more significant distinction lies between Socrates and Callias on the one hand and horses on the other.*[23]

What are we then to say about the substantiality of Socrates? What happens to the fleshy thing that argued, ate, and drank with his companions? This fleshy thing recedes from sight, and we are asked to focus our attention on the whatness of Socrates. Socrates's whatness is his substantial form, a form that makes him be this kind of a substance, a type common to Plato and every other human. But if all we seek is a way of distinguishing Socrates and Callias from horses, the appearances and the general set of practices such as language do the trick.

The Aristotelian grouping works fine if we take our definitions as clarifying our different perspectives on things. As long as our definitions are constructs that arise for a particular purpose and perspective, I do not think that they need create difficulties. The problem arises when we want to privilege the formal definition over the perception, or, in the present case, when we want to privilege the definition of substance over the investigation of things which are perceived to be substances, such as the human reality.

Indeed, I think that Balme's emphasis on the static aspect of a thing indirectly shows that the definitional approach to substance leads to insoluble problems. Aristotle is still caught up in Plato's conviction that the inner is more important than the outer and that the general is more important than the specific. Both a priori emphases arise from beginning with the definitional approach to substance. If, however, we begin our philosophical reflections, as I think we should, with the population question, then we base our concerns upon the concrete individual. From one perspective, the import of this present reflection is that our prime philosophical concerns should be directed to explaining the uniqueness of human life over all other existence and, correspondingly, the unique differences between individual human lives. The problem with the Aristotelian classification is that it makes moral differences among people to be an epiphenomena. I would hesitate to call the perspective that lumps Gandhi and Hitler together the only essential one possible to have on human existence.[24]

To return to the Aristotelian framework, we are still left with the question of just how to handle the substantiality of Socrates. The problem is most embarrassing when the related issue of personality is raised. Is the personhood of Socrates identified with the particular matter that happens to receive the form of humanity? But this matter, while essential to Socrates qua Socrates, is not essential to Socrates qua human. We encounter a strange split between Socrates the individual and Socrates the human, and it is not clear on which side of this split to place the personality of Socrates. If we place Socrates's personality on the side of his individuality, then his personality seems to be something incidental to his humanity. But this doesn't seem right. On the other hand, if we place Socrates's personhood on the side of his humanity, then it appears to be incidental to his flesh and bones, and then the concrete reality of Socrates recedes from sight.

Personality was a knotty problem for the Scholastics. Thomists, such as Jacques Maritain, saw the problem as insoluble in terms of matter and form alone. The entire composite substance, with all its individuating characteristics, is seen by Maritain to need a further determination in the order of substance. "Subsistence" is postulated as a unique mode of being that determines the composite Socrates to be this person rather than another.[25] The notion of subsistence appears to be another deus-ex-machina solution to the problem of individuation. What is important for our purposes is the recognition that individuality and personality do not fit comfortably within the matter-form distinction.

Rather than being a solution, Balme's distinction between the essence and the being of a thing highlights the Platonic roots in the definitional approach to substance. Nevertheless, I think that Balme has taken us about as far as we can go in giving due weight to the individuality of things, while remaining within the Aristotelian framework.[26]

Still, the fruitfulness of the reflection on Aristotle is that it shows, first, negatively, that there cannot be one essential perspective on Socrates that retains both his uniqueness and what he has in common with other people. In a more positive way, through Balme's insight, Aristotle's attempt to tighten the matter-form relation brings us to the distinction between the being of a thing and its essence, and in turn, this distinction opens the door on the kind of relational realism that has been my concern in this work.

What takes my perspective outside the Aristotelian tradition is my claim that there can be multiple essential perspectives which, while they are indeed united, are not united in any privileged way. The individuality and personality of Socrates are, from a commonsense perspective, just how he appeared to those who knew him for a long period of time. Socrates was the sum total of his actions as these were understood by him and by others; he was the way he gradually molded his body and reflections to be just who he was, and from a legitimate perspective, his personality was just the appearance of his flesh-and-blood body. Still, these observations are more a guide to reflection then a substantive discussion. Perhaps, however, the form of discussion of one's personality cannot be given in an ordinary philosophical mode. Here, I would suggest that Jean-Paul Sartre has given us an insight in how to capture the makeup of a personality in his studies of Genet and Flaubert cited in chapter 6.[27]

On Names

Neither Aristotle, Kripke, or Sartre have taken what Richard Rorty has called the "linguistic turn," limiting our philosophical concerns with language. I hope that I have made it clear that I think such a limited perspective creates more mystery than it solves. Nevertheless, all these thinkers are interested in the workability of our language, and specifically in explaining how our universal judgments work. We not only claim, admittedly somewhat awkwardly, that "Socrates is Socrates," but also that "Socrates is human," that "Socrates is an animal," and that "Socrates is a body." These predications seem to work in the sense that, in some way, Socrates does seem to belong simultaneously to the classes of things that we name as human, animal, and body. We may wonder, however, just how to interpret the import of the "is" in these predications. For example, *is* Socrates a body in the same sense that gold is a body? If he is, then how essential is his flesh to his being a body?

Again, I think that we can get clarification by beginning with Aristotle. However, since I am not interested in strict textual analysis, I find it useful to jump into the Aristotelian view of predications by way of a late-medieval interpretation that fruitfully develops aspects of Aristotle's views. The issue with which I am concerned is, in fact, related to the problem of tightening the matter-form relation so that *this* form is seen to need *that* matter. Admittedly, it may take some effort to see the relation of the problem of individuation to predications of the type "Socrates is a human," "Socrates is an animal," or "Socrates is a body." It may help to note that a reductionist would not need to squint, since no real issue would be at stake: Socrates *is* whatever he is supposed to be reduced to, C-fibers or subatomic particles. The other names, "human," "animal," or "body" are, at best, pragmatically useful or, at worst, "folksy," misleading ways of speaking about Socrates.

Thomas Aquinas, however, sees a problem with these seemingly innocent predications, and it is interesting to understand why. Like Aristotle, Aquinas sees a radical difference among the materialities of minerals, plants, mere animals, and rational animals. Given the difference in materialities, the problem then arises whether the animality in Socrates is the same, for example, as the animality in a lion. On the surface it seems that what makes the animality of Socrates essentially different from that of a lion is that Socrates is more intelligent. But I do not think that Aristotle can allow himself to move in this direction. A "rational animal" will never result by merely adding the quality of human intelligence onto a "brute" animality any more than a "Socrates" could become an individual by crafting specific characteristics to a general human nature. To move in this direction would be to destroy the substantial unity of the matter-form composite, and it would end by sliding over into Plotinus's view of multiple forms in matter.

It would seem that a proper Aristotelianism must insist that everything in a human being be human, and this is just the direction of thought that Aquinas develops. In that case, however, what sense are we to give to claims such as "Socrates *is* a body," or "Socrates *is* an animal"?

At first glance, the Aristotelian-Thomistic answer to this question of predication appears simple. The general outline is as follows: each substance is a composite formed from the union of one substantial form received in a matter properly suited to receive it. The explanation continues by noting that there is in nature an implicit hierarchy that rises from minerals and advances to plants, then to ordinary animals and beyond to rational animals, to substances that exist separated from matter but related to it, and then, finally, to that unique being who is totally complete because it is nothing but actuality, the Prime Mover, or for Aquinas, God. Even if we grant that this gradation is only a loose hierarchy, the higher realities are still essentially different from the lower ones. If we forget about those strange Aristotelian beings, the separated substances, beings whom Aquinas baptized as "angels," and concentrate on Aristotle's view of material nature, we are left with the implicit assumption that the kind of matter possessed by the higher beings differs from that of the lower. The flesh of an animal, for example, has a different material texture than that of plants, and plants have a different texture than do minerals.

But how different are these materialities and how are the differences related to our predictions of common properties? Let us recall that, for Aristotle, each thing can have only one substantial form that makes it this kind of thing. Socrates has one substantial form, and that form simultaneously makes him a body, an animal, a human, and an individual. Consequently, the flesh of Socrates is not the flesh of a lion, nor is Socrates extended in space as gold is extended in space. Socrates is an animal and extended in space precisely as he is—a fleshy, intelligent organism.

The more we insist on the unity of Socrates, however, the more mysterious predications of the type "Socrates is a body" and "Gold is a body" seem. We need to take a closer look at the Aristotelian-Thomistic answer. It consists of two parts: a claim that the "power" of the lower forms exists virtually in the higher forms, and a distinctive appeal to the abstractive function of the human intellect as this is considered a natural a priori ability of human nature.

Let us consider the first. We are told that, although the flesh of Socrates is distinctly human and ultimately distinctly Socrates, it can do virtually what a lion and a piece of gold can do. Socrates can eat, drink, and occupy space. To claim that he does these functions "virtually" means he is actually a higher and more noble perfection, namely a rational animal, and that this more noble perfection manages to accomplish similar effects as lower perfections, without formally being them. Now the second part of the Aristotelian-Thomistic solution comes forward. The human intellect can abstract the notion of body from Socrates, a lion, and a lump of gold. The intellect does this by focusing on the fact that while Socrates, a lion, and a piece of gold are formally different, they are nevertheless virtually identical. The power to affect similar results is sufficient to ground the notion of "body." Predications of the type "Socrates is an animal" and "Socrates is a body" are thereby true.

Aside from all the assumptions about how and why the nature abstracted from the individual should be the same as that possessed by the individual, that is, aside from the fact that the explanation works within a correspondence theory of truth, there are other more intrinsic difficulties. The real issue arises when we press just how these terms are predicated of their subject, and this brings us to the distinctions among univocal, analogous, and strictly equivocal predications.

The notion of body is supposed to be univocal; that is, Socrates and the planet Jupiter are supposed to be equally bodies. But we have already seen that, when pressed, an Aristotelian must answer that all of Socrates is Socrates and all of the planet Jupiter is Jupiter. How then can the predication be univocal; how can "body" have the same meaning when predicated of Socrates and the planet Jupiter? When the issue is put in this way, both Aristotle and Aquinas seem to hedge. They affirm the validity of univocal predication, and nevertheless, they speak of more or less perfect animals and, what is even stranger, more or less perfect bodies. The situation is particularly embarrassing when an attempt is made to explain how an animal such as Socrates or an element such as gold can be a body in the same way as one of the planets. Aristotle and Aquinas held that the matter that constituted all the bodies on Earth was corruptible while that of which the planets were composed was incorruptible.

The dilemma is met head-on by the Thomist Thomas Cajetan (1468–1534) in his *The Analogy of Names*. Cajetan reviews the different types of analogy described by Aquinas.[1] In his attempt to clarify Aquinas's position on analogy, Cajetan almost goes outside the Thomistic framework. We can start with a text of Aquinas:

> There are three ways in which something may be said by analogy. [In the first place,] according to intention only and not according to "to be." This happens when one intention refers to several things according to priority and posteriority, but has a "to be" in one only. For example, the intention *health* refers to animal, urine, and diet, in a different manner according to prior-

ity and posteriority, but not according to a diversity of "to be," because health has a "to be" only in animals.

[In the second place,] according to "to be" and not according to intention. This happens when several are considered equal in the intention of something they have in common, but this common element does not have a "to be" of the same kind in all. For example, all bodies are considered equally in the intention of *corporeity*. Hence the logician, who considers only intentions, says that the name *body* is predicated univocally of all bodies. However, the "to be" of this nature is not of the same character in corruptible and incorruptible bodies. Hence for the metaphysicist and the philosopher of nature, who consider things according to their "to be," neither the name *body* nor any other name is predicated univocally of corruptible and incorruptible bodies.[2]

The third analogy is according to intention and according to "to be," and both Aquinas and Cajetan agree that this type is analogy properly speaking. For example, the term "being" is analogously predicated of substance and accident, for example of a tree and the height of a tree. Thus, while neither the intention nor the "to be" are the same they are proportionately similar. In Aristotelian-Thomistic language, the substantial form is related to its "to be" proportionately to the way an accidental form is related to its "to be." Nevertheless, this analogy depends directly upon an Aristotelian matter-form distinction, and it does not provide an interesting focus for the point I wish to make.

Aquinas usually calls the first analogy "the analogy of attribution," the second, "the analogy of inequality," and the third, "the analogy of proper proportionality." The first two analogies are less closely tied to the Aristotelian matter-form context. In particular, it is the second, "according to 'to be' and not according to intention," that I believe can take us out of the Aristotelian-Thomistic context altogether.

When looked at carefully, the mere statement of this analogy is remarkable. According to this analogy, it is only when we decide to play at logic that the term "body" has the same meaning when predicated of the element gold and the planet Jupiter. The actual "to be," the actual existence of bodies such as a mineral and a planet, are different. The metaphysician and physicist are expected to take heed of this difference. The logician, however, can speak about a body as a three-dimensional object and claim that a mineral and a planet are *equally* three-dimensional. But if this is the case, what is the logician talking about, and what are we to say about the truth of statements of the type "Gold *is* a body" and "Jupiter *is* a body"? If the term "body" is univocal only for the logician and not for the metaphysician, then logic doesn't seem to connect with the world.

If our quandary occurred only in relation to the obsolete distinction between the earthly corruptible bodies and the heavenly incorruptible ones, it could perhaps be dismissed with the distinction itself. But it is clear that the problem arises in relation to every predication of a univocal term when applied to different kinds of things. In fact Aristotle does refer to a gradation in the perfection of being an animal, and in a more general way, the claim that each kind of thing has one specific substantial form implies that each kind of thing has a distinctive "to be." The "to be," or existence, of an element such as gold, and the "to be" of an animal such as a lion, are irreducibly different in nature. (We are dropping for the moment the question of individuation within species.)

Cajetan is clearly embarrassed by Aquinas's claim that the term "body" is univocal only for the logician. He quickly dismisses the so-called analogy of inequality as not being analogy at all, but simple univocation.[3] Distinguishing between the order of signification and the order of exercise, Cajetan attempts to connect the concept "body" with the world, while still claiming that, in some basic way, the term refers to irreducibly different things.[4]

> . . . since *animal* as predicated of man and horse implies univocation in the order of exercise, it does not predicate of man this whole, "a sensitive nature that is exactly the same in concept as the sensitive nature of a horse or an ox," but it predicates sensitive nature absolutely.[5]

Cajetan here cleverly appropriates Aquinas's answer to how a predication can be truthfully made concerning the individual Socrates and the general class of humanity: the nature of a thing is neither singular nor universal, and thus the nature of being human precisely as a nature can exist *identically* in the individual Socrates and in the general class of humanity.[6] In a similar way, Cajetan wants to maintain that the quality of animality *as such* is neutral; animality can thus exist equally in Socrates and a lion, even though they are formally different.

Cajetan sees that Aquinas cannot have his logical concepts floating about without a bond to nature, but it is hard to see how his distinction between the order of signification and the order of exercise saves the day. If what Socrates and a lion have in common is their sensitive nature absolutely speaking, what are we to make of the "existential" import of their differences? In the order of exercise, the "to be" of each is different. What Cajetan wants us to do is to look behind these differences to see a sensitive nature "absolutely speaking." In the final analysis, the notion of "body" is supposed to hook onto this common nature, but if that is the case, then the reality of "the order of exercise," the reality of the differences between the matter of gold and the flesh of Socrates, seems to evaporate into the more fundamental common quality of animality. Once again the ghost of Plato's World of Forms overshadows Aristotle's natural forms.

A healthy nominalism recommends that we retain the original intu-ition expressed in the analogy of inequality. This intuition recognizes the diverse materialities that we concretely experience in the world. I think that it is possible to hold onto these differences without recourse to the Aristotelian matter-form distinction or any kind of dualism. All that is required is that we see that essential structures exist in the world, but only as relations. There is no single perspective from which to glean *the* essen-tial structure of matter. We are free, for example, to view the human body as a neural complex or as a sophisticated computer, and in relation to the history of practices that make sense of such a perspective, the human body and the world it inhabits reveal a mechanical structure. That is, given a more or less Cartesian notion of the body, the world *is* itself more or less Cartesian. There is nothing wrong in such a perspective, and science has shown that a mechanistic view of the human body and the world works, within its limits. We go amiss only when we take this mechanistic perspec-tive on matter as privileged, as giving us *the* true nature of things. On the other hand, it is clear that we cannot simply make up perspectives on the human body and the world; some just don't seem to work.

I have been attempting to focus on an aspect of the human body and its relation to the world that I do consider viable and about which I believe we have lost sight, namely, the *fleshy* organic totality of the human organism and the corresponding world that emerges in relation to such a body. Specifically, I have been aiming to show that the so-called secondary qualities, such as color, sound, and odor, as well as gradations in matter, such as the textures of water, plants, and animals truly exist in the world in relation to the *fleshy* constitution of the body.

In a similar way I claim that Socrates *is* essentially the individual referred to by this name. His individuality emerges when we focus on the distinctness of his fleshy body and the way this flesh is related to the world. When we look upon Socrates as an individual, the statement "Socrates *is* a body" is *not* true. Socrates is not *a* body; Socrates is *this* body, and wholly this body. The predication "Socrates *is* a body" *can* be true if we choose to view Socrates in relation to the linguistic, philosophic, scientific, and cultural practices that practically ground these notions.

There are different holistic ways of looking at the world, depending on the different holistic ways of looking at our body. I want to part company somewhat with Putnam and Goodman by emphasizing that these different holistic ways of looking at the human body and the world are more than diverse language usages. Once we are given a certain holistic way of looking at the body, then a corresponding world truly exists. Further, different potencies and possibilities emerge from the different ways the organic body has of relating itself to the rest of the material universe. Insofar as the human body can be resolved into different holistic structures—for example, one of flesh or one of neurons—different potentialities of both the world and the body are revealed, and this gives us sufficient foundation for our counterfactual and modal predications. Of course, all these worlds are aspects of our one world, but they are viable aspects with a certain degree of independence from each other.

Notes

INTRODUCTION

1. Water can be ice or steam. We can learn to associate these as different states of a common substance, but it is clear that the individual aspects come first. Further, liquid, ice, and steam are, again, essentially the different ways water can relate to our fleshy body.

2. Donald Davidson, "Rational Animals," in *Actions and Events: Perspectives on the Philosophy of Donald Davidson*, ed. Ernest LePore and Brian McLaughlin (London and New York: Basil Blackwell, 1985), p. 473.

3. For similar reasons, I also do not find Daniel C. Dennett useful for my discussion. For example, Dennett seems to want to get to a definition of pain and then to see if other things, such as computers, can feel pain. A neurological explanation of pain assumes that one gets to the whole through the parts, but frequently the whole comes first, as when we attempt to understand the body in pain. See Daniel C. Dennett, *Brainstorms: Philosophical Essays on Mind and Psychology* (Cambridge, Mass.: M.I.T. Press, 1981), pp. 190–229. More generally, with all his differences from the Churchlands, Dennett also gives a privileged place to the kind of scientific materialism whose claims I relativize.

4. See my "The Body and the Book: Reading *Being and Nothingness*," in *The Debate Between Sartre and Merleau-Ponty*, ed. Jon Stewart (Evanston, Ill.: Northwestern University Press, 1998). For me, the paradigm of a work that is both ontological and historical is Sartre's five-volume (in English) study of Gustave Flaubert, *The Family Idiot* (Chicago: University of Chicago Press, 1981–1983) translated by

Carol Cosman, in which, through some three-thousand-odd pages, Sartre offers an explanation of Flaubert's passive-active consciousness that remains on the surface of bodily actions, for example, the mother's touch; the interaction of the child with the total family environment and the totality of French language as well as with its specific historical characteristics; and, finally, the way Flaubert interacted with his historical situation. As Sartre duly notes, a knowledge of Flaubert's inherited characteristics would have been useful for his study, but there is no a priori way to know that these would be primary, even if we had them. I do not give a study of Sartre's work, although I do at times refer to it (see chapter 6, notes 1 and 2).

5. See Edmund Husserl, *The Crisis of European Sciences and Transcendental Phenomenology*, translated by David Carr (Evanston, Ill.: Northwestern University Press, 1970), and Carr's introduction that focuses on the ambiguity of the pre-given status of the lived-world. See also my review article "Reinventing the Transcendental Ego," in *Continental Philosophical Reviews* (formerly *Man and World*), vol. 28, 1995, pp. 101–11.

CHAPTER ONE

1. See appendix II.

2. René Descartes, *Discourse on Method*, contained in *The Philosophical Writings of Descartes*, translated by John Cottingham, Robert Stoothoff, and Dugald Murdoch (Cambridge: Cambridge University Press, 1985), vol. I, pp. 114, 120. This collection hereafter referred to in notes as *Writings*.

3. See Tobias Dantzig's popular *Number: The Language of Science* (New York: MacMillan Co., 1939), pp. 19–35, and the more substantive work, Karl Menninger, *Number Words and Number Symbols* (Cambridge, Mass.: M.I.T. Press, 1970), pp. 400–45. These works remind us of the tremendous effort and time needed to perform even the simplest calculation until the Indian culture introduced the use of zero and until zero was recognized as an empty set. According to Menninger, the first mention of the empty set (*sunya*) was in Sanskrit sometime between the 6th and 8th centuries, but it took a long time for it be recognized for giving numbers a place-value, and longer still for this to be recognized for the great revolution that it was. "From all this we infer that the new numerals were adopted in the early Middle Ages not because of any conception of the advantages of place-value notation but merely as a new and exotic means of writing numbers" (p. 424). But by the 13th century, Leonardo of Pisa, in his *Liber Abaci* (1202) had been introduced to the new numeral by an Indian calculator, and wrote: "The nine numerals of the Indians are these: 9 8 7 6 5 4 3 2 1. With them and with this sign 0, which in Arabic is called *cephirum* [cipher], any desired number can be written" (quoted by Menninger, p. 425). Our present-day positional use of numbers, or what Menninger calls "place-value notation," is thus of relatively recent use. The important anthropocentric question is, was zero invented or discovered. I think it clear that it was invented, as was the entire

number system. Indeed, Menninger's book in particular makes this clear. As I note in chapter 7, I recommend reading these histories as recounting our efforts in crafting marks into meanings.

4. René Descartes, *The Principles of Philosophy*, contained in *Writings*, vol. I, p.221.

5. René Descartes, *Meditations on First Philosophy*, contained in *Writings*, vol. II, p. 22.

6. Ibid., pp. 22–3.

7. René Descartes, *The World, or Treatise on Light*, contained in *Writings*, vol. I, p. 89.

8. See Descartes, *Meditations*, contained in *Writings*, vol. II, pp. 123–24.

9. See Bernard Williams, *Descartes: The Project of Pure Enquiry* (Atlantic Highlands, N.J.: Humanities Press, 1978), chapters 2 and 3, particularly pp. 60–3, 73–4; Richard Rorty, *Philosophy and the Mirror of Nature* (Princeton, N.J.: Princeton University Press, 1979), pp. 45–61, especially pp. 54–5.

10. Rorty, *Mirror*, p. 38. On page 116, Rorty claims that J. J. C. Smart cannot explain the appearance of the mind-body problem as such. But, following Smart's materialism, Armstrong offers his own version of a topic-neutral materialism precisely as an attempt to show how dualism could have gotten started. See D. M. Armstrong, *A Materialist Theory of the Mind* (London: Routledge & Kegan Paul, 1968), p. 56.

11. Williams, *Projects*, pp. 70–1.

12. Ibid., p. 64. Williams continues in this vein throughout his study. For example, on p. 239, after noting that the distinction between primary and secondary qualities needs to be updated, he says: "The questions will still concern the association of the two notions, of the world as it is scientifically understood and of the world as it really is. They are questions about the role of natural science in forming what in this study I have been calling the 'absolute conception' of reality."

13. Armstrong, *Materialist Theory*, p. 91.

14. Martha Craven Nussbaum, *Aristotle's De Motu Animalium* (Princeton, N.J.: Princeton University Press, 1978), pp. 72–3. In a footnote Nussbaum refers to Hilary Putnam's functionalism. But Putnam has abandoned functionalism, although for reasons other than my own. See, for example, Hilary Putnam, *Representation and Reality* (Boston: M.I.T. Press, 1988).

15. Aristotle, *Metaphysics*, translated by W. D. Ross, contained in *The Complete Works of Aristotle*, ed. Jonathan Barnes (Princeton, N.J.: Princeton University Press, 1985), vol. II, p. 1636 (*Meta.*, 1036a43–67). Mary Louise Gill, in *Aristotle On Substance: The Paradox of Unity* (Princeton, N.J.: Princeton University Press, 1989), pp. 131–38, 151–70, also quotes this passage and seems at first to accept it as Aristotle's own opinion rather than a query. Later, however, she appears to qualify her acceptance. I discuss this issue more fully in appendix I.

16. The alienation from flesh and blood, implicit in a functionalist view of thought, is particularly evident in the last sections of Barrow and Tipler's provocative and controversial *The Anthropic Cosmological Principle* (Oxford: Oxford University Press, 1986). I am very sympathetic to the general intent of the book, which is to tie the laws of nature to the very possibility that made life possible. Unfortunately,

like many astronomers and cosmologists, Barrow and Tipler seem to regard the death of the universe predicted by the second law of thermodynamics billions of years in the future as too horrible to concede. Millions of people may die *now* because of poverty and greed, but the death of the universe, the demise of this grand spectacle of Nature, *that* is too much to concede to reality.

According to Barrow and Tipler, it might be possible to construct artificial intelligences that could reintroduce matter into black holes and thus provide an eternal existence for the Universe:

... if intelligent life were operating on a cosmic scale before any black holes approach their explosive state, these beings could intervene to keep the black holes from exploding by dumping matter down the black hole, at least in a short-lived closed universe. Thus ultimately life exists in order to prevent the Universe from destroying itself! We emphasize that we do not really want to defend this possibility, but we mention it to show that it is possible to imagine that intelligent life could play an essential global role in the universe (pp. 674–5).

Granting that Barrow and Tipler do not wish wholeheartedly to defend this particular view of how intelligent life might interact with the universe, a functionalist view of thought runs throughout their work. They turn our attention, properly, I think, to the degree to which the laws of nature are already constrained to make life possible. The life that they are talking about is *biological* life, cells and ultimately organisms, such as horses and humans. However, when we turn our attention to the makeup of human existence, we find that their analysis is particularly unfleshy. We trace the movement of bits of information, and the computer is the model. But what kind of thought and what kind of universe are we living in now? Where are the subtle interchanging colors of a sunset, the odor of a rose, the taste of a salad? In relation to a computer, colors, odors, and sounds are merely waves or particles of matter.

17. I do not concern myself here with morality. I have, however, made some initial anthropocentric approaches in that direction both in my *A Commentary on Jean-Paul Sartre's "Critique of Dialectical Reason"* (Chicago: University of Chicago Press, 1986), and in some of the essays in *Good Faith and Other Essays* (Lanham, Md.: Rowman & Littlefield, 1996).

CHAPTER TWO

1. René Descartes, *Meditations on First Philosophy*, contained in *The Philosophical Writings of Descartes*, translated by John Cottingham, Robert Stoothoff, and Dugald Murdoch (Cambridge, Mass.: Cambridge University Press, 1984), vol. II, p. 15.
2. Paul M. Churchland, *Matter and Consciousness*, revised edition (Cambridge, Mass.: M.I.T. Press, 1988), p. 26.
3. See Paul. M. Churchland, "Eliminative Materialism and Propositional Attitudes," *Journal of Philosophy* 78 (1981), p. 75. For a discussion of the Churchlands' views and a criticism as well a partial acceptance, see Stephen Stitch, *From Folk*

Psychology to Cognitive Science (Cambridge, Mass.: M.I.T. Press, 1983), chapter 10.

4. Churchland, "Eliminative," p. 75.
5. Patricia Smith Churchland, "Reduction and the Neurobiological Basis of Consciousness," in *Consciousness and Contemporary Science*, ed. A. J. Marcel and E. Bisiach (New York: Oxford University Press, 1988), p. 274.
6. Ibid., p. 277. On pp. 380–8 of *Neurophilosophy: Toward a Unified Science of the Mind/Brain* (Cambridge, Mass.: M.I.T. Press, 1990), Patricia Churchland at times forces the issue of a nonreductive materialism in the direction of one science not being reduced to another. She maintains that psychology rightly considers the importance of intentions, but wrongly supposes that they are irreducible to neuroscience. She acknowledges that one science *can* always be reduced to another just as neuroscience can, in principle, be reduced to mathematical physics. The point is what is lost in the reduction. But whenever this issue is raised, Churchland redefines an intention rather than showing how it is reduced to the function of neurons, and we are left with the impression that nothing is lost by the reduction.
7. In a somewhat different context in *A Neurocomputational Perspective: The Nature of Mind and the Structure of Science.* (Cambridge, Mass.: M.I.T. Press, 1989), pp. 285–6, Paul Churchland claims that

> ... our commonsense notions of hot, warm, and cold are empirically incoherent, in that they attempt to impose a one-dimensional continuum of properties where nature supplies three distinct and divergent continua— *degree* of heat energy, *amount* of heat energy, and *rate of flow* of heat energy— none of which corresponds adequately to commonsense conception. Our commonsense terms here are not just different in extension from the thermodynamic terms that displace them; they are entirely empty of extension, despite their usefulness in our quotidian affairs, since nothing in nature *answers* to the collected laws of "commonsense thermodynamics."

It is difficult to take Paul Churchland seriously. Common sense works perfectly well without any scientific understanding of degrees or amount of flow of heat. The knowledge needed to start a fire to boil water is perfectly accurate in its own domain: one learns pragmatically just how long to leave water on a fire in order to boil it.
8. Stitch, *Folk Psychology,* p. 212.
9. Churchland, *Neurocomputational,* p. 275.
10. Paul M. Churchland, *Scientific Realism and the Plasticity of Mind* (Cambridge: Cambridge University Press, 1979), p. 30.
11. Ibid.
12. D. M. Armstrong and Norman Malcolm, *Consciousness & Causality* (Oxford: Basil Blackwell, 1984), pp. 170, 178.
13. Ibid., p. 180. These remarks are similar to earlier comments made by Armstrong in his *A Materialist Theory of the Mind* (London: Routledge & Kegan Paul, 1968), pp. 270–90.
14. Armstrong and Malcolm, *Consciousness,* p. 182. Armstrong rejects a causal theory of explaining perception because it is a mere promissory note.
15. Ibid., p. 173.

16. Richard Rorty, *Philosophy and the Mirror of Nature* (Princeton, N.J.: Princeton University Press, 1979), pp. 70–1.
17. Ibid., p. 74.
18. "One vocabulary—that of particle physics—may work for *every* portion of the universe, whereas talk of mitochondria, emeroses, cabinet ministers, and intentions is called for only here and there. But the distinction between the universal and the specific is not the distinction between the factual and the 'empty' still less between the real and the apparent, or the theoretic and the practical, or nature and convention" (Rorty, *Mirror*, pp. 206–7).
19. Ibid., p. 110.
20. Ibid., p. 17.
21. See Jean-Paul Sartre's distinction between pain, on the one hand, and disease and illness on the other hand as given in *Being and Nothingness*, translated by Hazel E. Barnes (New York: Philosophical Library, 1956), pp. 331–8, 355–9. See also my exposition on these section in my *A Commentary on Jean-Paul Sartre's "Being and Nothingness"* (New York: Harper & Row, 1974; rev. ed., Chicago: University of Chicago Press, 1980).
22. See Richard Rorty's anthology with its perceptive introductory survey, *The Linguistic Turn* (Chicago: University of Chicago Press, 1967), pp. 1–39.

CHAPTER THREE

1. Daniel C. Dennett, *Brainstorms: Philosophical Essays on Mind and Psychology* (Cambridge, Mass.: M.I.T. Press, 1986), pp. 123–4, Dennett's italics.
2. Ibid., p. 73, Dennett's italics.
3. See Jean-Paul Sartre, *Being and Nothingness*, translated by Hazel E. Barnes (New York: Philosophical Library, 1956), part 2, chapter 3, section 4, "The Time of the World." Sartre's point is that a phenomenon is meaningful precisely by its relation to human consciousness. Time, as well as causality itself, are aspects of reality only because matter has an intrinsic relation to human consciousness. Sartre is not claiming that consciousness *causes* motion. Rather, I take his point to be that insofar as motion is a duration, its specific continuity over time arises from matter's relation to human consciousness. Nevertheless, Sartre is very careful not to dissolve matter into our relation to it. Consciousness does not really add anything to matter; rather, through a relation to consciousness, matter has a specific continuity over time that would otherwise not be present. "But in any case there is no doubt that the For-itself *adds nothing to being*. Here as elsewhere it is pure Nothing which provides the ground on which motion raises itself in relief. But while we are forbidden by the very nature of motion to *deduce* it, it is possible and even necessary for us to *describe* it," (p. 209, Sartre's italics). I will give an interpretation of Sartre's "nothingness" in chapter 6. While I am indebted to Sartre, I suspect that my anthropocentrism is more specific than his, especially in the way I emphasize the differentiation of the senses.
4. Richard Sorabji, *Time, Creation, and the Continuum: Theories in Antiquity and the Early Middle Ages* (Ithaca, N.Y.: Cornell University Press, 1983), p. 69.

5. Hilary Putnam, *Mind, Language and Reality: Philosophical Papers, Volume 2* (Cambridge: Cambridge University Press, 1975), pp. 215–71.
6. Ibid., p. 228.
7. Peter Clark and Bob Hale, editors, *Reading Putnam* (Cambridge and Oxford: Blackwell Publishers Inc., 1994), p. 243.
8. Andrew Pessin and Sanford Goldberg, editors, *The Twin Earth Chronicles: Twenty Years of Reflection on Hilary Putnam's "The Meaning of 'Meaning'"* (Armonk, N.Y. and London: M. E. Sharpe, Inc. 1996), p. xxi. Since I will not be considering the "molybdenum" example in the text proper, I will comment upon it briefly here. We are to imagine that Twin Earth has pots and pans made of molybdenum, and that these cannot be distinguished by our commonsense from pots and pans made of aluminum on our Earth. Further, we are to imagine that the terms have been switched in people's heads on each Earth: whenever I say "molybdenum," I am, in fact, referring to something made of aluminum, and whenever my double on Twin Earth says "aluminim," molybdenum is, in fact, the reference of the term. Putnam's point is that the extension of the terms work, even if their intentions are, from a scientific perspective, wrong. In each case, however, the proper natural kind can be determined by a metallugist in each Earth (see "Meanings" in *Papers*, vol. 3, pp. 225–6). There is, however, an ambiguity is Putnam's example. Both aluminum and molybdenum are technical terms, and as such they are properly identifies by a metallurgist. In practice, we rely on the manufacturer's label. However, in another sense, an aluminum pot is simply any old pot that looks more or less like aluminum, is relatively light like aluminum, and heats like aluminum. And, if the pot is like that, than, in relation to common sense, it *is* aluminum. Putnam *almost* says just that.
9. Ibid., p. ix. These comments arise in relation to Putnam's reply to John Searle. For while Searle acknowledges the importance of our public background language, this language is made conceptual by each individual, and, in this way, meanings, for Searle, are in the head, that is, in the brain.
10. Hilary Putnam, *The Many Faces of Realism* (La Salle, Ill.: Open Court, 1987), pp. 24–5.
11. Hilary Putnam, *Realism and Reason: Philosophical Papers, Volume 3* (Cambridge: Cambridge University Press, 1983), p. 214.
12. See David Lewis, "Causation," *Journal of Philosophy* LXX, 1973. I am indebted to Putnam for this reference (*Reason*, p. 217). Unlike Putnam, I am accepting Lewis's point here for the sake of argument.
13. Aristotle could refer to the efficient cause of a house as the builders who are here and now bringing the house into existence; but Aristotle *begins* with a universe, surrounded and guided by separated substances. No matter how tenuous the Aristotelian bond between the material and the immaterial, it seems clear that Aristotle *needs* to appeal to separated substances to guarantee the working of causality. Thus, the causality of the builders building the house can be justified because heavy elements seek their natural place and because the forms of things, however loosely, are ordered to intelligences related to but also transcendent of the world.

14. "Explanation is interest-relative and context-sensitive. We expect an explanation of a fact to cite the factors that are *important* (where our notion of importance depends on the reason for asking the Why-question). We also expect an explanation to support counterfactuals and, in contemporary theory, the truth of a counterfactual depends on what we take to be the most *similar* hypothetical situations to the actual ('similarity of possible worlds')" (Putnam, *Reason*, p. 297).

15. Putnam, *Philosophical Papers*, vol. 3, p. 295. See also pages 290–8. Putnam's point against Michael Devitt is that, even if one uses language or mechanism to eliminate reference and causality, there still exists an entire set of prior selections that fixed either the linguistic or mechanistic structure rather than a multitude of others. The appeal to causality to escape the epistemic properties in matter is simply another epistemic property in disguise.

    > On Michael Devitt's view, it is not the formal fact that *R*17 is in its own converse domain that matters; rather, it is this formal fact *plus* the fact that *R*17 *really is* reference (really is "causal connection"). . . . It is not that there aren't various naturalistic connections between the word "reference" and *R*17; it is the idea that one of these *declares itself* to have the honor of making *R*17 *be* the relation of reference independently from all operational and theoretical constraints that is entirely unintelligible (*Philosophical Papers*, vol. 3, p. 296, author's italics).

16. Hilary Putnam, *Realism and Reason*, pp. 220–1. For an interal criticim of Putnam's essentialism, see D. H. Mellor's "Natural Kinds" in *Twin Earth Chronicles*, pp. 69–80. Mellor considers Putnam's and Kripke's views together, but I do not think he sufficiently stresses the relational aspect of Putnam's essentialism.

17. Hilary Putnam, *Representation and Reality* (Cambridge: Mass.: M.I.T. Press, 1988), p. 115.

18. Putnam, *Realism and Reason*, pp. 85–6.

19. Putnam, *Faces*, p. 36.

20. Putnam, at least, comes very close to making this claim. See *Representation*, pp. 30–6.

21. See Putnam, *Representation*, p. 31; see also, *Philosophical Papers, vol 2*, pp. 232–47.

22. Still, from a broader perspective, Putnam is cautious and properly relative about the claims of science. "The price of taking the Weber-Habermas approach is to concede that the positivists have given essentially the right description of the natural sciences, the so-called "nomothetic" disciplines. This, it seems to me, we cannot and should not concede" (Putnam, *Reason*, p. 299).

23. Putnam, *Representation*, p. 32.

24. Putnam doesn't have to go in this direction. In *Realism and Reason*, he had earlier given us a more radical internal realism:

    > But the "essence of water" in *this* sense [Putnam's internal realist sense] is the product of our use of the word, the kinds of referential intentions we have: this sort of essence is not "built into the world" in the way required by an

essentialist theory of reference itself to get off the ground (*Realism and Reason,* p. 221).

If we stress this aspect of Putnam's internal realism, then we are lead to a deeper relational realism than what is expressed in the later *Representation and Reality.*

25. See: Israel Scheffler, "The Wonderful Worlds of Goodman," *Synthese* 45 (1980), pp. 201–9; and Goodman's reply on pages 211–5.

26. Nelson Goodman, *Ways of Worldmaking* (Indianapolis, Ind.: Hackett Publishing Co., 1978). Goodman writes:

Furthermore, the very distinction between internal and external properties is a notoriously muddled one. Presumably the color and shapes in a picture must be considered internal; but if an external property is one that relates the picture or object to something else, then color and shapes obviously must be counted as external; for the color or shape of an object not only may be shared by other objects but also relates the object to others having the same or different colors or shapes (p. 62).

27. Ibid., p. 199. See also Nelson Goodman, *Problems and Projections* (Indianapolis, Ind.: Bobbs-Merril Co., 1972), pp. 24–32.

28. Nelson Goodman, *On Mind and Other Matters* (Cambridge, Mass.: Harvard University Press, 1984), p. 36. Goodman here makes it clear that he is aware that, in some respects, his own position is close to the strong anthropic principle.

29. Ibid., pp. 41–2.

30. See Andrew Pickering, *Constructing Quarks: A Sociological History of Particle Physics* (Chicago: University of Chicago Press, 1984). I have some objection to Pickering's distinction between fact and meaning of fact, and I do not think that such a distinction is necessary to avoid idealism (p. 19, 19n.13). However, Pickering admirably brings out the intimate relation between the existence of quarks as meaningful entities and the relation of quarks to machines and mathematics. (See particularly chapter 2.) His emphasis, however, if not his intent, is different from the claims of my own relational realism. Pickering aims to show that the existence of quarks results from the day-to-day practice of science and that it is conceivable to imagine another history of practices that would not have revealed the existence of quarks. What Pickering does not consistently insist upon is that, without a history of these practices, quarks would not thereby exist (pp. 403–15).

31. Again I recommend Richard Rorty's anthology with its perceptive introductory survey, *The Linguistic Turn* (Chicago: University of Chicago Press, 1967), pp. 1–39.

32. George D. Ramanos gives a sustained and perceptive analysis of this particular aspect of Quine's thought in his *Quine and Analytic Philosophy: The Language of Language* (Cambridge, Mass.: M.I.T. Press, 1983), particularly pages 22–8.

33. Willard Van Orman Quine, *Word and Object* (Cambridge, Mass.: M.I.T. Press, 1960), pp. 21–2.

34. Willard Van Orman Quine, *Ontological Relativity and Other Essays* (New York: Columbia University Press, 1969), p. 33.

35. Thus, I suppose it would be consistent with Quine's double indeterminacy to claim that if one were converted from an Aristotelian correspondence theory of truth to a Hegelian coherence theory, one could train oneself to see that the rabbit running across the lawn was not, in truth, the real rabbit but merely a temporal stage in the true history of rabbit-life.

36. Quine, *Ontological*, pp. 54–5.

37. Quine states:

> Now it should be noted that even for the earlier examples the resort to a remote language was not really essential. On deeper reflection, radical translation begins at home. Must we equate our neighbor's English words with the same strings of phonemes in our own mouths? Certainly not; for sometimes we do not thus equate them. Sometimes we find it to be in the interests of communication to recognize that our neighbor's use of some word, such as "cool" or "square" or "hopefully," differs from ours, and so we translate that word of his into a different string of phonemes in our idiolect (*Ontological*, p. 46).

38. See Donald Davidson, *Inquiries into Truth & Interpretation* (New York: Oxford University Press, 1985), pp. 227–41. If I understand Davidson correctly, he is claiming that Quine's inscrutability of reference seems to contradict his own claim that there is "no fact of the matter." Quine should not call reference "inscrutable," because this label implies that there might be an underlying reality independent of our ways of referring to it. Quine, however, has already rejected such a notion, and thus reality is whatever reference *de facto* delivers to us. Davidson writes: "What we have shown, or tried to show, is not that reference is not relative, but that there is no intelligible way of relativizing it that mystifies the concept of ontological relativity" (*Inquiries*, p. 238).

39. Quine, *Ontological*, p. 47.

40. "It is important to think of what prompts the native's assent to *gavagai* as stimulations and not rabbits. Stimulation can remain the same though the rabbit be supplanted by a counterfeit" (Quine, *Word*, p. 31).

41. See Quine, *Word*, pp. 35–44, 73–9; and *Ontological*, pp. 1–25.

42. Quine, *Word*, p. 236.

43. Quine, *Ontological*, p. 93.

44. *Word*, p. 22. The point is brought home again when Smart attempts to push Quine toward a stronger realism. See *Words and Objections: Essays on the Work of W. V. Quine*, ed. Donald Davidson and Jaakko Hintikka (Dordrecht, Neth.: Reidel Publishing Co., 1968), pp. 292–3. In his reply to Smart's paper, Quine states: "In the first half of his paper Smart describes my position clearly, correctly, and approvingly. It is a pleasure to be thus understood and agreed with. A misunderstanding seems to emerge at the middle of his paper, where he finds me ambivalent on the paradigm-case-argument." Quine then goes on to reaffirm what he said about the importance of "posits" and to repeat the quote on posits from *Word and Object*. He adds: "The key consideration is rejection of the ideal of a first philosophy, somehow prior to science. . . . 'Posit' is a term proper to this methodological facet of science. To apply the term to molecules and wombats is not to deny that these are real; but declaring them real is left to other facets of science, namely, physics and zoology."

45. These remarks are given in Quine's reply to Chomsky in *Words and Objections,* p. 303.
46. See Quine, *Word,* p. 126.
47. See Barry Stroud, "Quine's Physicalism" in *Perspectives on Quine,* ed. Robert Barrett and Roger Gibson (Oxford: Basil Blackwell, 1990), pp. 324–5, 333. Quine replies to Stroud: "Firm evidence of extrasensory perception would and should send physicists back to the drawing boards, and no matter whether to call the resulting science physical" (p. 334). But how can we possibly receive such evidence except through the senses? If we allow the possibility that the senses may be the product of theory, then we dissolve away the materiality of the body. Quine, like Descartes and Armstrong, seems to be holding on to a neutral conception of thinking, one that can either be physical or spiritual depending upon how the evidence falls. But such a neutral conception is already an historically constituted notion, and it eliminates beforehand certain possibilities, for example, that knowledge may be a function of the organism in its flesh-and-blood constitution.
48. Quine, *Ontological,* pp. 126–7.
49. Quine, *Word,* p. 237. For a critique of Quine's "fall" from nominalism, see Goodman, *On Mind,* pp. 50–3.

CHAPTER FOUR

1. Again, I am developing only one part of this relational realism in this work; namely, that part that concentrates on the uniqueness of the human body in worldmaking. I plan to return to the study of the relational unity of things in a future work, *The Anthropocentric Universe.*
2. David Lewis, *On the Plurality of Worlds* (Oxford: Basil Blackwell, 1986), p. 1.
3. Idid., p. 17.
4. Idid., p. 22–3.
5. Idid., p. 142.
6. Idid., p. 164.
7. Idid., p. 15.
8. Idid., p. 213.
9. Idid., p. 63.
10. See David Lewis "Reduction of Mind" in *Papers in metaphysics and epistemology* (Cambridge: Cambridge University Press, 1999), pp. 291–324.
11. See Lewis, *Plurality,* pp. 92–3.
12. Jean-Paul Sartre, *Being and Nothingness,* translated by Hazel E. Barnes (New York: Philosophical Library, 1956), p. 5. It is frequently complained that Sartre minimizes the body, since the formal discussion of the body is not introduced until about halfway into the book. But I think that this criticism misses the formal structure of the book as a whole. It arises because readers project their own meaning of what a book should be onto Sartre's book. Most philosophical works are collections of essays, and the book itself has no internal logic as a whole. Dialectically announced works are an exception, but unity is there an explicit part

of the discourse. The unity in *Being and Nothingness*, however, is different and, I think, unique. It is recognized that Sartre is a literary writer as well as a philosophical one, but this is interpreted to mean merely that he sometimes lets his language become too flowery. It should, and I think it does, mean that he is very aware of the different styles required in each genre of writing. With this in mind, I again suggest that the entire book as a whole pivots around the chapter on the body wherein the notion of consciousness is given concrete meaning.

13. Sartre, *Being and Nothingness*, p. 7.
14. Sartre is here indebted to Heidegger; but, rightly or wrongly, Sartre accuses Heidegger of leaving non-being outside being rather than putting it at the heart of being. For a somewhat lengthy examination of Sartre's notion of non-being see my commentary on *Being and Nothingness* (Chicago: Chicago University Press, 1974, 1980), pp. 53–77.
15. Sartre, *Being and Nothingness*, p. 23.
16. Ibid., p. 24
17. Ibid., p. 99.
18. See Lewis's analysis of alien properties, *Plurality*, pp. 159–65. In these pages Lewis is hard pressed to talk about truly alien properties; it is clear that *we* are behind all these conjectures.
19. Sartre, *Being and Nothingness*, p. 305.
20. Ibid., p. 218.
21. Ibid., p. 330.
22. Ibid., p. 344.
23. Ibid.

CHAPTER FIVE

1. Saul A. Kripke, *Naming and Necessity* (Cambridge: Harvard University Press, 1972, 1980), p. 14. See also pp. 6–14, 30–2, 60–1.
2. One way of expressing this is to say that proper names indicate qualities that are true in all possible worlds. Unlike David Lewis, Kripke gives a modest interpretation of possible worlds: possible worlds are other possible states that arise from considering different aspects of an actual occurrence. If a die is thrown and two dots appear, the possible worlds are simply those other "worlds" in which one of the other five faces of the die would have been face up. See Kripke, *Naming*, pp. 18–20, 50–1.
3. Kripke, *Naming*, p. 83.
4. For example, "In general, our reference depends not just on what we think of ourselves, but on other people in the community, the history of how the name reached one, and things like that. It is by following such a history that one gets to the reference" (Kripke, *Naming*, p. 95).
5. Kripke, *Naming*, p. 51. These remarks occur in the context of Kripke's comments about transworld identification, but I think that this context gives additional weight to Kripke's remarks.

6. Kripke, *Naming.* p 52.

7. Ibid.

8. ". . . one should not confuse the type of essence involved in the question 'What properties must an object retain if it is not to cease to exist, and what properties of the object can change while the object endures?' which is a temporal question, with the question 'What (timeless) properties could the object not have failed to have, and what properties could it have lacked while still (timelessly) existing?' which concerns necessity and not time and which is our topic here" (Kripke, *Naming,* p. 114, n. 57).

9. Charlotte Witt, *Substance and Essence in Aristotle: An Interpretation of Metaphysics VII–IX* (Ithaca, N.Y.: Cornell University Press, 1989), pp. 190–1.

10. Kripke, *Naming,* p. 113. See also p. 114, n. 56, and Kripke's qualifications on the first page of the preface to the 1980 edition.

11. "If, on the other hand, it is demanded that I describe each counterfactual situation purely qualitatively, then I can only ask whether *a table*, of such and such a color, and so on, would have certain properties; whether the table in question would be *this* table, table *T*, is indeed moot, since all reference to objects, as opposed to qualities, has disappeared" (Kripke, *Naming,* p. 52). Also, "*This* table itself could not have had an origin different from the one it in fact had, but in a situation qualitatively identical to this one with respect to all the evidence I had in advance, the room could have contained *a table made of ice* in place of this one" (Kripke, *Naming,* p. 142).

12. Kripke, *Naming,* p. 47.

13. Ibid., p. 75.

14. Ibid., p. 124.

15. Ibid., p. 138.

16. Ibid., p. 155.

17. Jean-Paul Sartre, *Being and Nothingness,* translated by Hazel E. Barnes (New York: Philosophical Library, 1956), pp. 453–4, author's italics.

18. See for example my articles, "On the Possibility of Good Faith," and, "Successfully Lying to Oneself: A Sartrean Perspective," contained in my *Good Faith and Other Essays: Perspectives on a Sartrean Ethics* (Lanham, Md.: Rowman & Littlefield), 1996, pp. 77–99, 127–51. These articles were originally published in, respectively, *Continental Philosophical Review* (formerly *Man and World*) 13, no. 2, 1980, pp. 207–28; and *Philosophy and Phenomenological Research.* Vol L, No. 4, June 1990, pp. 673–93.

CHAPTER SIX

1. Andrew Pessin and Sanford Goldberg, editors, *The Twin Earth Chronicles: Twenty Years Reflection on Hilary Putnam's "The Meaning of 'Meaning'"* (Armonk, N.Y., and London: M. E. Sharpe, Inc., 1996), p. xviii.

2. Jean-Paul Sartre, *The Family Idiot: Gustave Flaubert: 1821–1857,* vols. 1–5, translated by Carol Cosman (Chicago: University of Chicago Press, 1981–1993). For a preliminary introduction to this massive work, I recommend Hazel Barnes's

excellent study, *Sartre and Flaubert* (Chicago: University of Chicago Press, 1981). See also my own remarks in *Good Faith and Other Essays: Perspectives on a Sartrean Ethics* (Lanham, Md.: Rowman & Littlefield, 1996), pp. 7–10, 12–5, 28–30, 169–70. My own remarks are rather general here, because at the time of writing I had not completed a detailed study of Sartre's own work. Since then, however, I have corrected this situation, but I have not as yet produced my own · study of Sartre's work.

3. See Sartre, *Family Idiot*, vol. 5, pp. 33–57. This entire last volume in the English translation is a study on the interaction of the world's web of meanings with Flaubert's writing project.

4. Karl Popper, *Objective Knowledge: An Evolutionary Approach* (Oxford: Oxford University Press, 1972), p. 74.

5. See Popper, *Objective*, pp. 122–26.

6. Ibid., p. 138.

7. Ibid., pp. 67–71.

8. See Popper, *Objective*, pp. 136–40. I think that Popper concedes too much to Brower's intuitionalism. "Although the third world is not identical with the world of linguistic forms, it arises together with argumentative language; it is a by-product of language" (p. 137). And yet in other contexts, Popper seems content to identify the third world with written language. I think that these apparent discrepancies can be explained, but what remains is the essential evolutionary perspective that is supposed to get us from matter to a consciousness as nonphysical. Even as a conjecture, this unnecessarily takes us outside the physical realm and mystifies our world.

9. Jean-Paul Sartre, *The Transcendence of the Ego*, translated and annotated with an introduction by Forrest Williams and Robert Kirkpatrick (New York: The Noonday Press, 1957). This work first appeared in French in *Recherches Philosophiques* VI, 1936–7.

10. Sartre, *Transcendence*, p. 80. This quote, of itself, overly simplifies Sartre's view. There is, for Sartre, an intimate connection between the "production" of the *I* and the way this ego tends to "weigh down" the spontaneity of consciousness on the one hand, and one's prereflective actions on the other hand. Another way of saying this is that there is a difference between the consciousness of our early childhood and that of our adult life. Sartre gradually becomes clearer about this issue in his later writings. See the introductory essay, "A Sketch of a Sartrean Ethics," in my *Good Faith and Other Essays*.

11. Sartre, *Transcendence*, p. 51.

12. Ibid., p. 104, Sartre's italics.

13. See Jean-Paul Sartre, *Being and Nothingness*, translated by Hazel Barnes (New York: Philosophical Library, 1956), pp. 600–15.

14. Jean-Paul Sartre, *Critique of Dialectical Reason, Part I: Theory of Practical Ensembles*, translated by Alan Sheridan-Smith (London: NLB, 1976), pp. 161–96. For an exposition of the section on inverted praxis, see Joseph S. Catalano, *A Commentary on Jean-Paul Sartre's Critique of Dialectical Reason, Volume I, Theory*

of Practical Ensembles (Chicago: University of Chicago Press, 1986), pp. 120–6.

15. Sartre, *Critique*, p. 179, Sartre's italics.

16. See Sartre, *Being and Nothingness*, pp. 186–95, and my commentary on the entire "Transcendence" section of part 2 of that work, in my *Commentary on Being and Nothingness*, pp. 132–147.

17. For a further discussion of this example see my *Commentary* on Sartre's *Critique*, pp. 68-79.

18. For a discussion of our Coca-Cola culture see William L. McBride's *Philosophical Reflections on the Changes in Eastern Europe* (London: Rowman & Littlefield, 1999), pp. 130-1.

CHAPTER SEVEN

1. W. V. O. Quine, *Quiddities: An Intermittently Philosophical Dictionary* (Cambridge: Harvard University Press, 1987), pp. 1–2.

2. I have developed this theme in two articles: "The Script Rose," *Philosophy and Literature*, April, 1995, pp. 85–93; and "Crafting Marks into Meanings," *Philosophy and Literature*, April, 1996, pp. 48–60. In the following discussion, I sometimes remain close to my remarks in these articles.

3. Frank Smith, *Reading* (Cambridge: Cambridge University Press, 1978), p. 58. In the final analysis, Smith forsakes this praiseworthy attention to the surface of the written word and opts for a deep structure. See my article, "Crafting Marks into Meanings," op. cit.

4. See David Diringer, *The Alphabet: A Key to the History of Mankind*, third edition, completely revised with the assistance of Reinhold Regensburger (New York: Funk & Wagnalls, 1968), volume I. As an introduction see pp. 1–13; 145–70. In this sense neither the Egyptian, the Chinese, nor other systems that use ideographic forms of writing are properly alphabetic.

> The prototype alphabet, which we have referred to as 'Proto-Semitic,' probably originated in the second quarter of the second millennium B.C., i.e., in the Hyksos period, now commonly dated 1730–1580 B.C. The political situation in the Near East at that period favored the creation of a "revolutionary" writing, a script which we can perhaps term "democratic" (or rather, a "people's" script), as against the "theocratic" scripts of Egypt, Mesopotamia, or China (p. 161).

5. Ibid., p. 10.

6. Ibid., p. 11.

7. Ibid., p. 12.

8. Florian Coulmas, *The Writing Systems of the World* (Oxford: Blackwell, 1989), p. 9.

9. In my articles cited above note 2, I acknowledged my indebtedness to Florian Coulmas's account, which I again here follow rather closely. See *Writing Systems*, pp. 23–36.

10. Julia Kristeva, *Language: The Unknown*, translated by Anne M. Menke (New York: Columbia University Press, 1989), p. 71.

11. Tobias Dantzig, *Number: The Language of Science*, third edition (New York: MacMillan, 1939), p. 27. See also my comments above in chapter 1, note 3.

12. Ibid., p. 30.

13. Ibid., p. 31.

14. See Dantzig, *Number*, pp. 30–35.

15. The simple expression "A=A" is the result of a long history of human attempts to refine written language. The seeming simplicity of the letter "A" and the apparent obviousness of the meaning of the "=" result from a series of historical developments which do not appear at all to have been necessary and which, once given, we tend to pass over. From the perspective of the historical practices that brought about the simplicity and neatness of the letter "A," the equation is not as obvious as it may seem. The one "A" can be a long "A" (ah) or a short "A" as in cat. This mathematical identity *instructs* us to abstract from these differences. We are supposed to read this identity to mean something like, "Substitute anything that you like for the A on the left and do the same for the A on the right and the two substitutions are equal to each other."

Apart from the ambiguity of whether this identity makes any sense, that is, whether the so-called principle of identity states anything at all, the substitution itself represents another degree of abstraction. This time the source is fairly clear, or at least it seems that Aristotle was the first to use the letters of the alphabet in this very abstract way in his logic. The Aristotelian "logic" is a construction that is itself a practical abstraction. By using letters to represent propositions, Aristotle is able to talk about the extension of predicates with a simplicity and formality that Socrates and Plato never achieved. But again, this abstraction was at a price. Imagine the Euthyphro or the Phaedo rewritten in Aristotelian terms.

16. Of course, the real question concerning the need for postulating classes concerns nondenumerable numbers. A denumerable infinite is one that can be put in a one-to-one correspondence with the infinite class of natural numbers. Cantor attempted to show that every infinite number had to be denumerably infinite, but he actually proved the opposite. There thus exist infinite classes, each of which cannot be put into a one-to-one correspondence with each "lower" infinite class. For example the real number system cannot be put into a one-to-one correspondence with the natural numbers. The workability of mathematics seem to require "positing," as Quine would say, the existence of these classes. My own naturalistic answer to the quest for the foundations for such numbers is that they are to be found in the efforts that effectively construct the classes and in the relation of these efforts to the books that embody these efforts.

17. My view of writing as a craft is far removed from Jacques Derrida's notion of writing as implying a relation to deep structures within things. I thus do not see how his objection against the repeatability of the text has any relation to my discussion. I have discussed some of Derrida's views on writing in my article, "Crafting Marks into Meaning," op. cit.

18. Crediting Aldus Manutius with the invention of the modern book is a simplification. My only point is that it took time to realize that the printed book was formally distinct from a manuscript.

19. For example, the books produced by William Morris at the Kelmscott Press and Robert Grabhorn at the Grabhorn Press are conscious attempts to "remake" the book into a thing of beauty as well as a medium of meaning.

APPENDIX I

1. Aristotle, *Metaphysics*, translated by W. D. Ross, contained in *The Complete Works of Aristotle*, ed. Jonathan Barnes (Princeton, N.J.: Princeton University Press, 1984), Vol. II, p. 1623 (*Meta.*, 1028b9–11). G.E.M. Anscombe writes: "Aristotle's prime examples of 'substance' are: *a* man. . . , *a* horse, or, I might add, *a* cabbage" ("The Principle of Individuation", contained in the *Collected Philosophical Papers of G.E.M. Anscombe, Vol I: From Parmenidies to Wittgenstein*, [Minneapolis: University of Minnesota Press, 1981], p. 61). Most scholars agree that animals are Aristotle's prime examples of substances; but, from different perspectives, either the elements or the Prime Mover can also be said to be exemplars of substances.
2. L. A. Kosman, "Animals and Other Beings in Aristotle," contained in Alan Gotthelf and James G. Lennox, *Philosophical Issues in Aristotle's Biology* (Cambridge: Cambridge University Press, 1987), p. 360; hereafter cited as *Philosophical Issues*. Kosman's observation may apply to the notion of species, but it hardly seems applicable to the notion of substance. The problem is that the kinds of individuals Aristotle examines to arrive at the notion of a biological species are picked because they are substances in the definitional sense of that word. Still, I think that Kosman is on the right track, although I suspect that, if we were to follow his insight, we would be forced to reject the matter-form distinction.
3. Charlotte Witt, *Substance and Essence in Aristotle: An Interpretation of Metaphysics VII-IX* (Ithaca, N.Y.: Cornell University Press, 1989), pp. 7–9, 53–62, 194–7. See also Mary Louis Gill, *Aristotle on Substance: The Paradox of Unity* (Princeton, N.J.: Princeton University Press, 1989). Gill's entire book is, in a sense, a discussion of this distinction, but see particularly pages 3–5, 13–6, 111–6, and 240–2.
4. Aristotle, *Meta.,* 1029a8.
5. See Richard Rorty, *Philosophy and the Mirror of Nature*, (Princeton, N.J.: Princeton University Press, 1979), pp. 49–51, together with notes 19 and 21. My emphasis here is somewhat different from that of Rorty's.
6. The trained Aristotelian or Thomist would no doubt attempt to avoid this conclusion by distinguishing between simple apprehension and judgement. The first is an intellectual process that is supposed to deliver to us the general nature of things without converting them into explicit universal notions. Our knowledge of Peter's substance is, from this perspective, unmediated. The issue of the definition and classification of Peter's substance is the job of reflection and judgment. Here we are admittedly on the level of mediated knowledge, but this mediation is rooted in acts of simple apprehension.

I don't think that this or any other similar distinction really helps either Aristotle or Aquinas. The fact is that this distinction hides two mysterious leaps. First, there is no way of justifying how the intellectual process of simple apprehension can deliver to us the nature of things, unless we accept Aquinas's view that nature as nature is neither universal nor singular. But this justification of the correspondence theory of truth is ultimately based upon the conformity of things to the Divine Mind.

Second, even if we had this natural connection with the things of the world, there would be no way of knowing whether our reflections upon them were "natural" or the result of historical training. The only recourse is to root the Aristotelian *Physics* in a Prime Mover and, again, to see the Prime Mover as in some way responsible for the fortuitous meshing of thought and thing. The eighth book of the *Physics* must then be seen to be integral with the entire movement of the *Physics*. But then we rightly wonder about Aristotle's naturalization of Plato.

7. Aristotle, *Meta.*, 1045b17–20. See Balme, "Aristotle's Biology Was Not Essentialistic," contained in *Philosophical Issues*, p. 295. Charlotte Witt takes a somewhat different approach. She insists that essences are individual, but that matter is not essential to the definition of a physical thing. Her reason is that Aristotle is seeking to explain how we define things rather than their physical unity. From this perspective, "Matter and form (or essence) are not two equal, independent factors in the constitution of an Aristotelian composite substance" (*Substance*, p. 192). Still it is difficult to see how to separate the demands for the unity of a thing from its definition. Witt's approach, however, has the advantage of being consistent, and I think that for the most part it reflects Aristotle's own intentions, at least as these are reflected in his primarily philosophical works.

8. Anscombe, *Philosophical Papers*, vol. 1, p. 62.

9. Aristotle, *Physics* II, 19a12–16. Translated by R. P Hardie and R. K. Gaye, contained in *Complete Works*, vol. I, p. 331. See also, *De Anima* III, 429b14; and *Meta.*, 1064a23.

10. Aristotle, *Meta.*, 1035a4.

11. D. W. Hamlyn, "Aristotle on Form," contained in *Aristotle On Nature and Living Things: Philosophical and Historical Studies*, ed. Allan Gotthelf (Pittsburgh: Mathesis Publications, and Bristol, Eng.: Bristol Classical Press, 1985), p. 61.

12. See Balme's excellent extended footnote in "Aristotle's Biology Was Not Essentialistic" contained in *Philosophical Issues*, pp. 302–6.

13. See the two appendices to his "Aristotle's Biology Was Not Essentialistic," contained in *Philosophical Issues*, pp. 302–12. In following Balme, I am bypassing the numerous attempts to solve the problem of individuation by considering the form as both singular and universal. Aquinas took this way out, and so do many commentators. However, the deus ex machina aspect of the distinction, if pressed, entails either the Aristotelian separated substances or the Christian God as fixing the fortuitous correspondence of the singular with the potentially universal.

14. Martha Craven Nussbaum, *Aristotle's De Motu Animalium*, (Princeton, N.J.: Princeton University Press, 1978), pp. 72–3.

15. Aristotle, *Meta.*, 1036a30–67, *Complete Works*, vol. 2, p. 1636. Gill also quotes this passage and seems at first to accept it as Aristotle's own view. Later, however, she appears to qualify this apparent acceptance by distinguishing between the way the generic matter is contained in the concrete singular. See Gill, *Substance*, pp. 131–8, 151–70.

16. Balme, *Philosophical Issues*, p. 309.

17. Ibid., p. 308.

18. The individuality of separated substances is brought out by Charlotte Witt as part of her general insistence that all forms are individual. See Witt, *Substance*, pp. 177–8.

19. See *Meta.* 1025b30. Aquinas also uses the notion that material things are more than their essence to avoid the paradox that singulars cannot be defined and yet only singulars exist. In his commentary on *Meta.* VII, he states: "Socrates is not identical with his own humanity but has humanity, for this reason he has in himself certain material parts which are not parts of his species but of this individual matter" (Thomas Aquinas, *Commentary on the Metaphysics of Aristotle*, translated by John P. Rowan [Chicago: Henery Regnery Co., 1961], vol. II, p. 572). Again, this leads to the strange distinction that nature as composite can be either universal or singular. "Yet it must be borne in mind that this composite, animal or man, can be taken in two ways: either as a universal or as a singular" (Ibid., p. 563).

I am not certain that Aquinas would include *this* flesh and *these* bones as necessary elements in the definition of the *being* of Socrates, but there are times when his thought seems to go in this direction. For example, he claims that differences in intelligence are due to the sensitivity of the flesh. Further, the distinction between essence and existence as well as the notion of subsistence also indicates an uneasiness with the notion of essence as capturing the true substantiality of an individual, such as Socrates.

20. See Balme, "Aristotle's Biology Was Not Essentialistic," contained in *Philosophical Issues*, p. 311.

21. Ibid.

22. Ibid., p. 312.

23. Ibid., my italics.

24. I do not think that oppression can be eliminated by appealing to some common inner nature that we all share. Indeed, if we focus on inner qualities, we can easily use our belief that others lack these inner qualities to justify oppression. Belief in the superiority of the male intellect and will rather than the obvious possession of a penis was used to justify the oppression of women. Of course, we can and still do use differences in color and behavior as justifications for slavery and the suppression of peoples, but I take this to imply that some of us need to base our own humanity on the a priori view that others are subhuman. Indeed, we confirm these views by actually stunting the growth of others so that they effectively become subhuman. Like war, oppression is a horrible work that we perform on others. True, universal notions of humanity can help us direct our actions; but these notions are themselves the collective result of those people who have struggled to get themselves and us to see that human dignity is incompatible with a hierarchal view of human nature. From this perspective of focusing on the population question before the definitional one, those who see the capitalistic marketplace as the natural forum through which true human dignity emerges, and who keep themselves blind to the oppression it causes, and who view those who do

not compete successfully in this market to be subhuman—*these* capitalists are further removed from true human dignity than is a horse. Thus, from the perspective of the population question, more separates Ghandi and Hitler than separates either from a horse. I have touched upon these themes in my *Good Faith and Other Essays: Perspectives on a Sartrean Ethics* (Lanham, Md.: Rowman & Littlefield, 1996), particularly the introductory survey; however, a full examination must await a future, planned work.

25. Jacques Maritain, *Distinguish to Unite or The Degrees of Knowledge,* translated under the supervision of Gerald B. Phelan (New York: Charles Scribner & Sons, 1959), p. 431. Subsistence is an aspect of the wider Thomistic distinction between essence and existence.

26. That is, unless we attempt to take seriously the cryptic remarks of Anscombe about matter as such. See Anscombe, *Collected Papers,* vol. I, pp. 57–77. I do not know what to make of her comments, except to note that perhaps she is overly straining to retain an Aristotelianism that she has effectively rejected.

27. See chapter 6, note 1.

APPENDIX II

1. Thomas Cajetan, *The Analogy of Names,* translated by Edward A. Bushinske with Henry J. Koren (Pittsburgh: Duquesne University Press, 1953).

2. Thomas Aquinas, *In I Sententia,* distinction 19, question 5, article 2, response 1. The reference is given by the translators of *Analogy* (p. 12), and I follow their translation. Aquinas repeats this division in different terms throughout his works. The translators give ample citations to Aquinas as well as to Aristotle for the basis of these distinctions.

3. In turn, the translators of Cajetan are embarrassed by his apparent departure from the words of Aquinas. See Cajetan, *Analogy,* p. 13, n. 19.

4. If my memory is correct, Cajetan uses this same distinction to show why the ontological argument doesn't work. I suspect that the reference would be found in his commentary on the early part of Aquinas's *Summa Theologica,* where he discusses the proofs for the existence of God.

5. Cajetan, *Analogy,* p. 55.

6. Thomists will note that I am sliding over the distinction between first- and second-order intentions here, but I don't think that the distinction is relevant for my purpose.

S e l e c t e d   B i b l i o g r a p h y

AQUINAS, ARISTOTLE, DESCARTES, AND RELATED TEXTS

Anscombe, G. E. M. *Collected Philosophical Papers of G. E. M. Anscombe, Vol. I: From Parmenidies to Wittgenstein.* Minneapolis: University of Minnesota Press, 1981.

Aquinas, Thomas. *Commentary on Aristotle's De Anima.* Translated by Kenelm Foster and Silvester Jumphries, with an introduction by Ivo Thomas. New Haven: Yale University Press, 1951.

———. *Commentary on Aristotle's Physics.* Translated by Richard J. Blackwell, Richard J. Spath, and W. Edmund Thirlkel, with an introduction by Vernon J. Bourke. London: Routledge & Kegan Paul, 1963.

———. *Commentary on the Metaphysics of Aristotle.* Translated by John P. Rowman. Chicago: Henry Regnery Co., 1961.

———. *In Aristotelis Libros De Caelo et Mundo, De Generatione et Corruptione, Meteorologicorum, Expositio.* Edited by Ramund Spiazzi. Rome: Marietti, 1952.

Aristotle. *The Complete Works, Volumes I and II.* Edited by Jonathan Barnes. Princeton: Princeton University Press, 1984, 1985.

———. *De Anima.* Translated with notes by Hugh Lawson-Tancred. Middlesex: Penguin Books, 1986.

———. *De Anima, Books II and III.* Translated with notes by D. W. Hamlyn. Oxford: Oxford University Press, 1968

―――. *De Generatione et Corruptione.* Translated with notes by C.J.F. Williams. Oxford: Oxford University Press, 1982.

―――. *Metaphysics, Books M and N.* Translated with notes by Julia Annas. Oxford: Oxford University Press, 1976.

―――. *Metaphysics, Books Tau, Delta, Epsilon.* Translated with notes Christopher Kirwan. Oxford: Oxford University Press, 1971.

―――. *Metaphysics, Books Zeta, Eta, Theta, Iota (VII–X).* Translated by Montgomery Furth. Indianapolis: Hackett, 1985.

―――. *Physics, Books I and II.* Translated with notes by W. Charlton. Oxford: Oxford University Press, 1970.

―――. *Physics, Books III and IV.* Translated with notes by Edward Hussey. Oxford: Oxford University Press, 1983.

Barnes, Jonathan. *Aristotle.* Oxford: Oxford University Press, 1982.

―――, Malcolm Schofield, and Richard Sorabji. *Articles on Aristotle, Vols. I–IV.* London: Duckworth, 1975–79.

Cajetan, Thomas. *The Analogy of Names.* Translated by Edward A. Bushinske with Henry J. Koren. Pittsburgh: Duquesne University Press, 1953.

Descartes, René. *Philosophical Writings of Descartes, Volumes I and II.* Translated by John Cottingham, Robert Stoothoff, and Dugald Murdoch. Cambridge: Cambridge University Press, 1985.

Gill, Mary Louise. *Aristotle on Substance: The Paradox of Unity.* Princeton: Princeton University Press, 1989.

Gotthelf, Alan, editor. *Aristotle on Nature and Living Things: Philosophical and Historical Studies.* Pittsburgh and Bristol: Mathesis Publications and Bristol Classical Press, 1985.

―――― and James G. Lennox, editors. *Philosophical Issues in Aristotle's Biology.* Cambridge: Cambridge University Press, 1987.

Hartman, Edwin. *Substance, Body, and Soul: Aristotelian Investigations.* Princeton: Princeton University Press, 1977.

Maritain, Jacques. *Distinguish to Unite or The Degrees of Knowledge.* Translated under the supervision of Gerald B. Phelan. New York: Charles Scribner & Sons, 1959.

Modrak, Deborah K. W. *Aristotle: The Power of Perception.* Chicago: University of Chicago Press, 1987.

Nussbaum, Martha Craven. *Aristotle's De Motu Animalium.* Princeton: Princeton University Press, 1978.

O'Hara, M. L., editor. *Substances and Things, Aristotle's Doctrine of Physical Substance in Recent Essays.* Washington: University Press of America, 1982.

Owens, Joseph. *The Doctrine of Being in the Aristotelian Meaphysics.* Toronto: Mediaeval Studies of Toronto, 1951.

Ross, Sir David. *Aristotle.* Fifth revised edition. London and New York: Methuen, 1949.

Simmons, George C., editor. *Phaedeia: Special Aristotle Issue.* Brockport and Buffalo: State University College at Brockport and Buffalo, 1978.

Sorabji, Richard. *Time, Creation, and the Continuum: Theories in Antiquity and the Early Middle Ages.* Ithaca: Cornell University Press, 1983.

Waterlow, Sarah. *Nature, Change, and Agency In Aristotle's Physics, A Philosophical Study.* Oxford: Clarendon Press, 1982.

———. *Passage and Possibility, A Study of Aristotle's Modal Concepts,* Oxford: Oxford University Press, 1982.

Williams, Bernard. *Descartes: the Project of Pure Enquiry.* New Jersey: Humanities Press, 1978.

Witt, Charlotte. *Substance and Essence in Aristotle: An Interpretation of Metaphysics VII–IX.* Ithaca: Cornell University Press, 1989.

PUTNAM AND SARTRE WITH TRANSITIONAL AND RELATED TEXTS

Armstrong, D. M. *A Materialist Theory of the Mind.* London: Routledge & Kegan Paul, 1968.

——— and Norman Malcolm. *Consciousness & Causality.* Oxford: Basil Blackwell, 1984.

Barnes, Hazel E. *Sartre and Flaubert.* Chicago: University of Chicago Press, 1981.

Barret, Robert and Roger Gibson, editors. *Perspectives on Quine.* Oxford: Basil Blackwell, 1990.

Barrow, John and Frank Tipler. *The Anthropic Cosmological Principle.* Oxford: Oxford University Press, 1986.

Catalano, Joseph S. *Commentary on Jean-Paul Sartre's "Being and Nothingness."* New York: Harper-Row, 1974; new preface, Chicago: University of Chicago Press, 1980.

———. *Commentary on Jean-Paul Sartre's "Critique of Dialectical Reason Vol. I, Theory of Practical Ensembles."* Chicago, University of Chicago Press, 1986.

———. *Good Faith and Other Essays.* Lanham: Rowman & Littlefield, 1996.

Churchland, Patricia S. *Neurophilosophy: Toward a Unified Science of the Mind/Brain.* Cambridge, Mass.: M.I.T. Press, 1990.

Churchland, Paul M. *Matter and Consciousness,* revised edition. Cambridge, Mass.: M.I.T. Press, 1988.

———. *A Neurocomputational Perspective: The Nature of Mind and the Structure of Science.* Cambridge, Mass.: M.I.T. Press, 1989.

———. *Scientific Realism and the Plasticity of Mind.* Cambridge: Cambridge University Press, 1979.

Clark, Peter and Bob Hall, editors. *Reading Putnam.* Oxford and Cambridge: Blackwell Publishers Ltd, 1995.

Coulmas, Florian. *The Writing Systems of the World.* Oxford: Basil Blackwell, 1989.

Dantzig, Tobias. *Number: The Language of Science.* New York: MacMillan Co., 1939.

Davidson, Donald. *Actions and Events: Perspectives on the Philosophy of Donald Davidson.* Edited by Ernest LePore and Brian McLaughlin. London and New York: Basil Blackwell, 1985.

———. *Inquiries into Truth & Interpretation*. New York: Oxford University Press, 1985.

Davidson, Donald and Jaakko Hintiikka, editors. *Words and Objections: Essays on the Work of W. V. Quine*. Dordrecht: Reidel Publishing Co., 1968.

Dennett, Daniel C. *Brainstorms: Philosophical Essays on Mind and Psychology*. Cambridge, Mass.: M.I.T. Press, 1981.

Diringer, David. *The Alphabet: A Key to the History of Mankind, Volumes I and II*. Third edition, revised with the assistance of Reinhold Regensburger. New York: Funk & Wagnalls, 1968.

———. *Writings*. London: Thames and Williams, 1962.

Goodman, Nelson. *On Mind and Other Matters*. Cambridge, Mass.: Harvard University Press, 1984.

———. *Problems and Projections*. Indianapolis: Bobbs-Merril Co., 1972.

———. *Ways of Worldmaking*. Indianapolis: Hackett Publishing Co., 1978.

Husserl, Edmund. *The Crisis of European Sciences and Transcendental Phenomenology*. Translated with an introduction by David Carr. Evanston: Northwestern University Press, 1970.

Kripke, Saul A. *Naming and Necessity*. Cambridge, Mass.: Harvard University Press, 1972, 1980.

Kristeva, Julia. *Language: The Unknown*. Translated by Anne M. Menke. New York: Columbia University Press, 1989.

Lewis, David. *On the Plurality of Worlds*. Oxford: Basil Blackwell, 1986.

———. *Papers in Metaphysics and Epistemology*. Cambridge: Cambridge University Press, 1999.

Marcel, A. J. and E. Bisiach, editors. *Consciousness and Contemporary Science*. New York: Oxford University Press, 1988.

McBride, William L. *Philosophical Refelctions on the Changes in Eastern Europe*. Lanham: Rowman & Littlefield, 1999.

Menninger, Karl. *Number Words and Number Symbols*. Cambridge, Mass.: M.I.T. Press, 1970.

Pessin, Andrew and Sanford Goldberg, editors. *The Twin Earth Chronicles: Twenty Years Reflection on Hilary Putnam's "The Meaning of Meaning"*. Armonk and London: M. E. Sharpe, 1996.

Pickering, Andrew. *Constructing Quarks: A Sociological History of Particle Physics*. Chicago: University of Chicago Press, 1984.

Popper, Karl. *Objective Knowledge: An Evolutionary Approach*. Oxford: Oxford University Press, 1972.

Putnam, Hilary. *The Many Faces of Realism*. La Salle: Open Court, 1987.

———. *Mind, Language and Reality, Philosophical Papers, Vol. II*. Cambridge: Cambridge University Press, 1975.

———. *Realism and Reason: Philosophical Papers, Vol. III*. Cambridge: Cambridge University Press, 1983.

———. *Representation and Reality*. Cambridge, Mass.: M.I.T. Press, 1988.

Quine, Willard Van Orman. *Ontological Relativity and Other Essays*. New York: Columbia University Press, 1969.

—————. *Quiddities: An Intermittently Philosophical Dictionary.* Cambridge: Harvard University Press, 1987.

—————. *Word and Object.* Cambridge, Mass.: M.I.T. Press, 1960.

Ramanos, George D. *Quine and Analytic Philosophy: The Language of Language.* Cambridge, Mass.: M.I.T. Press, 1983.

Rorty, Richard, editor, with introduction. *The Linguistic Turn.* Chicago: University of Chicago Press, 1967.

Rorty. Richard. *Philosophy and the Mirror of Nature.* Princeton: Princeton University Press, 1979.

Sartre, Jean-Paul. *Anti-Semite and Jew.* Translated by George J. Becker. New York: Schocken Books, 1948. (Published in England as *Portrait of the Anti-Semite.* Translated by Eric de Mauny. London: Secker & Warburg, 1948.)

—————. *Being and Nothingness.* Translated with an introduction by Hazel E. Barnes. New York: Philosophical Library, 1956.

—————. *Critique of Dialectical Reason, Vol. I: Theory of Practical Ensembles.* Translated by Alan Sheridan-Smith. London: New Left Books, 1976; Verso, 1982.

—————. *Existentialism Is a Humanism,* contained in Walter Kaufman, *Existentialism from Dostoevski to Sartre.* New York: New American Library, 1975.

—————. *The Family Idiot, Volumes I–V.* Translated by Carol Cosman. Chicago: University of Chicago Press, 1981; 1987; 1989; 1991; 1993.

—————. *Saint Genet, Actor and Martyr.* Translated by Bernard Frechtman. New York: George Braziller, 1963.

—————. *Search for a Method.* Translated by Hazel E. Barnes. New York: Alfred A. Knopf, 1963.

—————. *The Transcendence of the Ego.* Translated by Forrest William and Robert Kirkpatrick. New York: Noonday Press, 1957.

Schlipp, Paul A., editor. *The Philosophy of Jean-Paul Sartre.* La Salle: Open Court Publishing Co., 1981. (This work also contains an excellent bibliography both of primary and secondary sources.)

Schrag, Calvin O. *Radical Reflection and the Origin of the Human Sciences.* West Lafayette: Purdue University Press, 1980.

Stich, Stephen. *From Folk Psychology to Cognitive Science.* Cambridge, Mass.: M.I.T. Press, 1983.

Index